Coaching
SOFTBALL
Technical and
Tactical Skills

**American Sport
Education Program**

HUMAN KINETICS

Library of Congress Cataloging-in-Publication Data

Coaching softball technical and tactical skills / American Sport Education Program.

   p. cm.

Includes index.

ISBN-13: 978-0-7360-5376-1 (soft cover)

ISBN-10: 0-7360-5376-X (soft cover)

1. Softball--Coaching. I. American Sport Education Program.

GV881.4.C6C62 2009

796.357'8--dc22

2008030204

ISBN-10: 0-7360-5376-X

ISBN-13: 978-0-7360-5376-1

The Web addresses cited in this text were current as of August 2008 unless otherwise noted.

Acquisitions Editors: Amy Tocco and Jenny Maddox; **Project Writers:** Mona Stevens and Kirk Walker; **Developmental Editor:** Laura Floch; **Assistant Editors:** Cory Weber and Elizabeth Watson; **Copyeditor:** Robert Replinger; **Proofreader:** Jim Burns; **Indexers:** Robert and Cynthia Swanson; **Permission Managers:** Carly Breeding and Martha Gullo; **Graphic Designer:** Nancy Rasmus; **Cover Designer:** Keith Blomberg; **Cover Photo:** © Human Kinetics; **Photographer (interior):** Ryan Gardner; **Visual Production Assistant:** Joyce Brumfield; **Photo Production Manager:** Jason Allen; **Art Manager:** Kelly Hendren; **Associate Art Manager:** Alan L. Wilborn; **Illustrator:** Jennifer Gibas; **Printer:** Sheridan Books

We thank Oregon State University in Corvallis, Oregon, for assistance in providing the location for the photo shoot for this book.

Copies of this book are available at special discounts for bulk purchase for sales promotions, premiums, fund-raising, or educational use. Special editions or book excerpts can also be created to specifications. For details, contact the Special Sales Manager at Human Kinetics.

Printed in the United States of America   10 9 8 7 6 5 4 3 2 1

Human Kinetics

Web site: www.HumanKinetics.com

United States: Human Kinetics
P.O. Box 5076
Champaign, IL 61825-5076
800-747-4457
e-mail: humank@hkusa.com

Canada: Human Kinetics
475 Devonshire Road Unit 100
Windsor, ON N8Y 2L5
800-465-7301 (in Canada only)
e-mail: info@hkcanada.com

Europe: Human Kinetics
107 Bradford Road
Stanningley
Leeds LS28 6AT, United Kingdom
+44 (0) 113 255 5665
e-mail: hk@hkeurope.com

Australia: Human Kinetics
57A Price Avenue
Lower Mitcham, South Australia 5062
08 8372 0999
e-mail: info@hkaustralia.com

New Zealand: Human Kinetics
Division of Sports Distributors NZ Ltd.
P.O. Box 300 226 Albany
North Shore City
Auckland
0064 9 448 1207
e-mail: info@humankinetics.co.nz

contents

preface

If you are a seasoned softball coach, surely you have experienced the frustration of watching your players perform well in practice, only to find them underperforming in games. In your playing days, you likely saw the same events unfold. Teammates, or perhaps even you, could tear the cover off the ball in batting practice and snag every ground ball in drills but could not transfer that kind of performance to games. Although this book will not provide you with a magical quick fix to your team's problems, it will help you prepare your players for game day. Whether you are a veteran coach or a new coach, *Coaching Softball Technical and Tactical Skills* will help you take your game to the next level by providing you with the tools that you need to teach your team the game of softball.

Every softball coach knows the importance of technical skills. The ability of a player to field a fly ball, make a strong throw, block a pitch in the dirt, lay down a bunt or throw a curveball can significantly affect the outcome of a game. The book discusses the basic and intermediate technical skills necessary for your team's success, including both offensive and defensive skills. You will learn how to detect and correct errors in your athletes' performance of those skills and then help them transfer the knowledge and ability that they gain in practice to execution in games.

Besides covering technical skills, the book explains tactical skills, including offensive skills like the sacrifice bunt, getting out of a rundown and stealing third base and defensive skills such as pickoff plays, defending the first-and-third double steal and double-play defenses. The book discusses the "tactical triangle," an approach that teaches players to read a situation, acquire the knowledge that they need to make a tactical decision and apply decision-making skills to the problem. To advance this method, the book covers important cues that help athletes respond appropriately when they see a play developing, including important rules, game strategies and the strengths and weaknesses of opponents.

Although rigorous technical and tactical training prepares athletes for game situations, you can improve their game performance by incorporating gamelike situations into daily training. The book offers many traditional drills that can be effective but also shows you how to shape, focus and enhance scrimmages and minigames to help your players transfer their technical skills to tactical situations that occur during games. For example, you can add realism to the infielders' work on the double play by including base runners or timing the fielders with a stopwatch.

The book also covers planning at several levels—the season plan, practice plans and game plans. Sample games approach practice and season plans are offered. The season plan lays out a season based on the skills in this book, and the practice plans include a description of eight practice sessions, covering elements such as the length of the practice session, the objective of the practice, equipment needed, warm-up, practice of previously taught skills, teaching and practicing new skills, cool-down and evaluation. Sample traditional approach season and practice plans can be found in the *Coaching Softball Technical and Tactical Skills* online course.

Of course, playing the games is what your practices eventually lead to. The book shows you how to prepare long before the first game, including issues such as communicating with players, parents, officials and the media; scouting your opponent; and motivating your players. You will learn how to control your team's performance on game day by establishing routines and how to make decisions during the game, such as how to deal with removing pitchers, making substitutions and setting a batting order.

PART I

Teaching and Evaluating

Being a good coach takes more than knowing the sport of softball. You have to find a way to teach your athletes how to be better ballplayers, and you need to know how to evaluate your players to find ways to improve their performance.

In chapter 1 we go over the fundamentals of teaching sport skills. We first provide you with a general overview of your sport and talk with you about the importance of being an effective teacher. Next, we define some important skills to improve your understanding of technical and tactical skills and the traditional and games approaches to coaching.

We build on the knowledge of how to teach sport skills with the evaluation of technical and tactical skills in chapter 2. We discuss the importance of evaluating athletes, review the core skills that you should assess and describe how you can assess them. Chapter 2 stresses the importance of preseason, in-season and postseason evaluation and provides you with sample tools that you can use to evaluate your players.

By learning how to teach and evaluate your players, you will be better prepared to help them improve their performance.

chapter 1

Teaching Sport Skills

Although its rules and the look of the playing field have changed over the years, the basic concept of softball has not—the team that scores the most runs wins. The basic concepts of softball are ingrained so deeply into America that its terms have become part of our everyday language. Many states' judicial codes have "three strike" laws on the books for repeat criminals. Goofy people are said to be "out in left field." And when a young romantic says that he "struck out," everyone knows what he means.

A certain uniformity exists at all levels as far as rules are concerned. A playing field in Indiana looks the same as one in Washington. Youth fields are merely shrunken versions of their high school and collegiate counterparts. Infields are diamond shaped, and the center field fence is usually farther from the plate than the fence in left or right. The pitching circle is 8 feet in diameter. Depending on the age of participants, the pitching rubber is 38 to 46 feet from the plate.

Although competitive and recreational softball has been played for years, its heyday may be occurring right now. With women's softball being played in the Olympics, names like Lisa Fernandez, Jenny Finch, Dot Richardson and Sheila Douty have become familiar to millions of softball enthusiasts. The NCAA has recognized softball as a sport, allowing scholarships in colleges from the beginning of the organization's involvement in women's athletics. Even so, no longer can the assumption be made that most Americans know the game; too many diversions are available to them. So, too, it cannot be taken for granted that youth will know how to perform the skills of softball as soon as they step out of the cradle. Today those skills have to be taught.

Effective Teaching

A commonly held fallacy is that an athlete who excelled as a player can excel at coaching too. Great players often play instinctively and don't know why they do what they do. They just do it. Players who are not as skilled sometimes try to make up for their limited skills by becoming more knowledgeable about the tactics and techniques needed to become good softball players. These players, although never able to perform at a high level themselves, learned enough about the game to know how to pass on that knowledge of skills to others. This is not to say that good players cannot be good coaches. Rather, you should realize that just because you were a good player you will not naturally become a good coach. You will need to work at it.

Good coaching is good teaching. There is no simpler way to put it! Coaches who discover the best way to help all their players succeed become the best coaches. Coaches must recognize this fact and be responsible for their athletes' learning. Coaching requires teaching.

Good coaches, then, not only teach the mechanics of the game but also understand the way that athletes learn. Rather than tell players how to play, good coaches teach them how to learn the game for themselves. This approach demands that you do more than just work with the *X*s and *O*s. The great player is the sum of many parts: technical skill, tactical skill, physical ability, mental acuity, communication proficiency and strength of character (Rainer Martens, *Successful Coaching, Third Edition*, Champaign, IL: Human Kinetics, 2004, pp. 186–188). Although all these skills are important, this book focuses on the technical and tactical skills that you need to be aware of in coaching softball. To learn more about other skills that should be part of the makeup of a great athlete, refer to Rainer Martens' *Successful Coaching, Third Edition*.

A softball player could master literally thousands of technical and tactical skills. Covering every aspect of the game—from the simple act of gripping and holding a softball to the complexity of successfully executing a suicide squeeze—would be impossible. Instead, this book focuses on the essential basic and intermediate technical and tactical skills, developed from a list of skills compiled with the cooperation and assistance of the National Fastpitch Coaches' Association (NFCA).

Technical Skills

Everyone involved in coaching softball knows the importance of technical skills. The way a player fields a ground ball, lays down a bunt, throws a fastball or executes a bent-leg slide has a big effect on the outcome of a game. Technical skills are "the specific procedures to move one's body to perform the task that needs to be accomplished" (Martens, *Successful Coaching*, p. 169). The execution of technical skills, the capability to teach athletes how to perform them, the flair to detect errors and correct them and the ability to recognize when those skills come into play in a game are all things that you will develop over time with the accumulation of experience. You may need years and hundreds of games to acquire the knowledge necessary to know instinctively what to do. This book will help you reach that stage more quickly, taking you from your current level of knowledge to a higher plane by showing you how to o focus on the key points of the skill,

o detect errors in an athlete's performance of those skills,

o correct the errors that athletes make, and

o help athletes transfer the knowledge and ability that they gain in practice to execution in games.

Developed from the expertise of the NFCA, the plan outlined in this book will help you learn how to teach athletes to become masters of the basic to intermediate technical skills of softball and will assist you in providing athletes with the resources necessary for success.

Tactical Skills

Although mastering the technical skills of softball is important, it is not enough. Softball players need to know not only how to play the game technically but also how to choose the tactics necessary to achieve success. Many softball texts overlook the tactical aspects of the game. Coaches even omit tactical considerations from practice because they focus so intently on teaching technical skills. Teaching tactics is much harder and takes much more effort than teaching techniques, but the resulting dividends are substantial.

Tactical skills can best be defined as "the decisions and actions of players in the contest to gain an advantage over the opposing team or players" (Martens, *Successful Coaching*, p. 170). One way that coaches can approach teaching tactical skills is by focusing on three critical aspects, the "tactical triangle":*

o Reading the play or situation

o Acquiring the knowledge needed to make an appropriate tactical decision

o Applying decision-making skills to the problem

This book as a whole provides you with the knowledge you need to teach players how to use the tactical triangle. Part III covers important cues that help athletes respond appropriately when they see a play developing, including important rules, game strategies, and the strengths and weaknesses of opponents that affect game situations, as well as ways to teach athletes how to acquire and use that knowledge. Part III will help you teach athletes how to make appropriate choices in a given situation and will show you how to empower players to recognize emerging situations on their own and make sound judgments.

Anyone who has observed softball for any length of time has seen players make errors in games on plays that they have practiced many times in training sessions. Such situations can cause tremendous frustration, for both players and coaches. As you will see, however, these errors can be prevented!

---

*Reprinted, by permission, from R. Martens, 2004, *Successful coaching*, 3rd ed. (Champaign, IL: Human Kinetics), 215.

Traditional Versus Games Approach to Coaching

As mentioned previously, transferring skills from practice to games can be difficult. A sound background of technical and tactical training prepares athletes for game situations. But you can surpass this level by incorporating gamelike situations into daily training, further enhancing the likelihood that players will transfer skills from practices to games. To understand how to accomplish this, you must be aware of two approaches to coaching: the traditional approach and the games approach.

Traditional Approach

Most coaches are comfortable with the traditional approach to coaching. This method often begins with a warm-up period followed by a set of drills, a scrimmage and finally a cool-down period. This approach can be useful in teaching the technical skills of softball, but unless coaches shape, focus and enhance the scrimmages or drills, the athletes may not successfully translate the skills to game situations, leaving coaches to ponder why their team practices better than it plays.

Games Approach

Using the tactical triangle in practice supplies athletes with the tools that they need to make appropriate and quick decisions. But unless they can employ these tools in game situations, they are of little value.

You have surely seen players jump into the batting cage in practice and tear the cover off the ball on the tees or the pitching machine but then have trouble making good contact after the game begins. This type of hitter has learned the art of performing well in drills but has not learned how to transfer those technical skills to tactical situations that occur during a game. Some people call this choking, but a more accurate description would be failure to adapt. The same sort of thing happens to the player who can field every ground ball flawlessly in practice but bobbles easy grounders in a game or lets them go through her legs.

The best way to prevent this scenario is to use the games approach to coaching, which provides athletes with real-time, gamelike situations in training that allow them to practice and learn the skills at game speed. This philosophy stresses the importance of putting technical skills rehearsed in drills into use in practice. You can drill players in a skill like bunting until they are sore, but if they never get the opportunity to use the skill in a gamelike setting, they will not be able to perform when it really counts—in an actual game. When players make mistakes in game-speed situations, they learn. You have to provide gamelike opportunities in which players can feel secure about making mistakes so that they can file those mistakes in the "softball sense" parts of their brains. By doing so, the chances of their making the same mistakes in games will lessen.

The games approach emphasizes the use of games and minigames to provide athletes with situations that are as close to a real game as possible (Alan G.

Launder, *Play Practice*, Champaign, IL: Human Kinetics, 2001). This approach requires more than just putting the team on the field, throwing them a ball and letting them play. Rather, according to Launder, the games approach includes three components that make each minigame educational:

1. Shaping
2. Focusing
3. Enhancing

Shaping play means modifying the game in a way that is conducive to learning the skills that you want to teach in that particular setting. The games approach shapes play by modifying the rules, the environment (playing area), the objectives of the game and the number of players used (Launder, p. 56). In a typical scrimmage situation, the stronger players dominate and the weaker players rarely get a chance to play an active role. When play is shaped, for example, by reducing the number of players—the weaker players are put into positions where they will have more opportunities to play active roles. But you cannot simply shape the play and expect miracles to happen. You need to focus your athletes' attention on the specific objectives that you are trying to achieve with the game. Young players are more apt to learn, or at least to reduce their reluctance to learn, if they know why you are asking them to grasp new tactical information.

Knowing how the tactic fits into the team's game plan or season plan also helps players buy into the tactic. You can assist your athletes with this phase by providing them with clear objectives and explaining how learning those objectives elevates their capability to play and helps their team win games. Shaping play and focusing players on objectives, however, cannot be successful unless you play an active role and work on enhancing their play. You can enhance minigames by adding challenges to make the contests between the sides equal. You can also enhance play by encouraging your players and give them confidence by frequently pointing out their progress. Minigames also give you an opportunity to stop the game whenever you recognize an opportunity to teach something that will improve their play even further.

Most coaches have used aspects of the games approach one way or another in their training sessions. Although you may already have a basic understanding of how to use this approach, this book takes the concept further by presenting a games approach season plan as well as sample practices for you to use with your team.

Both the traditional and the games approach are sound coaching practices. Part IV examines both approaches to teaching the skills in softball. Although both approaches have value, the philosophy of this book slants toward the latter. Providing athletes with game-speed, real-time situations that have clear objectives creates a productive, fun-filled learning environment. Athletes who have learned to think of training as a necessary evil will be more motivated to come to practice if they are engaged on a daily basis. More important, if they sense that they have ownership over what they learn in practice, they become more responsible team members. An added benefit is that softball players who learn through the games approach will be better prepared for competition because they have already faced stiff challenges in their everyday practice sessions.

Knowing how to teach the technical and tactical skills of softball is important, but you will never know how your players are performing unless you create good assessment systems. Next, you must learn how to evaluate players.

chapter 2

Evaluating Technical and Tactical Skills

Softball is a team sport. In building your team, you should use specific evaluation tools to assess the development of the individual parts that make up the whole of the team. You must remember that basic physical skills contribute to the performance of technical and tactical skills. In addition, an array of nonphysical skills, such as mental capacity, communication skills and character training, overlay athletic performance and affect its development (Rainer Martens, *Successful Coaching, Third Edition*). In this chapter we examine evaluation guidelines by exploring the specific skills that should be evaluated and the tools used to accomplish that evaluation. Evaluations as described in this chapter will help you produce critiques of your players that are more objective, a goal that you should continually strive to attain.

Guidelines for Evaluation

Regardless of the skill that you are measuring and the evaluation tool that you are using, you should observe the basic guidelines that govern the testing and evaluation process. First, the athletes need to know and understand the purpose of the test and its relationship to the sport. If you are evaluating a technical skill, the correlation should be easy. But when you are evaluating physical skills, or mental, communication or character skills, you must explain the correlation between the skill and the aspect of the game that will benefit.

Second, you must motivate the athlete to improve. The player will benefit by understanding the correlation of testing to her game, but sometimes the games seem a long ways away during practices and training. In the physical skills area, elevating the status of the testing process can help inspire your athletes. If you can create a game-day atmosphere by having many players present and watching as you conduct the testing, athletes will compete with more energy and enthusiasm than they would if you ran the tests in a more clinical fashion. Goal boards and record boards with all-time best performances can also motivate athletes. The best of these boards have several categories (separating the quicker players from the more powerful players, for example, to give the smaller and often quicker players a chance to compete in strength contests and to allow the often slower and more powerful players a chance to compete in speed tests) and list several places, such as the top 5 or top 10 performances, to give more athletes a reasonable chance to compete for a spot on the board.

The best motivation, though, is the concept of striving for a personal best effort in physical skills testing, or an improved score, compared with a previous evaluation, on measurement of technical, tactical, communication and mental skills. When the athlete compares herself today to herself yesterday, she can always succeed and make progress, regardless of the achievements of her teammates. And when she sees herself making progress, she will be motivated to continue to practice and train. This concept, while focusing on the individual, is not antithetical to the team concept. You simply need to remind the team that if every player gets better every day, the team will be getting better every day!

Third, all testing must be unbiased, formal and consistent. Athletes will easily recognize flaws in the testing process and subsequently lose confidence in the results. You must be systematic and accurate, treating every athlete the same way, for the test to have any integrity. No athlete can be credited with a test result on a physical skill if she does not execute the test regimen perfectly. You must mandate good form and attention to the details of the test. The same is true of evaluation tools that are not quantitatively measured. A coach who wants to evaluate technical skills must use the same tool for all athletes playing the same position and score them fairly and consistently if they are to trust the conclusions reached.

Fourth, you must convey the feedback to the athletes professionally and, if possible, personally. No athlete wants to fail, and all are self-conscious to a certain extent when they don't perform to their expectations or the expectations of their coach. At the same time, all athletes have areas that they need to improve, and you must communicate those needs to the athlete, especially if she doesn't see or understand the need to make the improvement! Personal, private meetings with athletes are crucial to the exchange of this information. Factual results, comparative charts ranking the athlete, historical records of previous test results and even study of videotape of the athlete's performances can discretely communicate both the positive areas of improvement and the areas where progress needs to be made. If you have a large number of athletes, you can accomplish these individual meetings in occasional and subtle ways—by asking the athlete to stay for a few minutes in the office after a team meeting, by finding the athlete after practice or after a workout in the locker room, by going out to practice early and creating an opportunity to talk to the player individually or by calling the player into the office at random times just to talk. These in-person, one-on-one meetings are by far the best method to communicate to athletes the areas in which they need to improve.

Finally, you must apply the principles that you are asking of your players to the process of evaluating them. You must be knowledgeable about the technical and tactical skills of your sport so that you can accurately and consistently evaluate the skill that you see your players perform. You must understand the value and importance of the physical skills (perhaps even in your personal lifestyle and health habits!) to convey the importance of these skills to the game. You must exhibit outstanding communication skills to be effective in your teaching, and you must exhibit those same skills in your dealings with other staff members, especially when you are visible to the players, so that you can establish credibility with the players regarding communication.

Evaluating Skills

Clearly, players must know the technical skills demanded by their sport, and they must know how to apply those skills in tactical situations when they compete. You must remember, however, that basic physical skills contribute to the performance of the technical and tactical skills, and must be consciously incorporated into the athlete's training plan. In addition, an array of nonphysical skills such as mental capacity, communication skills and character training also overlay athletic performance and affect its development.

As you evaluate your athletes, one concept is crucial: Each athlete should focus on trying to improve her own previous performance, as opposed to comparing her performance with those of her teammates. Certainly, comparative data helps an athlete see where she ranks on the team and perhaps among other players in her position, and this data may motivate her or help her set goals. But all rankings place some athletes on the team below others, and the danger of focusing on this type of system is that athletes can easily become discouraged if they consistently rank in the bottom part of the team or skill group. Conversely, if the focus of the evaluation is for every player to improve, compared with herself at the last testing, then every player on the team can be successful every time tests are conducted. Whether you are looking at physical skills or nonphysical skills, encourage your athletes to achieve their own personal bests.

Evaluating Physical Skills

The essential physical skills for softball are strength, speed, agility, power and flexibility. The training and evaluation of those five physical skills is especially important in the off-season and preseason periods, when athletes are concentrating on overall improvement. In-season evaluation, however, is also important to ensure that any off-season gains, especially in strength, do not deteriorate because the players and coaches are devoting much of their time and attention to game-plan preparation and practice.

Testing should occur at least three times a year—once immediately before the softball season begins to gauge the athlete's readiness for the season, once after the season ends to measure the retention of physical skills during competition and once in the preseason to evaluate the athlete's progress and development in the off-season program. In addition, you will constantly be evaluating your athletes throughout the season to make slight adjustments, as you will learn more about in chapter 9.

Of course, training programs can positively affect several skills. For example, improvements in leg strength and flexibility will almost certainly improve speed. Furthermore, no specific workout program will ensure gains for every athlete in each of the five skill areas. Consequently, testing and measurement of gains in these areas is critical in showing you and the athlete where she is making gains and what you should emphasize in subsequent training programs.

Strength

Strength testing can be done safely and efficiently using multiple-rep projections of the athlete's maximum performance. The risk of injury for the athlete is minimal because she is working with a weight that is less than her maximum load. After a proper warm-up, the athlete should select a weight that she believes she can rep at least three times but no more than seven times. Using a chart of projected totals, the number of reps that she accomplishes will yield her max. This type of test is slightly less accurate than a one-rep max, in which the athlete continues to work with heavier weights until she finds the highest load that she can rep one time. But the one-rep test takes much longer to administer and is less safe because the athletes are working with peak loads. Furthermore, the accuracy of the test would be critical only if the athletes were competing with each other. Because the focus of the off-season training program is the development and improvement of each athlete, the multiple-rep projection is adequate for determining comparisons for each athlete with her own previous performances.

Core Strength

Like the proverbial chain that is only as strong as its weakest link, the core ultimately determines whether the athlete can put it all together and translate her strength, speed or agility into successful softball performance. The core refers to the midsection of the body—the abdominal muscles, the lower-back muscles and the muscles of the hip girdle—that connect lower-body strength and functions with upper-body strength and functions. Core strength, then, is essential for softball, but at the same time it is extremely difficult to isolate and test.

Softball coaches repeatedly emphasize the importance of keeping the legs bent and the center of gravity close to the ground for improved balance, leverage and transition from one direction to another. Without a strong core, the softball athlete will experience great difficulty in staying low and transitioning quickly. The core also must be strong for the softball athlete to be able to play with explosiveness—combining strength, power and speed into decisive and effective throws, swings, leads and fielding technique. Every physical training program for softball, therefore, must include exercises that strengthen and develop the core. This training program must go beyond sit-ups and crunches, which are important but not comprehensive enough to develop true core strength. Softball athletes must incorporate active exercises such as lunges, step-ups and jump squats to focus on development of the core.

As mentioned before, isolating core strength is difficult because it is involved in the performance of every physical skill. But any exercise that recruits one or more large-muscle areas and two or more primary joints (such as the bench press) can be used to test core strength (NSCA, *Essentials of Personal Training*). The ultimate evaluation of core strength, however, is the athlete's performance of softball skills in practice and on game day on the field.

Speed

Speed testing for softball typically focuses on the 20-yard dash—the distance between the bases and a distance that exceeds the ground that fielders cover when making most defensive plays. In some instances, longer sprints are required, such as when running down a long fly ball or running an extra-base hit. But these events do not define the speed needed to play the game. Most sprinting that a softball player performs in a game occurs in short bursts, so a test of the player's initial 10-yard speed from a standing start also correlates well with the type of speed needed to play the game. The 10- and 20-yard tests can be administered simultaneously, with a coach or electronic timer stationed at each of those distances to record times for both yardages on the same trial. You want the test situation to resemble the game situation as closely as possible, so, for example, you should test the players on the field in cleats rather than in shoes that would be appropriate for the basketball court.

Agility

Softball also requires the athlete to change direction quickly in short spaces and use quality footwork to get into proper position to field ground balls, make throws, block pitches, catch fly balls and make tags. So agility and footwork are physical skills that must be trained and measured. The most common agility test for softball is the pro shuttle, a 20-yard lateral shuttle run. In this test, the athlete starts on a designated line, runs 5 yards to her left or right, returns through her starting point to a spot 5 yards on the other side of the starting point and then moves back to finish at the point where she started (yardage run is 5, 10 and 5). This test measures the athlete's ability to plant and change directions and requires her to keep the core low, in the athletic body position frequently mentioned throughout the skills in this book. The time on the pro shuttle should be about two-tenths of a second less than the athlete's 40-yard dash time. If the margin is greater, the athlete should emphasize speed development in her program; if the margin is less, the athlete should emphasize agility drills in her training program.

Power

Power is the fourth primary skill required for softball. The emphasis here is on the lower-body explosiveness that helps the softball athlete transition into throws, explode off the mound, redirect body movements or jump to catch a throw. The two simplest and best tests for power are the standing long jump and the vertical jump. Administer both tests with the athlete in a stationary position so that the test measures pure explosiveness unassisted by a running start. Allow the athlete to take several trials at each event. Record her best effort as her score.

Flexibility

Flexibility is the most neglected physical skill but one of the most important. Increases in flexibility will help the athlete improve her performance in just about every other physical skill. Off-season programs should stress stretching, and you should encourage, or mandate, athletes to stretch for at least 15 minutes each day. In addition, the training program should include exercises that require the athlete to bend and move, such as lunges, step-ups and so on, so that the athlete is stretching and training the hip girdle and lower-back area as she works on strength and power. Flexibility is difficult to measure, but the classic sit-and-reach test provides a reasonable indication of the athlete's range and gives her a standard to improve on.

Evaluating Nonphysical Skills

Athletic performance is not purely physical. A number of other factors influence it. You must recognize and emphasize mental skills, communication skills and character skills to enable your athletes to reach peak athletic performance.

Despite the importance of the physical, mental, communication and character skills, however, the emphasis in this book is on the coaching of essential technical and tactical skills. For an in-depth discussion of how to teach and develop both physical and nonphysical skills, refer to chapters 9 through 12 in Rainer Martens' *Successful Coaching, Third Edition*.

Mental Skills

Softball is a complex game because of the large number of players on the field at one time, the vast number of defensive responses, and the diversity of athletic types and abilities that make up a team. In addition, the long interval between plays can cause an athlete to lose focus or talk herself into tension and stress. Consequently, softball requires excellent mental skills.

The successful softball player must have the mental ability to sort out and isolate the cues that allow her to execute the skills of the game. Corner players must focus on the batter's hands and react in unison. Middle infielders do the same while also focusing on the runners and subtle cues from the coach and the hitter so that they can anticipate the play and know how to react. Pitchers must focus on the target so that they can throw the ball effectively. Outfielders must focus on the swing. Catchers must focus on catching the pitch and resisting the temptation to peek at the runners after the pitch is on the way. And hitters must focus entirely on the ball and ignore the pitcher and defense so that they can execute their swing successfully. The performance of these skills takes study, discipline, focus and belief that the system of cues will produce the desired results. The term mental toughness might be the best and simplest way to describe the concentration and determination required to perform these skills.

Communication Skills

Softball also requires communication skills at several levels—among the players on the field and between the coaches and players in classrooms, in practices and in the dugout during games—to get the desired skills accomplished. Softball teams use numerous and specific forms of communication to get all players on the same page on every play. Coaches send plays on to the field using hand signals or oral signals; catchers give signals to the pitcher or to the defense for pickoffs; infielders signal to the outfield that the pitch is being thrown; coaches communicate to runners during a play; and fielders communicate the direction of throws and location of runners. You have to convey adjustments to the game plan and strategy between innings. All these communication skills are essential to softball, and you must spend considerable time coordinating your system of communication.

Character Skills

Finally, character skills help shape the performance of the team. Although the game has many variables, officials regulate it so that it is fair and as safe as possible within the rules. Softball athletes must play hard and aggressively, but they also must stop at the call of the umpire. Failure to follow the rules results in outs or runs scored, and both outcomes clearly affect the team's performance. Softball players also must avoid becoming distracted by any talking from the other team or from the stands that might occur between plays. In all these cases, the team that has the most character among its players will have the best chance for success.

Evaluation Tools

Softball coaches are beginning to use videotape of practices and games to evaluate athletes' performance of basic technical and tactical skills. Taping is useful because so many players are participating at one time and watching each of them on every play is difficult, if not impossible. The problem is compounded, especially on game days, because the players are a considerable distance away and you cannot see from your position precisely what is happening in the outfield and the infield at the same time. Videotape allows you to review reps in practice or plays in a game repeatedly, enabling you to evaluate each player on each play. The tape also becomes an excellent teaching tool in individual, group or team meetings because the players can see themselves perform and listen to your evaluation of their performance.

You can use many different systems to evaluate what you see on tape. The most common system isn't really a system at all—it is the subjective impression that you get when you watch the tape, without taking notes or systematically evaluating every player on every play. Because of limitations of time and staff, many coaches use the tape in this manner, previewing the tape, gathering impressions and then sharing those impressions with the player or players as they watch the tape together later.

Other coaches systematically grade the tape, evaluating the athlete's performance on every play as to whether she executed the correct reaction, technique and tactical decision. The grading process can be simple. For example, you can simply give the athlete a plus or a minus on each play and score the total number of plusses versus the total number of minuses for the game. Alternatively, you can score the athlete on each aspect of the play, giving her a grade for her reaction, a grade for her technique and a grade for her tactical decision making.

Regardless of the level of sophistication or detail of the grading instrument, most coaches use a grading system of some kind for evaluating game tape. Most grading systems are based on a play-by-play (or rep-by-rep in practices) analysis of performance. Rarely does a coach systematically evaluate the technical and tactical skills required for softball on a skill-by-skill basis.

Furthermore, when coaches evaluate a skill, they generally evaluate only the result (did the outfielder catch the ball or not?), not the key elements that determine the player's ability to catch the ball (tracking the ball, glove position and so on).

Figure 2.1, *a* and *b* are examples of an evaluation tool that allows you to isolate technical and tactical skills. By breaking down the whole skill into its component parts, this tool enables a more objective assessment of an athlete's performance in a skill than can be produced by statistics. By using these figures and the technical and tactical skills described in parts II and III as a guide, you can create an evaluation tool for each of the technical and tactical skills that you want to evaluate during your season. In figure 2.1*a*, using the technical skill of throwing as an example, we have broken down the skill by pulling out each of the key points from the skills found in chapters 3 through 5 so that you can rate your players' execution of the skill in specific targeted areas.

As you may already know, evaluating tactical skills is more difficult than evaluating technical skills because many outside influences factor into how and when the skill comes into play. But as a coach, you can evaluate your players' execution of tactical skills using a format similar to the one that you used for assessing technical skills. You will need to do the legwork of breaking down the skill into targeted areas. In figure 2.1*b* we have used a generic format to show you how you can break tactical skills down using the skills found in chapters 6 through 8 as a guideline.

Figure 2.1a Throwing Technical Skill Evaluation

Key focal points	Weak 1	2	3	4	Strong 5	Notes
Grip	1	2	3	4	5	
Line of force	1	2	3	4	5	
Initial shoulder and hip rotation	1	2	3	4	5	
Weight transfer	1	2	3	4	5	
Arm action	1	2	3	4	5	
Wrist snap	1	2	3	4	5	
Follow-through	1	2	3	4	5	

From ASEP, 2009, *Coaching softball technical and tactical skills* (Champaign, IL: Human Kinetics).

Figure 2.1b Stealing a Base Tactical Skill Evaluation

Player's ability	Weak 1	2	3	4	Strong 5	Notes
Reads the situation	1	2	3	4	5	
Understands rules and uses them appropriately	1	2	3	4	5	
Understands physical playing conditions and reacts appropriately	1	2	3	4	5	
Recognizes the skill level of opponents and reacts appropriately	1	2	3	4	5	
Recognizes own skill level and reacts appropriately	1	2	3	4	5	
Makes appropriate decisions based on the game situation	1	2	3	4	5	

From ASEP, 2009, *Coaching softball technical and tactical skills* (Champaign, IL: Human Kinetics).

This evaluation tool, and the process of scoring that it advocates, may help you avoid the common pitfall of becoming preoccupied with the result of the skill and coaching and evaluating only the final outcome. This tool will help you pinpoint where errors are occurring and enable you to focus on correcting those errors with your athletes.

The tool is admittedly somewhat subjective because it asks the evaluator to rate on a scale of 1 to 5 how well the athlete executes the basic elements of each technical or tactical skill. Ratings would simply be an opinion based on observation. But you can add some statistical weight to the process by scoring the player on each play in which the skill came into use. For example, during a game, an infielder might have six opportunities to field a ground ball. You could then score the player on each of those six opportunities and calculate an average score. Most coaches would simply grade the infielder on whether or not she fielded the ball successfully, but this tool allows you to organize your evaluation of the elements of fielding. You can pinpoint where the player is making mistakes by breaking down the skill and analyzing the component parts.

Likewise, if a catcher who handles every pitch has five opportunities to block a pitch in the dirt, you could use the evaluation tool to grade each of those five plays on the tactical skill of recognition, speed of movement, correct positioning and keeping the ball in front. This score would give both you and the catcher an excellent evaluation of her ability to perform this tactical skill, regardless of whether she successfully blocked the ball.

You must go beyond the result and focus your teaching on the cues and knowledge needed to execute a specific skill, giving the athlete an evaluation that alerts her to the key elements of the skills that need improvement. An important corollary to this teaching and evaluation strategy is that even when the result is positive, the evaluation of the athlete's technique might be substantially critical.

For example, if the center fielder is working in a practice session on catching the fly ball with two hands instead of one, you need to reinforce the key point of using both hands, whether or not she catches the ball. If the fielder drops the ball but uses both hands, you must be positive about her effort to use that technique and avoid making comments about her dropping the ball. Likewise, if the fielder catches the ball but uses one hand, you need to tell her that she is using an unacceptable technique. You cannot give the fielder mixed messages; you must focus on the process of catching with two hands, not the result, if you truly want the fielder to catch the ball with two hands.

The importance, and the challenge, of learning to focus on the skills of the game is graphically illustrated in many softball games. For example, assume that your team is playing a home game at the beginning of the season. In the top of the first inning your pitcher's adrenaline is pumping and she is a bit nervous. The first four pitches are too high, so the first batter walks. The next batter steps in, and the first two pitches are also high. By now, the pitcher's teammates and more than a few parents are shouting advice: "Don't walk her!" or "Get the ball down!" The pitcher usually knows that she needs to throw strikes, and it is not her intention to walk the hitter! The comments that she hears are not helpful and only add to her anxiety. What the pitcher needs is some advice from the coach on how to get the ball down—some instruction and refocusing on the key points of the technical skill of pitching a softball.

The sample evaluation tool shown in figure 2.1, *a* and *b* constitutes a simple way to use the details of each technical and tactical skill. It provides an outline for both the player and you to review and a mechanism for understanding the areas in which improvement is needed. The tool also can be used as a summary exercise. After a game, after a week of practice or after a preseason or spring practice segment, the athlete can score herself on all her essential technical and tactical skills, including all the cues and focal points, and on as many of the corollary skills as desired. You can also score the athlete and then compare the two score sheets. The ensuing discussion will provide both the player and you with a direction for future practices and drills, and help you decide where the immediate focus of attention needs to be for the athlete to improve her performance. You can repeat this process later, so that the athlete can look for improvement in the areas in which she has been concentrating her workouts.

As the process unfolds, a better consensus between the athlete's score sheet and your score sheet should occur.

You must display the identical mental skills that you ask your athletes to demonstrate—skills such as emotional control, self-confidence and motivation to achieve—because the players will mirror your mental outlook. Likewise, players will model your character, in terms of your trustworthiness, fairness and ability to earn respect. You are a role model, whether you want to be or not, and athletes will develop the proper mental and character skills only if you display those skills.

You must evaluate athletes in many areas and in many ways. This process of teaching, evaluating and motivating the athlete to improve her performance defines the job of the coach: to take the athlete somewhere that she could not get to by herself. Without you, the athlete would not have a clear direction of the steps that she needs to take, or how she should proceed, to become a better player. You provide the expertise, guidance and incentive for the athlete to make progress.

One final rule caps the discussion of evaluating athletes. Athletes in every sport want to know how much you care before they care how much you know. You need to keep in mind that at times you must suspend the process of teaching and evaluating to deal with the athlete as a person. You must spend time with your athletes discussing topics other than softball and their performance. You must show each athlete that you have an interest and a concern for her as a person, that you are willing to listen to her issues and that you are willing to assist her if doing so is legal and she wishes to be helped. Events in the athlete's personal life can overshadow her athletic quests, and you must be sensitive to that reality.

Another reality is that athletes will play their best and their hardest for the coach who cares. Their skills will improve, and their performance will improve, because they want to reward the coach's caring attitude for them with inspired performance. They will finish their athletic careers for that coach having learned a lifelong lesson that care and concern are as important as any skill in the game of softball.

PART II

Teaching Technical Skills

Now that you know how to teach and evaluate sport skills, you are ready to dive into the specific skills necessary for success in softball. This part focuses on the basic and intermediate skills necessary for your team's success, including offensive technical skills related to hitting, bunting, stealing and sliding and defensive technical skills related to throwing, catching and the basics for various positions and pitching variations.

Chapters 3 and 4 present the material in a way that is clear and easy to understand so that you can immediately incorporate the information into your practices. Whether you are a seasoned veteran or a new coach, you will find the presentation of skills in this part helpful as you work with your athletes.

For each skill we first present what we call the "Key Points" for the particular skill. These points highlight the most important aspects of the skill, providing you and your players with a roadmap to proper execution of the skill. The remainder of the presentation of the skill is a detailed explanation of these essential components, including instructional photos and diagrams to guide you along the way.

At the end of each skill presentation we include a table to help you detect common errors and correct them in your athletes. To close each skill presentation, we include a useful "At a Glance" element to guide you to other tools in the book that will help you teach your athletes this particular skill—whether it is another technical skill that they need to be able to perform, a tactical skill that uses this technical skill or a practice plan or drill that helps you teach the skill.

chapter 3

Offensive Technical Skills

This chapter will cover the offensive technical skills that you and your players must know in order to be successful. In this chapter you will find:

Hitting

KEY POINTS

The most important components of hitting are

○ proper grip and stance,

○ stride,

○ rotating into the swing, and

○ controlling the bat.

Hitting is arguably the most challenging and exciting skill in the sport of softball. Physically it involves quickness, strength and hand–eye coordination. Hitting requires some amount of natural ability, but everyone can improve with practice. The mechanics of hitting occur in such close timing that they all appear to happen at once; however, the better the timing of the sequence is, the better the result is. The proper sequence of motion creates efficient strength and quickness without extra motion and tension. The more the body moves unnecessarily, the greater the eye movement is and the greater the chance is to swing and miss.

PROPER GRIP AND STANCE

When preparing to hit, the batter grips the bat with her fingers, not deep in the palm. The second line of the knuckles for both hands is lined up (see figure 3.1). With this grip, the hands and wrists can snap the bat forward with sufficient bat speed during contact. The hands are loose and hold the bat over the back shoulder at about ear level (see figure 3.2).

In addition, the head and eyes should be as level as possible. The athlete should be sure that she can see the ball with both eyes. The challenge in seeing the ball is to recognize the pitch as a ball or strike as the ball approaches and as the body begins the hitting motion. This is the do-or-don't part of the sequence. To see the ball well, the hitter must focus on the release point with both eyes. To accomplish this, the hitter may have to rotate the head slightly more than she realizes to allow the back eye a full view of the release point. The eyes can be trained to follow the ball and see small but significant changes in pitches. But to begin, the hitter should just focus on the release point and follow the ball as long as possible to the contact point.

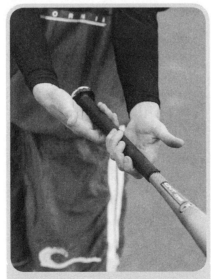

Figure 3.1 Proper grip for hitting.

Figure 3.2 Bat position when preparing to hit.

When hitting, comfort and the ability to move are key, so the athlete's stance is an important aspect of this skill. In the batter's box, the feet should be shoulder-width or slightly wider apart. The weight is on the balls of the feet, and the knees are slightly bent and positioned inside the feet for good balance. The feet should be positioned so that they are parallel with each other (see figure 3.3a) or slightly pigeon toed (see figure 3.3b). For most hitters, standing even with home plate in the batter's box is sufficient to hit most pitches. The hitter wants to be just close enough to the plate to hit the outside pitch. A quick test is to have the hitter reach out with the bat, bend at the waist and tap the outside edge of the plate. If the hitter can reach it, as she straightens up you will notice that the sweet spot of the bat is still over the outside corner (see figure 3.4).

a   b

Figure 3.3 Foot positioning for hitting: (*a*) parallel and (*b*) pigeon toed.

Figure 3.4 Distance from the plate for proper plate coverage.

(continued)

At some point before the initial stride into the swing, discussed in the next section, the weight should be distributed with approximately 75 percent of the body weight on the back foot and 25 percent on the front foot. During the swing, the weight shifts forward. The hitter can either begin with the weight back or shift it back as the pitcher begins her motion. Either way, the hitter needs to be back before going forward.

STRIDE

The stride is a linear shift that happens before rotation. It is a controlled forward move, in the direction of the pitcher, that helps the hitter transfer her weight during the swing, letting her drive the ball farther. A good stride is one that is long enough to balance the force of the swing and still allows weight transfer and proper rotation.

When striding, the shoulders should be level and knees evenly bent. The upper body and hips are as quiet as possible until the rotation and actual swing phase. The stride foot, which is the front foot (left foot for right-handed batters and right foot for left-handed batters) touches the ground with a toe touch first (see figure 3.5a), followed by a heel plant (see figure 3.5b), ensuring that the foot and knee remain in a closed position. On the heel plant the weight should be shifted back to center (the transfer of weight will continue forward as the body finishes the swing, as discussed in the next section, "Rotating Into the Swing"). If the stride is too long, the athlete will be unable to transfer her weight correctly, which will end up slowing down the swing. Note that a no-stride method is acceptable, although using this technique makes the transfer of weight more difficult.

a   b

Figure 3.5   **Stride: (a) toe touch and (b) heel plant.**

ROTATING INTO THE SWING

After the stride-foot heel plant, as discussed in the previous section, the hands start forward, immediately followed by the rotation of the back hip so that the chest is facing the contact point (see figure 3.6). These movements almost appear to occur together, but they're independent of each other. The body continues to shift the weight forward onto the ball or toe of the back foot, and the heel lifts. The foot may even come off the ground.

The extent of rotation on contact differs depending on the type of pitch. For example, if the pitch is an inside pitch, the body rotates farther than it would for an outside pitch. The rotation is complete when the arms wrap around the body after reaching full extension forward (see figure 3.7)

Figure 3.6 Rotation into the swing.

Figure 3.7 Completing the rotation.

CONTROLLING THE BAT

The hands move on a short track from their initial starting position over the back shoulder, as shown previously in figure 3.5*a*, to the center of the body, as shown previously in figure 3.5*b*. The distance the hands are held from the body stays the same whether the pitch is inside or outside; only the contact point and amount of rotation must be adjusted when preparing to swing. The barrel of the bat is held above the hands and tipped slightly back (see figure 3.8*a*). If the bat is held too flat, it will feel heavy, causing the wrists and hands to tighten the grip, creating a slow snap of the bat. Athletes should be taught to keep the barrel of the bat above the hands for as long as they can before contact. The back elbow then moves in toward the back hip as the hands move to the center of the body (see figure 3.8*b*). When the hands

(continued)

reach the center of the body, the wrist snaps, throwing the bat head forward, putting it on a level plane with the ball. Timing varies with the location of the pitch and its speed, but proper timing should have the batter in midsnap at contact (see figure 3.8c). Releasing or snapping the wrists too early (back by the shoulder) will result in a long, loopy swing and a loss of power and control.

On contact, the elbows are bent, the top hand (this would be the right hand if the athlete is right-handed) should be in a palm-up position and the bottom hand should be in a palm-down position. After contact, the elbows extend (see figure 3.8d), creating power and keeping the bat on the path of the ball as long as possible so that the hitter has a greater chance of making contact.

Once the hitter has extended the arms fully after contact, the swing will continue into the follow-through with the wrists beginning to roll and the bat wrapping around the back of the hitter. Rolling the wrists too early creates a very weak hand position on contact and should only be done after full extension of the arms. When the bat wraps around the hitter on the follow-through, some hitters prefer to release the top hand from the bat, while others keep both hands gripping the bat. Either method is correct, but if the hitter releases the top hand, it shouldn't be done until the wrists begin to roll in the follow-through. If the hitter releases the top hand any sooner than that, it becomes too easy for the hitter to release the bat during contact. Releasing the hand is comfortable for some hitters and helps them feel as if they can lengthen through the ball, creating more power. Again, the key is to not release the hand until after contact and full extension.

a   b

Figure 3.8 **Upper-body movement on the swing.**

c   d

Figure 3.8 *(continued)*

Common Errors

Following are several common errors that you might run into when teaching your athletes how to hit.

Error	Error Correction
The grip is too tight, causing weak contact with the ball.	Teach athletes to place the bat in the fingers, not the palm. Also, ensure that players choose a bat of appropriate weight; if the bat is too heavy, players will grip it too tightly to control it.
The hitter rotates during the stride phase, causing her to pull off the ball.	Teach athletes to keep the knees, hips and shoulders linear until the heel plant of the stride foot.
The hitter swings under the ball.	Be sure that the bat is not too heavy to control. Athletes should focus on getting the bat on an even plane with the ball and moving through the ball after contact.
The hitter pops up.	Pop-ups typically occur when the athlete does not transfer the weight during the swing and sits back on the leg during rotation. Teach players to transfer the weight through the swing with a balanced stance and level shoulders and hips.

KEY POINTS

The most important components of the sacrifice bunt are

o proper stance,

o bat position and angle,

o hand position on the bat, and

o contacting the ball.

The main purpose of the sacrifice bunt is to advance a runner on base into a scoring position by sacrificing an out by the batter. But advancing runners isn't the only purpose of the sacrifice bunt. It can also be used in other offensive strategies because a team with an effective short game puts pressure on the defense and increases the team's chances to score. Outstanding hitters might overlook the need to learn how to bunt, but teams that win championships move hitters into scoring position successfully. A great hitter with a batting average of .400 is less likely to advance a runner than a great bunter, who will advance a runner with a bunt approximately 80 percent of the time.

PROPER STANCE

The batter initially positions in the stance learned previously in "Hitting" on page 22. The feet are shoulder-width or slightly wider apart, the weight is on the balls of the feet and the knees are slightly bent and positioned inside the feet for good balance. The feet should be positioned so that they are parallel with each other or slightly pigeon toed. When preparing to sacrifice bunt, a bunter can take either of two positions in the box, depending on her comfort and more important on the chances for success. The first position, called tandem, is simply a pivot of the feet so that they are front and back in the box, not square to the pitcher (see figure 3.9*a*). The second is a movement of the feet to a side-to-side position (see figure 3.9*b*). In both cases, the knees are flexed, moving the bunter's eyes lower and closer to the strike zone,

a   b

Figure 3.9 Stances for the sacrifice bunt: (a) tandem and (b) side to side.

and the upper body leans forward. The batter must learn to hold the initial hitting stance as long as possible. Moving into the sacrifice bunt stance early will tip off the defense and give them time to set up for the bunt. On the other hand, the batter should not be too late with the move because she needs to be set by the time she needs to contact the ball.

In addition, note that the farther up in the box the bunter moves, the better the angle is to keep the ball fair. The batter has a lot more room for error if she is positioned near the front of the box.

BAT POSITION AND ANGLE

Initially, the batter should always hold the bat out in front of the body and at the top of the strike zone. The bat head should always be pointing forward. A slight angle of the bat (bat head above the hands) helps the bunter keep from dropping the bat head and popping the ball up (see figure 3.10). When preparing to contact the ball, the bunter should extend the hands forward to begin, which will help her see the ball hit the bat (see figure 3.11).

Figure 3.10 Initial bat position for a sacrifice bunt.

Figure 3.11 Holding the bat out from the body when contacting the ball.

HAND POSITION ON THE BAT

Hand position on the bat for the sacrifice bunt is extremely important because it determines the bunter's control of the bat. The bat should be shortened by choking up with one hand. The bottom hand is on the knob of the bat, and the top hand is halfway up the bat (see figure 3.12a). Alternatively, the player can move both hands up the bat (see figure 3.12b). The bunter will have much more control of the bat if the hands are split a few inches because both hands are used equally in pushing the ball. In addition, the fingers of the top hand should be positioned to the sides and back of the bat, not on the front, so that the ball doesn't hit them.

(continued)

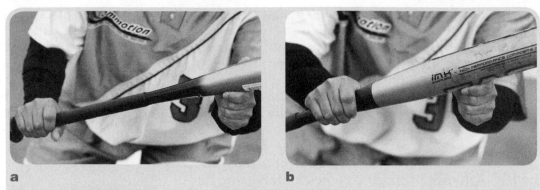

Figure 3.12 Choking up on the bat for the sacrifice bunt: (*a*) one hand or (*b*) two hands.

CONTACTING THE BALL

Contact with the ball for a bunter is more of a "catch and drop" action than it is a gentle tap, which many assume. The bunter should get the bat on plane with the ball as early as possible. When the ball makes contact with the bat, the bunter gives slightly with both hands to cushion the speed of the ball. To increase the chances that the bunt will be fair, the bunter should give with the ball on contact so that the bat moves to square (see figure 3.13*a*) and does not angle back (see figure 3.13*b*).

Figure 3.13 Moving the bat on contact: (*a*) correct and (*b*) incorrect.

Another way to take some power away from the ball coming off the bat is to use the end of the bat more than the sweet spot because the end of the bat is less responsive to the ball. The sweet spot is the area in the middle of the barrel of the bat that has the most rebound. When a ball hits the sweet spot of the bat it will bounce farther and faster than it would if it hits the end of the bat. The bunter should make every effort to make contact with a pitched ball on a bunt. But to keep the ball from going too far into the infield, the bunter should make contact toward the end of the bat. Achieving this goal comes largely from hand–eye coordination, but choking up on the bat can help the batter feel the location better. As a coach, you can place tape on the end of the bat during batting practice to help the bunter learn where this area is.

At a Glance

The following parts of the text offer additional information on the sacrifice bunt.

Common Errors

Following are several common errors that you might run into when teaching your athletes how to sacrifice bunt.

Error	Error Correction
The bunt goes foul.	Check the bat head on setup. It should be slightly forward. If only the top hand gives, the bat head will drop back behind the hands and the player is likely to bunt the ball foul.
The bunter often misses the ball.	The initial setup is usually the key. First, be sure that the bunter is bent down closer to the strike zone. To see the ball well, the eyes need to be right over the top of the bat and the bat should be extended forward out in front of the body.
The bunt is too hard.	A hard bunt usually occurs because the bat is still moving forward on contact or the bunter is punching at the ball instead of using a catch-and-drop action. Work with the athlete so that she gets the bat forward and still, on plane, and then gives slightly with both hands.

Slap Hit and Hard Bunt

KEY POINTS

The most important components of the slap hit and hard bunt are

o proper stance,

o hand position on the bat, and

o contacting the ball.

The slap hit and hard bunt are deceptive hits that are hit slightly harder than a bunt. The batter pushes or punches the ball just past the defensive players who are coming in to field what they think is going to be a bunt. Both hits are effective against a team that is overaggressive or that charges out of control to field bunts. Knowing that, when using either the slap hit or hard bunt, the batter should try to look as if she is going to bunt for as long as possible, drawing the defense as close as she can.

PROPER STANCE

Because the hitter is trying to be deceptive and fool the defense into thinking that she is bunting, the stance for the slap hit or hard bunt needs to be identical to that of the sacrifice bunt. Again, the bunter should be positioned toward the front of the batter's box. A bunter can take two common positions in the box—a simple pivot of the feet so that they are tandem or a movement of the feet to a side-by-side position, as shown in figure 3.9 on page 28. For the slap hit, the shoulders should be square to the pitcher. No rotation is necessary, so they should stay that way throughout the skill. This isn't a powerful hit; the batter should use just enough force so that the ball is too quick for the defense.

HAND POSITION ON THE BAT

Hand position on the bat should be the same as the initial setup for the sacrifice bunt. For the hard bunt, the batter should shorten up the bat by choking up with one hand. The bottom hand is on the knob of the bat, and the top hand is halfway up the bat. For the slap hit, the batter should shorten up by choking up with two hands so that both hands move up the bat (see figure 3.12 on page 30). The bunter will have much more control of the bat if the hands are split a few inches because both hands are used equally in pushing the ball. The motion on contact, however, depends on the location of the hands on the bat, as discussed in the next section.

CONTACTING THE BALL

For the hard bunt, the batter chokes up on the bat with one hand, before the pitcher releases the ball, and sets the angle of the bat in the direction that she wants the ball to go. For example, if the bat had eyes on it, the eyes would be looking in the desired direction. Anticipating contact, the hitter takes a slight step forward, shifting her weight forward (see figure 3.14*a*) and extending her arms through the ball (see figure 3.14*b*). This action is a smooth glide and extension through contact, not a jerky punch. The bunter wants to contact the ball during the move, not after reaching full extension. The bunter's grip on the bat becomes firm on contact, creating a quick, solid punch when meeting the ball.

Figure 3.14 **Contacting the ball when choking up with one hand.**

For the slap hit, the bunter chokes up on the bat with two hands. The top-hand wrist needs to be more active than the bottom. The bunter sets up as if she will bunt, but as the ball approaches, she pulls the bat head back very slightly with the top hand. The shoulders stay square to the pitcher (see figure 3.15a). The hands are firm on contact using a tight palm-up, palm-down grip. The wrist of the top hand snaps and punches the ball at contact as if hitting it with a hammer (see figure 3.15b). Many hitters shift their weight slightly forward during contact to create a little more power, but a hitter can produce sufficient power by using just the hands. Teach hitters that the smaller the move is, the more control they have in directing the ball. The key to controlling the direction of the ball is controlling the wrist snap. The bat head should snap to the angle where the hitter wants the ball to go and not move beyond.

Figure 3.15 **Contacting the ball when choking up on the bat with two hands.**

(continued)

In addition, athletes may use different methods to direct the ball to the right side or the left. For example, they may choose to hard bunt to one side but slap to the other. The key is fooling the defense and contacting the ball correctly.

At a Glance

The following parts of the text offer additional information on the slap hit and hard bunt.

Common Errors

Following are several common errors that you might run into when teaching your athletes how to slap hit and hard bunt.

Error	Error Correction
There is no force behind the ball.	Most likely the snap or push was too early. Be sure that the timing has the bat still moving on contact.
The ball goes right to a fielder.	The bat needs to be angled at the alleys on contact.
The bunter misses the ball.	Too much movement is occurring. Work with the athlete to keep the eyes steady with a small move of the hands.
The bunter pops up.	Check to make sure that the player starts the bat at the top of the strike zone and that hand position on contact is palm up, palm down.

A correctly executed squeeze bunt almost guarantees that a runner on third will score. This offensive tactic is also called a suicide squeeze because it is an all-out gamble by the offense, risking the runner at third. The squeeze bunt is different from the sacrifice bunt in timing and purpose, although the technique is the same. In a squeeze bunt the hitter squares to bunt later than she does for a sacrifice to add an element of surprise. Meanwhile, the runner on third leaves the base in an all-out sprint home with no hesitation, timed with the pitcher's release of the ball. The bunter's role here is to bunt any ball, whether a strike or a ball. If the hitter misses the ball or doesn't at least foul it off, the runner will be caught far off base and will most likely be tagged out. If the ball is bunted fair, however, the runner generally beats the toss home and scores. If the pitch is difficult to bunt fair, the hitter should at least foul the ball off to protect the runner from being caught and thrown out.

KEY POINTS

The most important components of the squeeze bunt are

○ proper stance,
○ timing of the stance,
○ location in the box, and
○ angle of the bat.

A variation of the suicide squeeze is the safety squeeze. The difference between them is the timing of the runner's commitment to running home. On a suicide squeeze the runner leaves on the pitched ball, whereas on a safety squeeze the runner waits until the fielder picks up the ball to throw to first and then runs home. The safety squeeze is a great tool if the fielders don't throw well or if you are not sure about your team's ability to bunt. With either type of squeeze, suicide or safety, the element of surprise puts pressure on the defense, creating a high-percentage scoring attack. If the opposing pitcher is difficult to hit, a bunt might help you manufacture a run. If a pitcher is difficult to hit, however, she may be difficult to bunt as well. As a coach, you will have to choose the play that you think has the highest percentage of success.

PROPER STANCE

The batter will initially position in the stance learned previously in "Hitting" on page 22. The feet are shoulder-width or slightly wider apart, the weight is on the balls of the feet and the knees are slightly bent and positioned inside the feet for good balance. The feet should be positioned so that they are parallel with each other or slightly pigeon toed. When preparing to squeeze bunt, a bunter can take two positions in the box, depending on her comfort and more important on the chances for success. The first position, called tandem, is simply a pivot of the feet so that they are front and back in the box, not square to the pitcher. The second is a movement of the feet to a side-to-side position (see figure 3.9b on page 28). In both cases, the knees are flexed, moving the bunter's eyes lower and closer to the strike zone, and the upper body leans forward.

TIMING OF THE STANCE

The bunter needs to wait until the last minute so that she can square around and use her preferred bunting style. Because the purpose is to surprise the defense, most successful squeeze bunters wait until the ball has left the pitcher's hand. If the opposing pitcher throws extremely hard, the hitter has less time to be set and not moving. Therefore,

(continued)

she needs to start squaring up as the pitcher's arm is moving down toward the release. If the pitcher throws more slowly, the bunter can wait until the ball is much closer. The key is to be set and not moving the bat forward as close to the actual contact time as possible.

LOCATION IN THE BOX

Because the ball must be bunted fair, the bunter should move up in the box as shown in figure 3.9 on page 28 of "Sacrifice Bunt." But if moving up early alerts the defense, the bunter should stay in a position in the box that she typically hits from and make an effort to shift her weight and the bat forward when she squares around to get the best angle to bunt fair.

CONTACTING THE BALL

Because a pop-up would be disastrous, the bunter may choose to angle the bat head slightly higher and more forward more than she does on a sacrifice bunt to help her put a downward angle on the ball. But if altering the bat angle causes the bunter to move the bat too much on contact, thus making it difficult to bunt the ball fair, the angle is pointless. A bunter may choose to adjust the angle if it helps, but many players don't need to change anything from their sacrifice bunt technique with the exception of timing.

Common Errors

Following are several common errors that you might run into when teaching your athletes how to squeeze bunt.

Error	Error Correction
The bunt is too hard.	A hard bunt usually occurs because the bat is still moving forward and not stationary before contact.
The bunter misses the ball on the bunt.	Quick movement can prevent the player from getting to the proper bunting position. Be sure that the bat is at the top of the strike zone and out in front where the hitter can see the ball make contact with the bat.
The bunter cues the defense.	Because this is a possible hitting situation, the hitter should keep the corners back from the plate by going through the same routine that she would use before swinging away. The hitter should call no attention to the play.

A hitter executes a running slap by running forward before contacting the ball. The hitter can be either right-handed or left-handed, but this technique is done exclusively from the left side of the batter's box. The running slap adds pressure to the defense because the batter essentially has a running start. The defense will need to be perfect in their execution and extremely quick to get the batter out.

Because the running slap is a speed-based skill, only athletes who have an average speed from home to first under 3.0 seconds should learn it (timing is measured from contact of the ball with the bat to contact at first base). A good time is around 2.8, but if you have a slapper who approaches 2.6 or lower, you have something special. A player with this kind of speed will be extremely hard for the defense to get out. Having a strong running slapper or two on your team can put a lot of pressure on any defense. The best candidates are athletes who may not be your best hitters but have this kind of speed. After they have mastered the running slap, they can add other skills such as bunting, hard bunts and even swinging away.

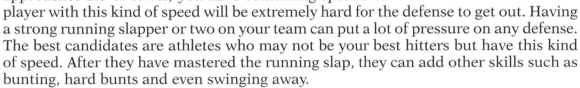

KEY POINTS

The most important components of the running slap are

- proper footwork,
- hip and shoulder rotation,
- contacting the ball, and
- slapper options.

PROPER FOOTWORK

A slap hitter needs to set up in the box to allow for a comfortable first step forward. By positioning herself so that it looks as if she is going to swing away, she can deceive the defense (see figure 3.16). Some slap hitters, however, like to position farther back in the box or farther away from the plate. The key is to set up so that the stride forward lands as close to the front corner of the batter's box as possible without stepping out.

While learning the footwork for the running slap, timing will be difficult at first, but it will become easier with practice. The first key to timing the steps is to be sure to start soon enough to enable the left foot to be planted at the front of the box before contact is made. If the foot is still in the process of stepping forward, the slapper isn't as stable and able to make last-second adjustments with the body. The second key to timing is to be sure the slapper doesn't start too soon and have to stop momentum once the left foot has been planted. Correct timing for the running slap means players will have the left foot planted and the body still moving smoothly forward on contact.

Figure 3.16 Positioning in the batter's box for a slap hit.

(continued)

a   b

Figure 3.17   Initial footwork for a slap hit.

Figure 3.18   Crossover step for the running slap.

To begin the running slap, the slapper first slides the front foot back while opening the toe toward the pitcher (see figure 3.17a) or simply shifts the weight completely to the front foot while opening the toe (see figure 3.17b). The next step is typically a crossover step so that the left foot lands as close to the front inside corner of the box as possible (see figure 3.18). The upper body stays slightly forward of the hips as the weight shifts during the crossover step and then moves forward into the contact phase. If the shoulders are too far back, the slapper will probably not be able to hit the top of the ball and drive it into the ground (see the next section, "Hip and Shoulder Rotation," for more information).

HIP AND SHOULDER ROTATION

Figure 3.19 Hip and shoulder rotation for the slap hit.

As the slap hitter moves forward to make contact during the crossover step, the hips rotate open toward the pitcher, allowing the slap hitter to move forward easily (see figure 3.19). The shoulders need to stay closed or square to the plate, meaning that the front shoulder points toward the pitcher, so that the slapper can still reach an outside pitch. This action will feel slightly unnatural because the hips are open, but when players feel the correct motion they can easily master it. Because the motion is linear and not rotational, the upper torso doesn't need to turn to hit the pitch unless it is a good inside pitch. The shoulders then rotate just enough to allow the hands to get inside the ball.

CONTACTING THE BALL

The swing and contact for the running slap is different from a full swing in several ways. The most significant is that any power (which should be minimal) comes from the forward movement of the body and a quick, slight flick of the wrists on contact. To do this successfully, the player moves the hands forward to make contact by getting inside the ball so that the meat of the bat can contact the ball. The hitter must keep the hands up while moving forward so that she can contact the top of the ball and hit it into the ground. The swing then continues out, or forward, and doesn't pull or rotate around the body (see figure 3.20, a–c).

(continued)

Figure 3.20 **Contacting the ball for a slap hit.**

It's easy for an inexperienced slapper to try to put more punch behind her swing. That often causes her to over rotate the torso and lose ability to hit the ball where she desires. Once the player's technique is perfected, the ability to hit the ball effectively and with the correct power will be a result of timing, forward momentum and wrist snap.

Common Errors

Following are several common errors that you might run into when teaching your athletes the running slap.

Error	Error Correction
Balance is too upright or back on contact.	Have the slapper get into the position that she should be in on contact. The left foot should be forward and the player should lean slightly forward. Using either a toss or a tee, have the slapper hit the ball without moving. Balance should remain constant. After the player has mastered balance in a stationary position, she can begin with a slow forward movement to contact the ball until it becomes routine for her to be in balance. Eventually, progress the process to game speed.
The shoulders rotate in an attempt to help hit the ball.	Place a ball on a tee low and outside. Work with the athlete to keep the shoulder pointed toward the tee until just before contact.
The ball is bunted too hard.	Make sure that the left foot is down and the bat has stopped forward movement just before contact. Hands should be gentle on contact, not hard.
The ball is constantly bunted foul.	The slapper should keep the bat head forward of the hands until contact. A slight give with the bat on contact will bring it back to square and not angled toward foul territory.

KEY POINTS

The most important components of baserunning are

o running from home to first,

o running pattern for an extra-base hit,

o leading off,

o direction of the leadoff, and

o tagging up on fly balls.

Teams whose players run the bases aggressively keep their opponents on edge and create pressure that causes errors and hurried, out-of-sync performance. Every player can be a threat on the bases. Correct running technique can improve any player's speed, but unless players master the finer points of baserunning, speed alone won't be a threat. By being aware of what is happening in the moment, knowing where the ball is at all times, reacting quickly and having proper technique, players will gain the confidence that they need to be effective.

RUNNING FROM HOME TO FIRST

The first key to baserunning is getting out of the box. These first few steps are often the most passive steps that a runner takes, yet those steps often determine how far a runner can advance or how fast she reaches any base. To keep it simple, short steps and a forward lean will help the runner get out of the box faster than longer strides will (see figure 3.21). As the runner gains speed, the stride will lengthen and the player will become more upright. Unless the ball is hit or bunted very close to home plate, the runner should run directly down the line toward first base. Runners have a tendency to start on the inside of the line, but running on a natural path to the outside is important. If a player is inside the line and is hit by a thrown ball, she will be out. If the player is outside the line and is hit, the ball is considered live and play continues.

Figure 3.21   Getting out of the box.

The runner should maintain speed through first base and make sure to touch it as she passes it. The runner should get into the habit of glancing quickly to the right into foul territory after touching the base so that she can see whether the ball was overthrown. If she sees it immediately, she has a much greater chance of being able to advance. If she always waits for the first-base coach to tell her about an overthrown ball, her reaction will be much slower and she won't be able to take advantage of an overthrow as often. After passing the base, the runner should slow down, stay right on the foul line and turn toward the infield when turning around to return to first. This technique allows her to see the infield and keep an eye on what the fielders are doing. Many outstanding base runners take their time returning to first, all the while watching the defense. If the defense vacates second base and isn't paying attention, the base runner may be able to steal second as long as she hasn't completely returned to first. If she has reached first on the return, she can't advance.

RUNNING PATTERN FOR AN EXTRA-BASE HIT

After a hit ball has cleared the infield and it is apparent that the hitter has hit at least a single and possibly more, the running lane to first changes. The runner rounds first base and heads toward second base in the quickest and most efficient manner possible. Whether the runner advances to second or third depends on the defense and the depth of the ball, but the runner should always be ready to go farther if possible. Therefore, rounding first puts the runner in a position to take advantage of a bobble or a poor throw by an outfielder.

When rounding first, the running path should be as tight a circle as possible (see figure 3.22). A few feet after the hitter has gotten out of the box, she should run in a straight line to foul territory to begin the tight circle. If she continues in a straight line down the foul line, she will end up running in a large circle from first to second, taking more time to reach second base. To round first correctly, the runner swings out to foul territory early,

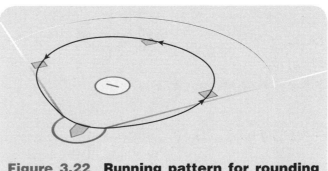

Figure 3.22 **Running pattern for rounding the bases.**

touches first base and uses it to push herself toward second. The rule of thumb is to go as far as the defense allows. The runner rounds as far as she can without risking being picked off at first and then watches carefully to see whether she can possibly advance to second. She should take advantage of any hesitation or bobble. Not being in the right position or not paying attention might mean the difference between remaining at first and advancing to scoring position at second.

LEADING OFF

A runner can accomplish several objectives with a leadoff. First, the rule in softball states that the runner can't leave the base until the ball leaves the pitcher's hand. A good base runner tries to make that timing exact. The runner also wants to be able to create momentum toward the base and at the same time be in control of her body weight. The runner uses a slightly different lead at each base, but all of them require either a conventional start or a rocker start. The start that a runner uses depends on which one she can master, which is more comfortable and which is quicker.

For the conventional start, the runner's back foot is on the base (see figure 3.23a). The move is a shifting of weight from the back foot to the front foot. Almost simultaneously, the back foot quickly drives forward, leaving the base at the same time that the pitcher releases the ball (see figure 3.23b). The conventional start has the advantage of being easier to time because the first move happens at the same time that the back foot leaves the base. The disadvantage is that the conventional start doesn't produce much momentum because it is a still start. The rocker start uses momentum to produce a quicker start, resulting in a faster time from base to base. Remember, however, that if the runner's timing is late with the rocker start, the advantage is negated.

(continued)

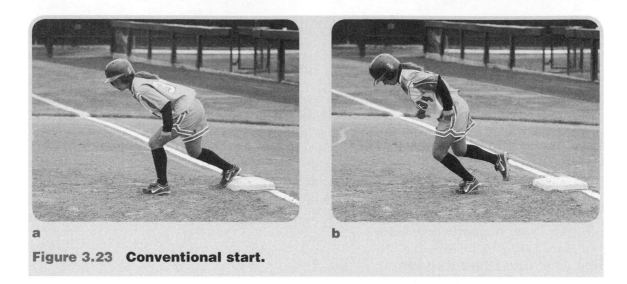

Figure 3.23 Conventional start.

For the rocker start, the runner begins with the front foot on the front edge of the base (see figure 3.24a). The side of the base on which the runner begins the rocker start depends on which foot is forward (if it is the right foot, the runner will be on the side of the base closer to the infield, and if it is the left foot, the runner will be on the side of the base closer to the outfield). The runner uses the base as a starting block and pushes off as the back foot moves forward (see figure 3.24b). The back foot doesn't move over the top of the base because doing so can interfere with the motion. Instead, the back foot moves along the side. The advantage of the rocker start is that it produces momentum because it is a moving start instead of a still start. Be aware, though, that the timing of the first move will need to be earlier in the pitcher's motion than it is with the conventional start. Still, the runner cannot leave the base until the ball leaves the pitcher's hand.

Figure 3.24 Rocker start.

DIRECTION OF THE LEADOFF

When leading off using either of the starts discussed in the previous section, the hips should be pointing toward the base that the runner is running to when the ball crosses the plate, so that if the ball is hit, the runner is already in position to advance as quickly as possible. The steps should be small to aid in control of body weight in case the runner needs to return quickly. If the runner leads off too hard and can't control her movement forward or back, she becomes an easy target to be picked off.

When the runner is at first base, the leadoff is directly toward second. The first few steps are short, quick and aggressive so that it looks as if the runner may be attempting to steal. The runner then slows slightly while still facing second when the ball crosses the plate. Immediately after the catcher catches the ball, the runner squares to the infield, reads the situation and returns to first.

When the runner is at second base and a runner is also at first, making it a force situation at third, the lead is much like the lead at first, but it can be slightly longer because the pickoff throw is longer. But when no runner is at first and a force situation is not present, the most effective lead angles toward the shortstop and initiates the tightest circle possible to reach home. On a base hit, the runner has a good jump on the path to score.

When the runner is at third base, the path on the lead should be angled out toward foul territory. Any hit ball that contacts the runner in fair territory results in an automatic out, so the runner should be in foul territory because reaction time is limited at third base. The mechanics are similar to first-base mechanics in that the hips are square to the plate when the pitch crosses, and a controlled movement forward should occur. The runner should consider a rolling, or slower, movement at the beginning of the lead at third and increase the speed as the ball crosses the plate. Again, control of body weight is necessary to put the base runner in the best position to score on a slow-rolling ground ball to the middle infield. Reaction time is increased because the runner is already moving toward the plate and not trying to return instantly to third. The runner should have the mind-set of always thinking about scoring and not just getting back to third. Still, the runner must control her body weight and not be caught with momentum out of control toward home.

TAGGING UP ON FLY BALLS

The key points to advancing on a fly ball are knowing which balls to advance on, having the right technique and knowing the rules about when the runner can leave. When a fly ball is hit, the runner, with the help of the base coach, needs to determine whether the ball is deep enough for her to beat the throw from the outfielder to the base that she is trying to advance to. The key factors are the speed of the runner, the depth of the fly ball and the strength of the outfielder's arm. If the runner or coach determines that advancing on a tag isn't possible, the runner should go as far toward the forward base as she can without risking being put out with a throw after the catch. If the outfielder drops the ball, the runner can then advance. If the outfielder catches the ball, the runner can safely return.

(continued)

If the runner or coach determines that a tag is possible, the runner returns to the base quickly after the leadoff, assumes a conventional start position and watches the outfielder catching the ball. The runner can time when to leave the base much better by watching the ball approach the fielder than she can by anticipating a coach's telling her when to go. The important thing to remember is that the runner can leave the base as soon as the ball has been touched or hits the ground. The ball doesn't need to be caught. If the outfielder bobbles the ball, the runner doesn't need to wait for the fielder to control or catch the ball.

At a Glance

The following parts of the text offer additional information on baserunning.

Common Errors

Following are several common errors that you might run into when teaching your athletes how to run the bases.

Error	Error Correction
The runner runs in a large circle for extra-base hits.	The circle route usually results from running directly to first base and not moving out into foul territory soon enough. Teach athletes the desired path by placing cones along the path until they learn it.
The runner is slow getting out of the box.	Emphasize short steps and body lean.
The runner leaves the base too early or too late.	Have one coach blow a whistle when the runner's foot leaves the base and another blow a second whistle when the ball leaves the pitcher's hand. Repetitions will help the runner hear and adjust to the correct time.
The runner is out of control and easily picked off.	Emphasize a controlled creep in the leadoff after the first short steps.

The bent-leg slide is typically the first slide that players learn because it is the most commonly used and leads up to the pop-up slide. Players most often use the bent-leg slide in an attempt to avoid tags and reach the base safely or to break up double plays. Players may also use a bent-leg slide on close plays when they need to stop forward motion on the base quickly without slowing down. A good rule of thumb is to slide when in doubt.

Although sliding is a skill that intimidates some softball players, sliding with the correct technique limits the abrasions and injuries provoked by sliding without proper technique. Most sliding injuries occur because of players' hesitation after they begin the sliding motion. When this happens the skill breaks down.

KEY POINTS

The most important components of the bent-leg slide are

- timing and distance,
- leg positioning, and
- contacting the ground.

TIMING AND DISTANCE

When first learning the bent-leg slide, players must understand that if their timing is too late, they increase their chances of injury by jamming into the base. Players should start the slide at a distance from the base of roughly their body length plus a few extra feet. As a coach, you can mark that spot in practice until the athlete has gone through enough repetitions to know the correct distance.

LEG POSITIONING

When beginning the bent-leg slide, the player's front leg and foot will thrust out and the knee will be slightly bent to absorb the impact with the base. The front leg is typically the leg that is in front when the person sits cross-legged. The front leg is different for each player, but in most cases it is the left leg. If a player happens to use the right leg, however, there is no need to change it. Comfort for the player is most important. When the leg is thrust out, the foot must not touch the ground until it reaches the base.

The bent leg for the bent-leg slide is typically the right leg (or the leg opposite the thrust leg), and it bends under the knee of the thrust leg. The first impact with the ground generally takes place on the side of the bent leg. Protecting this part of the leg with some form of padding is recommended. See figure 3.25 for an example of the bent-leg slide.

At a Glance

The following parts of the text offer additional information on the bent-leg slide.

(continued)

CONTACTING THE GROUND

Immediately after the initial contact with the ground by the bent leg, the player should roll back, going from the leg, to the hip, to the back. This laying out of the body in the slide will distribute the weight and keep one spot from taking all the pressure, as shown in figure 3.25, *a* and *b*. In addition, your players should not use their hands to try to ease impact. The hands don't touch the ground to initiate the slide. Instead, they are up and off the ground. As the weight goes back, the arms and hands reach back to help the weight roll back, as shown in figure 3.25*c*. The chin and head are tucked into the chest so that the player doesn't hit her head on the ground behind her.

a　　　　　　　　　　b　　　　　　　　　　c

Figure 3.25　Bent-leg positioning.

Common Errors

Following are several common errors that you might run into when teaching your athletes the bent-leg slide.

Error	Error Correction
Both legs thrust forward.	Focus on the impact site of the bent leg.
The thrust leg stays in contact with the ground.	Excessive contact with the ground is a big concern for injury. Put the athlete on a slippery surface and have two coaches hold the opposite ends of a bat or rod of some kind. The athlete can hold on to the bat and slide under it. This method eliminates the fear of contact and promotes a controlled movement that helps the athlete understand which leg does what.
Player sits too upright (the primary cause of abrasions on the upper thigh).	Players can learn to slide on a slippery surface. Have them slide under a low barrier that requires them to lie back but still allows for a tuck of the chin. Be sure that the barrier is soft!

After mastering the bent-leg slide, players should learn the pop-up slide, a variation that is extremely effective for a quick slide. In force or tag situations at second or third when the runner needs to get to the base as quickly as possible and not overrun it, the pop-up slide is the best choice. This slide is consistent with the bent-leg slide with a few differences noted here. The advantage of this slide is that the runner never slows, reaches the base as quickly as possible and pops up into a standing position so that she can advance to the next base if circumstances allow.

KEY POINTS

The most important components of the pop-up slide are

o timing and distance,
o leg positioning, and
o contacting the ground.

TIMING AND DISTANCE

A successful pop-up slide requires that both legs be able to redirect the forward motion into an upright motion, which requires momentum. If a player slides the same distance in a pop-up slide as in the bent-leg slide, the body stops too early and no momentum is available to work with. For the pop-up slide, players need to slide late so that they have enough speed to execute the skill.

LEG POSITIONING

The thrust leg for the pop-up slide is the same one used in the bent-leg slide. As discussed in "Bent-Leg Slide" on page 47, this leg is typically the leg that is in front when a person sits cross-legged. The front leg is different for each player, but in most cases it is the left leg. In the pop-up slide, the thrust leg has the added role of absorbing a greater impact and redirecting the motion from forward to upward. To do this, the thrust foot needs to plant firmly on the base. The knee will bend, and when the body slides up close to the feet, it straightens to assist in standing up.

The bent leg takes the initial impact, just as it does in the bent-leg slide. But the body weight stays on the leg and hip. After the hips slide forward to the feet, the bent leg pushes against the ground to push the slider up to the standing position. This slide is so quick that the body never fully leans back. The pop-up slide is a brief slide in a sitting position. The body rolls slightly to the bent-leg side so that it is square over the leg. See figure 3.26 for an example of the pop-up slide.

At a Glance

The following parts of the text offer additional information on the pop-up slide.

(continued)

Figure 3.26   Pop-up slide.

Common Errors

Following are several common errors that you might run into when teaching your athletes the pop-up slide.

Error	Error Correction
The runner can't get to a standing position.	Check to see whether the hips slide up to the bent leg before the runner attempts to stand up. Also ensure that the player is keeping her speed through the slide. A body that is moving quickly is easier to redirect.
The runner slides over the top and past the base.	The runner should plant the thrust foot firmly against the front edge of the base. The knee is bent and uses the base as the barrier to redirect the motion.

The headfirst slide is the most common and most effective slide when stealing any base because it is the quickest sliding skill. In softball, sliding is necessary on all steal attempts because time is always a factor, and the headfirst slide is the most successful in these situations. Although this slide looks difficult and attempting it may make some players nervous, it is easy to perform once perfected and is generally the most widely used slide by aggressive base runners.

RUNNING AGGRESSIVELY INTO THE SLIDE

When preparing to slide, many runners make the mistake of slowing down immediately before beginning to slide. Just as runners should slide every time they steal a base, they should continue running hard and gradually lower themselves into the base, not stopping, jumping or leaping at the base. A good base runner will get low, lean forward and have a controlled fall into the slide while continuing to run. Because it is easier to lean forward while running into a slide, this slide is quicker to the base than the bent-leg slide, which requires the runner to lean backward to slide. See figure 3.27, *a* and *b* for an example of running aggressively into the slide.

KEY POINTS

The most important components of the headfirst slide are

- running aggressively into the slide,
- maintaining contact points,
- receiving the base, and
- knowing when to use the headfirst slide.

Figure 3.27   Headfirst slide.

(continued)

MAINTAINING CONTACT POINTS

When executed correctly, the heels of the player's palms touch the ground first and the chest (diaphragm high) and the thighs contact the ground immediately thereafter. The player extends her arms toward the base, making certain to point the fingers slightly upward to avoid jamming them into the base on contact. The player should also keep her head up to see the situation. The back is arched to keep the chin off the ground, and the friction points are the belly and thighs. Players should be discouraged from jumping or belly flopping into the headfirst slide. These techniques are slower and can cause injury from the downward force of the body. See figure 3.27c for an example of contacting the ground.

RECEIVING THE BASE

To avoid injury, the runner should relax the joints in the shoulders, arms, wrists and fingers. As the player slides into the base, the arms bend, allowing the body to slide closer to the base. The player, in essence, absorbs the base into the body. As stated earlier, the fingers are pointing more upward and the palms of the hands contact the base. See figure 3.27d for an example of receiving the base.

c

d

Figure 3.27 *(continued)*

KNOWING WHEN TO USE THE HEADFIRST SLIDE

Although the headfirst slide is the quickest slide, it isn't the best in every situation. The disadvantage to the headfirst slide versus the pop-up slide is the time required to stand back up. But if the play is extremely close and will more than likely end after the tag attempt, the headfirst is the preferred option. In no situation, however, should a player use a headfirst slide when sliding into home with a catcher wearing shinguards. A good rule of thumb is always to slide feet first into home. If the infield dirt is wet, the runner will not slide as far, making it necessary to start the slide closer to the base.

At a Glance

The following parts of the text offer additional information on the headfirst slide.

Common Errors

Following are several common errors that you might run into when teaching your athletes the headfirst slide.

Error	Error Correction
The player slows down when beginning to slide.	Players must keep running and lean forward into a controlled fall.
The player flops or jumps into the slide.	Emphasize that players should get low and feel as if they are running under an imaginary bar or rope.
The runner stops short of the base.	The runner who fails to reach the base is usually not running aggressively enough or is sliding too early. Players should move into the slide about 10 feet before the base.

chapter 4

Defensive Technical Skills

This chapter will cover the defensive technical skills that you and your players must know to be successful. In this chapter, you will find:

KEY POINTS

The most important components of throwing are

- grip,
- line of force,
- initial shoulder and hip rotation,
- weight transfer,
- arm action,
- wrist snap, and
- follow-through.

Figure 4.1 Proper grip for a throw.

Throwing is perhaps the most important skill in softball because most defensive plays involve throwing. Poor throws can allow offensive players to reach base, give them extra bases or even allow runs to score. More games are lost on a player's inability to throw than on any other error. Even so, many coaches overlook throwing, assuming that their players have mastered the skill somewhere along the line. Teams who work at this skill play the game with more confidence and can handle surprise situations with more ease.

GRIP

When preparing to throw, the player should hold the ball on the length of the fingers, not in the palm (see figure 4.1). The fingers should be spread comfortably, and the finger pads should grip a seam on the ball. The thumb is under the ball opposite the middle and ring fingers. The little finger isn't a critical part of the grip, so it may curl or just lie alongside the ball. The hand and wrist should be loose and relaxed until release.

LINE OF FORCE

Accuracy is an obvious desire for any throw. Much of it comes from proper wrist snap and arm motion, but if your athletes don't understand the line of force, the body and mind will compete against each other. The body will dictate that the athlete will throw one direction, while the mind knows better and tries to compensate by making adjustments.

The line of force is the imaginary line extending from the back, or pivot, foot directly toward the target. The player wants to stride directly down that line and have the arm "circle" move back along the line. When beginning the throw, the throwing-hand foot rotates and establishes the thrust point, which is the point that the foot pushes against the ground to drive the body forward into the throw and which is also the beginning of the line of force (see figure 4.2a) The glove-hand foot then strides along this line toward the target (see figure 4.2b). As the body is turning to begin the throwing action, the throwing hand drops back along the line and the glove hand or elbow points forward down this line toward the target. This point is the most critical for your athletes to focus on in the initial setup for the throw: They must stride down the line and make sure that the backswing of the arm is on the line of force to ensure accuracy. Reaching or extending the glove hand toward the target will create some variation in the amount of bend in the elbow, but the critical point is to extend it forward in line toward the target. After the throwing arm is in place on line behind the body, correct movement of the arm will take the arm accurately toward the target.

a   b

Figure 4.2   **Line of force.**

INITIAL SHOULDER AND HIP ROTATION

When preparing to throw, the shoulders and hips rotate open simultaneously. To begin the rotation, the throwing-hand foot turns so that the instep is square to the target, which in turn causes the hips to rotate almost automatically (see figure 4.3a). As the foot turns, the throwing arm goes back and the body turns sideways, or opens, to the target. The glove-hand shoulder and arm should now be pointing in the direction of the target. After your athlete has rotated properly, her body weight should be almost completely on the back, or throwing-hand, foot (see figure 4.3b).

a   b

Figure 4.3   **Shoulder and hip rotation when preparing to throw.**

(continued)

WEIGHT TRANSFER

Power in the throw is generated in part by the amount of leg drive that throwers can develop. After the weight is on the back leg, the back knee should be bent, putting the leg in a position to extend and drive the body forward down the line, transferring the weight to the front leg.

The forward stride is linear, as discussed in "Line of Force," and transfers the body weight from the back leg to the front leg (see figure 4.4a). After the foot is planted on the ground, the hips and then the shoulders, staying in a direct line, rotate to finish the actual throw (see figure 4.4b). Note that bending the waist is common and acceptable at this point for a throw that is hard or covers a long distance.

a   b

Figure 4.4   Weight transfer into the throw.

ARM ACTION

Arm action is the most important aspect of the throwing motion because the upper body can overcome mistakes with the lower body, but incorrect arm action of the throw is almost impossible to overcome. The result is typically an inaccurate throw. As the athlete is transferring her weight and taking the stride, the throwing arm is back in preparation to throw and the thumb is under the ball with the palm facing back or toward the ground as shown in figure 4.3a. After the stride foot has been planted, the hips and shoulders rotate forward to initiate the throw and rotation of the shoulder girdle pulls the arm forward. When the shoulders are square to the target, the arm should be directly to the side. The elbow must be at shoulder height and positioned at 90 degrees from the target or to the side of the body; the throwing elbow never points at the target. If the forearm is bent toward the head or away from the head, throwing accuracy is severely affected and the potential for injury to the elbow is heightened.

When the throwing arm moves forward, the hand rotates from a position with the palm facing down in the back to a position with the palm facing forward toward the target (see figure 4.5a). As this rotation occurs, the elbow leads the forearm, creating forearm lag, meaning that the hand and ball will drag behind the elbow. Note that the hand never drops in toward the head. It should stay on a path directly below the elbow at 90 degrees. After the body is square, the elbow slows and catapults the forearm and hand forward down the line of force (see figure 4.5).

a   b

Figure 4.5   Arm action for the throw.

When rotation of the body starts forward, the glove hand does not pull back to increase torque. Instead, it acts as a counterbalance to the throwing arm. The glove hand will find its way to a place that feels comfortable to the thrower, most commonly somewhere toward the shoulder of the glove arm, as shown previously in figure 4.3b, and acts as a pivotal point for the body to rotate against. The placement of the glove arm is generally natural and automatic. It usually doesn't need to be taught, but its role should be discussed.

WRIST SNAP

An athlete with good wrist snap has added power and accuracy. A strong wrist snap is necessary to throw the ball well. To have a great snap, first, a proper grip is necessary, as discussed previously. The forearm lag will make the hand drag behind the arm, which naturally cocks the wrist back without any tension in the forearm. If the wrist is cocked back deliberately, the tension will not allow the wrist to snap with full potential, and tightness in the forearm will cause it to slow in response.

(continued)

The wrist snap consists of the full length of the fingers flinging the ball forward. The ball rolls down the fingers until just before it reaches the finger pads. At that point the finger pads finish the snap through the ball using the seam, and the ball will spin off the fingers in the direction of the target. If the fingers are directly behind the ball, the spin will be close to a 12 o'clock–6 o'clock rotation. Little curve will result in the path of the ball, so the throw will be much more accurate.

FOLLOW-THROUGH

To release the tension of the throw and help maintain arm health, the arm should continue forward after release, decelerating as it pulls across the line of force and moves toward the midline of the body. A bend at the waist aids the lower back in releasing tension. The amount of bend in the waist determines the motion of the back leg. The leg may kick up in back when the thrower bends deeply at the waist to finish the release. The back leg then recovers and steps to the side to help regain balance. Remind your athletes that if they fail to follow through, the abrupt stop of the arm can injure the muscles in the back of the shoulder.

Common Errors

Following are several common errors that you might run into when teaching your athletes how to throw.

Error	Error Correction
The player is striding off line.	To help the player practice staying on the line of force, have her throw down an actual line during warm-ups for practice.
The player has no rotation when beginning the throwing motion.	Have the player start from a sideways position and make the throw. Check to see that she is turning her foot to begin the motion.
The elbow is below the shoulder when it is to the side of the body just before release.	Isolate the arm action of the throw by having the player kneel on the throwing-hand knee. The player should start the arm back and then throw forward. Hold a soft pad just below the shoulder in the correct path of the elbow. If the elbow drops, it will hit this pad. You can now teach the player to get the elbow up so that she can throw over the top of the pad.
The player has no wrist snap on the throw.	Isolate this portion of the throw by having the athlete stand or kneel, facing the target with the arm to the side of the body. The elbow begins the motion forward, and the wrist finishes with a quick fling of the ball forward. Check the player's grip. If the ball is in the palm, the fingers cannot throw the ball.

Players must often slightly alter the basic throwing motion because of the needs of their specific positions. Whereas outfielders always want a big arm circle so that they can throw over the top, infielders and catchers need a quicker release. After fielding a ground ball, an infielder might find herself in a position that requires her to release the ball without the time to set up for a normal throwing motion. The following throwing variations are the most common for throws in the infield. By learning specific fundamentals, athletes can make more accurate throws.

KEY POINTS

The most important components of infield throws are the

- forehand flip,
- backhand flip,
- scoop throw, and
- three-quarter throw.

FOREHAND FLIP

The forehand flip is a throw that a fielder uses to make a short, quick throw to a player on her glove-hand side. For example, assume that the second-base player fields a ground ball close to first base with her shoulders square to home plate (see figure 4.6*a*). Because the player is close to the target and doesn't have enough time to reposition for a throw, she simply stays in the same position she was in when fielding the ball. After fielding the ball, the fielder doesn't stand up. Instead, she keeps her shoulders and hips down, moves her hands slightly toward the throwing-hand side (see figure 4.6*b*) and flips the ball across the front of her body to the player making the catch (see figure 4.6*c*). Around the time of release, the throwing-hand knee may drop to the ground, or it can turn inward to help stabilize the body, as shown in figure 4.6*c*. The player then follows through toward the target after the release to help the accuracy of the throw (see figure 4.6*d*). In this case, the follow-through is only with the arm, because the body isn't as involved in the throw as it is for a regular full throw.

a   b

Figure 4.6   Forehand flip.

(continued)

(continued)

c

d

Figure 4.6 *(continued)*

BACKHAND FLIP

A backhand flip is a throw that a fielder uses for a close, quick throw to a player on her throwing-hand side. The backhand flip is similar to the forehand flip in that the player uses it when in proximity to the target, but the target is now on the opposite side of the body. After fielding the ball, the fielder doesn't stand up. Instead, she keeps her shoulders and hips down and moves her hands slightly toward the glove-hand side (see figure 4.7a). She initiates the flip with the throwing-hand elbow moving toward and pointing at the target (see figure 4.7b). The forearm then moves in the same direction and ends with a snap of the wrist and with the fingers pointing toward the target (see figure 4.7c). Accuracy results from the control of the ball by the wrist, a follow-through toward the target and a weight shift or movement toward the target (see figure 4.7d).

Some athletes find it easier to control the backhand flip by keeping the wrist from snapping and using only the forward momentum of the body and the elbow snap. The advantage to a slightly stiffer wrist is often added accuracy. The disadvantage could be the loss of power. Both the wrist snap method and the stiffer wrist and more elbow snap methods are correct, and fielders should work with both to get a feel as to what is most comfortable and consistent for them. The intended purpose is a quick and accurate toss without taking time to rotate the body. How the hand releases the ball in this toss might vary and a good infielder can usually master both.

Figure 4.7 **Backhand flip.**

(continued)

SCOOP THROW

A scoop throw is a quick, close throw that a fielder makes directly in front of herself, usually when on the run. A good example occurs when a corner player fields a bunt on a squeeze play or when an infielder fields a ground ball on the run when moving toward the base that she wants to throw to. In either case, the fielder continues forward after fielding the ground ball, takes the ball out of the glove with the hand under the ball (see figure 4.8a) and flips or scoops the ball, using a slight underhand swing of the arm to the receiver (see figure 4.8b).

a   b

Figure 4.8   Scoop throw.

When teaching the scoop throw, you must emphasize two points. First, the fielder should be sure to show the ball to the receiver for a split second before releasing it because the ball arrives quickly and the receiver may have difficulty seeing it. Second, the fielder needs to continue her forward motion while releasing the ball and for a short distance thereafter. If the fielder stops, the ball often flies out of control with no accuracy. The speed of the toss results from the slight swing of the arm and the forward movement. Any extra effort usually results in a wild throw or toss.

THREE-QUARTER THROW

A three-quarter throw is generally used when the target is too far for a flip throw but the throw still needs to be quick. First, you must emphasize the position of the elbow in relation to the shoulder to preserve the safety and the health of the player's throwing arm. The throwing motion is similar to that used in the overhand throw as discussed in "Throwing" on page 56; a line drawn across the shoulders should continue straight to the throwing-hand elbow. But the three-quarter throw is done with the shoulders at an angle to the ground, not parallel to the ground. If the elbow falls below the line drawn across the shoulders, injury may occur when the athlete attempts to throw hard.

For the three-quarter throw, if the fielder's feet aren't in alignment with the target after she fields the ball, she quickly adjusts so that the instep of the throwing-hand foot faces the target and the glove foot is on the line of force (see figure 4.9*a*). The player shifts her body weight to the throwing-hand side of the body, and the hands also move to the throwing-hand side (see figure 4.9*b*). The shoulders should be on an angle. The throwing-hand shoulder should be lower than the glove-hand shoulder, and the forearm should be lifted to a 90-degree angle (see figure 4.9*c*). The throw is initiated by the weight shifting forward, the shoulders rotating the elbow, creating a forearm lag (see figure 4.9*d*), and then the wrist snapping to release the ball (see figure 4.9*e*). The throwing-hand knee often drops to the ground on the three-quarter throw to help stabilize the body and give the fielder a solid foundation for a throw that requires a little more force. The follow-through for the three-quarter throw is directly at the target, as shown in figure 4.9*e*, or slightly across the body.

a   b

Figure 4.9 Three-quarter throw.

(continued)

(continued)

c

d

e

Figure 4.9 *(continued)*

Common Errors

Following are several common errors that you might run into when teaching your athletes infield throws.

Error	Error Correction
The athlete has no wrist snap when using the forehand flip or three-quarter throw.	Teach players to focus on having the ball roll down the fingers and then pushing with the pads of the fingers when the middle of the ball reaches them. When done correctly, the ball will spin off the fingers.
The athlete has no accuracy on the backhand flip.	Be sure that the player begins with the elbow pointing at the target.
The athlete has pain in the elbow when using a three-quarter throw.	This common occurrence must be watched! The key is aligning the elbow with and not below an imaginary line that extends across the shoulders.

Fielding Balls on the Forehand or Backhand Side

Although a player always wants to get into a position to field the ball in the middle of her body, at times the ball will be moving too quickly or be too far away for the fielder to get in front of it. In these situations, when a ball is hit to the side, the fielder uses a forehand or backhand to field the ball, depending on which side is the fielder's glove hand.

KEY POINTS

The most important components of fielding balls with a forehand or backhand are

- moving to the ball,
- positioning the glove properly, and
- transitioning into the throw.

MOVING TO THE BALL

As suggested, fielders use a forehand or backhand in two situations. The first occurs when the ball is hit to the side of the fielder and is moving too quickly for the fielder to get in front of it. The fielder will have time to perform only a simple rotation of the body toward the path of the ball so that the glove can reach toward the ball. The fielder must field the ball with little or no footwork to the side because the ball is hit hard and close to the fielder. Note that the corner players in softball use the forehand and backhand from this stationary position more than baseball players do because they play closer to the plate and don't have as much time to get in position.

In this situation, if the ball is hit to the glove-hand side, the fielder should use a forehand. From a ready position, the fielder's first movement is to rotate the shoulders and hips so that the glove hand opens to the side and to place her body weight on the ball of the glove-hand foot (see figure 4.10*a*). Accomplishing this may require pivoting out the toe of the glove-hand foot to allow free rotation of the shoulders and hips. If the ball is hit to the throwing-hand side, the fielder should use a backhand. From a ready position, the fielder's first movement is to rotate the shoulders, keeping them low so that the elbow of the glove hand is facing the ground, and to place her body weight on the ball of the throwing-hand foot (see figure 4.10*b*). Doing this may require pivoting out the toe of the throwing-hand foot to allow free rotation of the shoulders and hips.

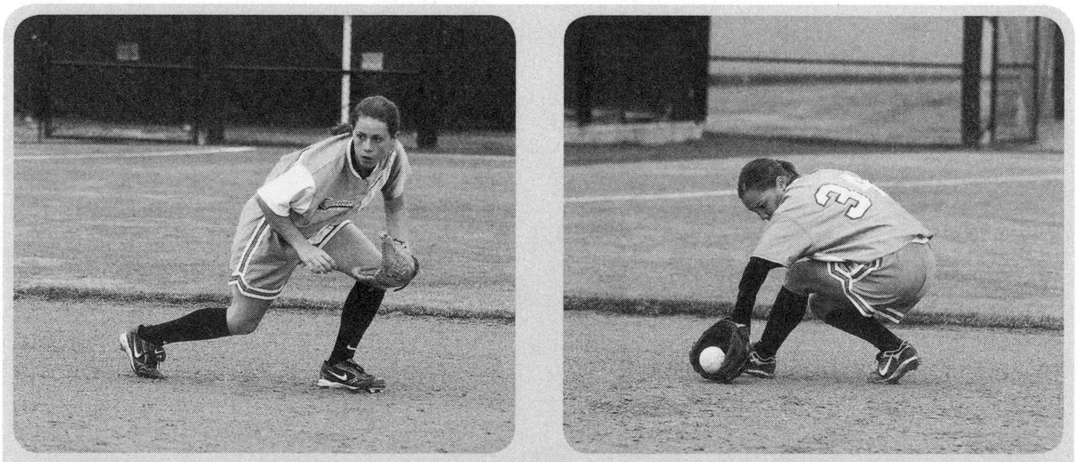

a b

Figure 4.10 When the ball is hit to the side and is moving quickly, use (*a*) a forehand or (*b*) a backhand.

(continued)

The second situation in which a fielder uses a forehand or backhand occurs when the ball is farther from the fielder and she needs to sprint to the ball and field it on the run. When the ball is hit away from the fielder on the glove-hand side, the fielder should use a forehand and field the ball on the run. The fielder first rotates her shoulders and glove-hand foot in the direction of the ball (see figure 4.11a). To be as quick as possible, the fielder should turn the foot closer to the ball open as she shifts her weight to it rather than pick up the foot. Using a crossover step with the throwing-hand foot, the player runs to where she anticipates fielding the ball (see figure 4.11b). As she gets closer to the ball, she should bend at the waist to lower the shoulders, allowing the glove to be low for a better reach (see figure 4.11c).

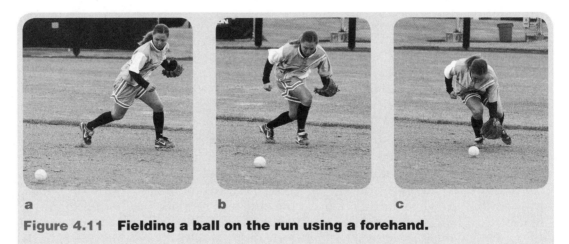

Figure 4.11   Fielding a ball on the run using a forehand.

When the ball is hit away from the fielder on the throwing-hand side, she should use a backhand and field the ball on the run. The fielder first rotates her shoulders and foot in the direction of the ball (see figure 4.12a). To be as quick as possible, the fielder should turn the foot closer to the ball open as she shifts her weight to it rather than pick up the foot. Using a crossover step with the back foot, the player runs to where she anticipates fielding the ball (see figure 4.12b). As she gets closer to the ball, she should bend at the waist to lower the shoulders, allowing the glove to be low for a better reach (see figure 4.12c).

Figure 4.12   Fielding a ball on the run using a backhand.

POSITIONING THE GLOVE PROPERLY

When fielding a ball on the forehand side, the glove naturally opens in the direction that the fielder is going. The pocket of the glove is open and facing the ball (see figure 4.13). Although the movement is natural for most infielders, staying low still needs to be emphasized.

The fielder should bend at the waist so that the chest is closer to the thigh, and the knees should be bent so that the hips are low. The fielder then fields the ball forward of the body and in front of either foot while keeping the hands still. In addition, fielders should learn to let the glove stay down for a moment after fielding the ball to avoid trying to pick it up at the same time that they are fielding it.

If possible, the fielder should field the ball with the throwing-side foot planted (see figure 4.13). This will give the athlete a little more reach as well as eliminate the possibility of kicking the ball while trying to field it. However, it is important to remain smooth and comfortable while moving to the ball. If fielding the ball with the throwing-side foot forward makes footwork choppy and slows down the fielder, the glove-side foot forward will work. The fielder should be proficient at both.

When fielding a ball on the backhand side, the glove-hand elbow, staying loose, points forward in the direction that the ball came from. The pocket of the glove is open and facing the ball (see figure 4.14). The most successful technique is to slide the glove lightly across the ground for a few inches before reaching the ball, rather than stab at the ball by dropping the glove directly down to field it. The fielder's shoulders should stay down so that the glove is close to the ground. The fielder then fields the ball in front of the body and in front of the glove-hand foot. In addition, fielders should learn to let the glove stay down for a moment after fielding the ball to avoid trying to pick it up at the same time that they are fielding it.

Figure 4.13 Glove positioning when fielding a ball on the forehand side.

Figure 4.14 Glove positioning when fielding a ball on the backhand side.

(continued)

TRANSITIONING INTO THE THROW

After fielding the ball, the fielder takes the fewest steps possible to stop momentum and move into the throw. If fielding the ball takes the fielder away from the throwing target, she should take the fewest steps possible through the ball (see figure 4.15a), plant the throwing-hand foot (see figure 4.15b), pivot and throw (see figure 4.15c). The fielder may actually turn her back to the infield when making this throw. If fielding the ball takes the fielder close to the target, the fielder continues through the ball (see figure 4.16a) and uses an underhand toss to the target (see figure 4.16b)

a   b   c

Figure 4.15 **Fielding a ball when the fielder is moving away from the target.**

a   b

Figure 4.16 **Fielding a ball when the fielder is moving toward the target.**

Common Errors

Following are several common errors that you might run into when teaching your athletes how to field balls on the forehand and backhand side.

Error	Error Correction
The athlete's shoulders are too high and her body is erect.	The player should bend at the waist, getting the chest close to the thigh. The athlete should not be sitting up. Rather, she should be leaning toward the thigh.
The athlete is stabbing her glove at the ball, going from high to low.	Rotate the fielder and turn the elbow toward the batter's box or origin of the ball. Roll or hit the ball toward the backhand. Have the fielder slide the glove lightly along the ground, keeping the glove open for 6 to 12 inches before fielding the ball. The player should keep the glove still and in place for a moment after fielding the ball.
The athlete is stopping the ball but leaving it on the ground when moving into the throw.	The fielder is not moving through the ball. She is reaching for it as she shifts back toward the throwing target. In almost every case the fielder will leave the ball behind when she pulls back from it.
The athlete is constantly bobbling the backhand.	The fielder must keep the glove quiet when fielding the ball. She should not try to pick it up. She should field it and hold it for a moment. Pushing the glove very slightly into the ball and along the path of the ball may help the player control the hop.
The ball is going under the athlete's glove.	Moving to the forehand side is easy, but players may need to focus on staying low enough to reach the ball out front and not directly down from the shoulder. Staying too high is more natural. Teach players to lean so that the chest is closer to the thigh with the knees bent and hips low.

Fielding Ground Balls in the Infield

KEY POINTS

The most important components of fielding ground balls in the infield are

o being in the ready position,

o approaching the ball,

o controlling weight distribution and balance,

o using proper glove work, and

o moving into the throw.

Fielding ground balls in the infield is key for a sound defense. A team that can field ground balls well creates outs, not errors. If your team fields ground balls successfully, your pitchers have more confidence and your team has a better chance to win. If infielders have confidence in their ability to field ground balls, they can be more aggressive and will be more assertive on defense.

BEING IN THE READY POSITION

The ready position for fielding ground balls in the infield is an athletic balanced stance. The feet should be a little more than shoulder-width apart, and the knees should be slightly bent with the weight on the balls of the feet (see figure 4.17). The glove foot is slightly in front of the throwing foot to promote a quick start for moving in any direction. This stance also enables fielders to reach farther from the body for balls hit sharply directly at them. Players should also bend at the waist so that their forearms can rest on their thighs and they can lift their heads comfortably to look straight ahead.

Figure 4.17 Ready position for fielding ground balls in the infield.

APPROACHING THE BALL

When fielding ground balls in the infield, the approach to the ball relies on proper footwork to get the glove and throwing hand in position to field the ball. The fielder moves quickly from the ready position (see figure 4.18a) to the line of the path of the ball. The fielder's feet move quickly to get the body—shoulders, feet and hips—square to the path of the ball and to center the ball on the body (see figure 4.18b). The steps taken depend on the distance that the fielder has to cover to reach the ball. The fielder can shuffle if the ball is nearby (see figure 4.19, a and b) or use a crossover step and run if the ball is farther away (see figure 4.20, a–c). As the fielder gets closer to the ball, she lowers her body and then slows into a controlled glide through the ball.

a   b

Figure 4.18   **Moving from the ready position toward the ball.**

a   b

Figure 4.19   **Shuffle step to the ball when it is nearby.**

(continued)

a   b   c

Figure 4.20   **Crossover step to the ball when it is farther away.**

CONTROLLING WEIGHT DISTRIBUTION AND BALANCE

When the fielder is ready to field the ball, her weight should be in the balls of the feet. As learned previously, the player fields the ball in the middle of the body if possible, in front of the head. To ensure a good move through the ball with proper balance, the feet are spread at least shoulder-width apart and the glove foot is in front of the throwing foot (see figure 4.21a), allowing the proper shifting of the weight forward during the actual fielding motion (see figure 4.21b). When she reaches the ball, the fielder's weight is on the throwing-hand foot (see figure 4.21c) and moves naturally onto the glove-hand foot (see figure 4.21d). The fielder's upper body is bent at the waist, with the back flattened, so that she can reach forward to field the ball out in front of her feet. The fielder's head should stay as still and as level as possible throughout the entire motion.

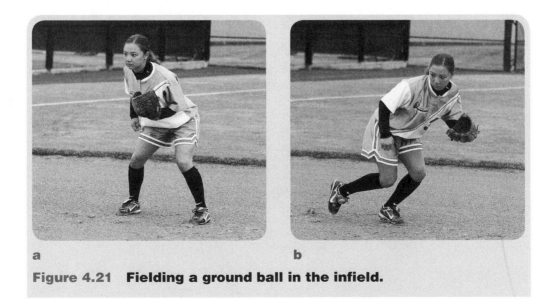

a   b

Figure 4.21   **Fielding a ground ball in the infield.**

c   d

Figure 4.21 *(continued)*

Balance and weight distribution are essential to being a consistent fielder and allow the fielder to make last-second adjustments to an unpredictable hop of the ball. The hands are the quickest part of the body and the fielder's greatest asset in fielding grounders. With proper balance and weight distribution, the player consistently puts the body into a position that allows the hands to move in a familiar pattern. If the body is not in correct position, the hands have to adjust and are out of position.

USING PROPER GLOVE WORK

Training your players' hands is the easiest way to make them better fielders. The hands should be down and out in front of the eyes. The glove should be open by the time the ball is 5 or 6 feet in front of the fielder so that she has time to adjust to the movement of the ball. The throwing hand should be held over the glove or to the side of the glove, and the palm should be facing the ball. Having the throwing hand close to the glove aids the fielder both in fielding correctly and in making a quick transition into the throw.

The player places the hands in line with the ball and holds them still (but not hard) as the body glides through the ball. The hands are still but appear to move forward as the body moves. The quieter the hands are, the better and more consistent the fielder is. The glove should always be out in front of the eyes, and the pocket should be facing out rather than facing backward or outside the player's feet. These two common mistakes can cause players to make quick, sudden movements when attempting to field the ball, often resulting in errors.

(continued)

MOVING THROUGH THE BALL

Fielding a ground ball is a dynamic movement. The player never comes to a stop until after she throws the ball. As stated earlier, the hands are still and the body glides through the fielding of the ball. Balls can take three kinds of hops—the short hop, the medium hop and the long hop. Your players need to learn how to anticipate each kind.

Short Hop

The short hop is easy if the fielder pushes the glove as close to the bounce as possible, enabling her to field the ball immediately after the hop and eliminating the chance that the ball will go anywhere but the glove.

Medium Hop

The medium hop is the most difficult play because the fielder doesn't have time to adjust to the bounce of the ball. Players need to move either forward or backward to field the ball successfully. Fielders should be aggressive when approaching a medium hop by reaching with the glove and essentially making it more of a short hop so that they can field it more cleanly

Long Hop

The long hop is the easiest to field because it hangs in the air the longest and is easy to judge and react to.

When fielding, players should move directly through the path of the oncoming ground ball while they are fielding it and shift their movement to the direction of the throw quickly after fielding the ball. Although outstanding fielders have mastered the technique of fielding the ball while moving toward the throwing target, when players are learning or beginning their season they should begin by staying through the path of the ball. If the ball is hit so hard that the player cannot center the ball and move forward through it, have your fielder at least center the ball and then just keep her weight forward on the balls of her feet.

After successfully fielding the ground ball, the fielder prepares to throw by bringing both hands to the throwing-hand ear and stepping with the throwing-hand foot toward the target (see figure 4.22*a*). The foot should then turn (instep facing the target) to allow the body to rotate to throw. The glove-hand shoulder and hip should now point at the target (see figure 4.22*b*). The glove-hand foot steps directly toward the target to aid in producing an accurate throw (see figure 4.22*c*).

At a Glance

The following parts of the text offer additional information on fielding ground balls in the infield.

Playing First Base	102
Playing Second Base	108
Playing Third Base	114
Playing Shortstop	121
Fielding Balls on the Fore-hand or Backhand Side	67

a   b   c

Figure 4.22   Making a throw after fielding a ground ball.

Common Errors

Following are several common errors that you might run into when teaching your athletes how to field ground balls in the infield.

Error	Error Correction
The athlete is sitting upright in more of a squat to field the ball and dropping the hands between the feet where the fielder can't see them or the ball.	Have the fielder spread her feet and flatten the back so that the hands reach out to the ball.
The athlete's hands are too hard and stiff when fielding the ball.	The elbows should be slightly bent and not locked. When the arms are extended forward, the muscles should be loose. The fielder should be in position to field the ball before it reaches her. Hard hands can also be the result when a fielder charges out of control through the ball.
The athlete is fielding the ball outside the feet.	A player who fields the ball outside the feet is usually afraid of the ball. Work with the fielder slowly at first, rolling the ball while she works at proper hand positioning and gains trust in her ability to field the ball. As she gains confidence, move her back farther and either throw the grounder or hit it. Progress as the fielder feels comfortable and be sure that she uses proper technique.
The athlete is not rotating to throw the ball after fielding it.	The instep of the throwing-hand foot must be facing the target. It is almost impossible not to rotate the body in the direction dictated by the feet. If the feet are correct, the body generally follows.

Fielding Ground Balls in the Outfield

The outfield is considered the last line of defense because a ball that gets past an outfielder may go all the way to the fence. An outfielder can field the ball two ways. First is the safety, in which the outfielder lowers onto one knee to become a wall that the ball cannot pass through. This technique is a conservative, sure way to secure the ball. The second method is the run-through, which, as the name suggests, is running through the ball while fielding it. This method has more risk associated with it but has the advantage of being quicker and allowing the fielder to move quickly into a throw. The outfielder must consider many factors when deciding which method to use to field the ball (see Outfield Defensive Responsibilities in chapter 6 for more information).

MOVING TO THE BALL

Just as an infielder centers her body on the ball when fielding, so does an outfielder. Generally, outfielders have more time, but they also have more distance to cover. Even so, an outfielder may get to the ball just in time to stop it or to attempt to field it as she cuts across its path. In this circumstance, she doesn't have enough time to square up or move through the path of the ball. She will also need more time to move into the potential throw to a base. In either case, the outfielder should sprint to the path of the ball to have the best chance to field the ball cleanly and quickly and make a good throw. A good offense will recognize lazy outfielders and try to take extra bases because those players will need more time to get the ball back into the infield.

APPROACHING THE BALL

As discussed earlier, an outfielder should do everything in her power to field ground balls in the center of the body. To do so, the fielder should run to a point behind the ball that is in a direct line with the path of the ball. If the fielder runs directly to the path of the ball, she will more than likely cut across the path. The fielder should work to be behind the ball in time to move forward toward it as it approaches. If the ball is moving quickly, the fielder may have to run deeper in the outfield to get behind the ball (see figure 4.23a). If the ball is moving slowly, the fielder can run on a shallower angle (see figure 4.23b). The fielder will then need to turn a rounded corner into the path of the ball, allowing her to control her speed and balance, and then move directly in line with the path of the ball. If the ball is moving too fast for the fielder to get behind it, she should take the best possible angle to intercept it and attempt to use a backhand or forehand to field the ball. Another player should be available to back her up.

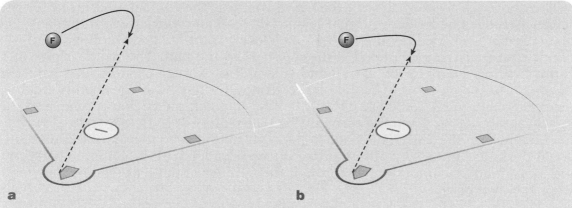

Figure 4.23 Outfielder's path to the ball when it is moving (*a*) quickly or (*b*) more slowly.

FIELDING THE BALL

The safety method of fielding involves making a human wall that, in theory, the ball can't pass through. The fielder centers on the ball and approaches it in a direct line. As the fielder gets within a few feet of fielding the ball, she puts one knee (generally the throwing-hand knee) on the ground and places the lower leg out to the side to create as much of a barrier as possible with the leg (see figure 4.24). The knee is tucked in close to the foot of the other leg and the hips and shoulders are square to the ball, which also helps create the wall. The glove hand and throwing hand are down and in front of the small gap that may occur between the knee and the foot. The player then rounds the shoulders and turns squarely into the ball to keep it from glancing off and going past. If the ball takes a bad hop and doesn't hit the glove, it should make contact with the body and drop right in front of the fielder. The safety method is the most widely used and preferred because the ball is unlikely to get past the fielder, but it doesn't allow the fielder to return the ball quickly. If the situation calls for a quick return of the ball for a potential game-winning play, the fielder must execute the run-through.

Figure 4.24 Safety method of fielding ground balls in the outfield.

(continued)

The approach to the ball with the run-through is the same as that used for the safety method. The fielder must get behind the ball and move toward it in a direct line (see figure 4.25a). As the fielder gets closer to the ball, she shifts slightly to the side so that the glove hand is directly behind the ball. The fielder slows to a controlled jog, leans to the glove-hand side and forward, far enough to have the fingertips of the glove drag lightly on the ground for 6 to 12 inches before fielding the ball (see figure 4.25b). The glove is behind the ball, the pocket is open and the fingertips are down. Running through the ball requires the fielder to be down, to field the ball on the glove-hand side of the body and to keep the shoulders and arm down for at least one step after fielding it (see figure 4.25c). When done correctly, the movement is a smooth glide through the fielding of the ball. The fielder never stops forward progress.

a   b   c

Figure 4.25 **The run-through method of fielding ground balls.**

PREPARING TO THROW

When preparing to throw after fielding a ground ball, the safety method is more challenging because the fielder is in a stationary, low position. From the knee (see figure 4.26a), the fielder stands and steps immediately with the throwing-hand foot, rotating the instep to face the target (see figure 4.26b). This movement allows proper rotation of the shoulders and hips to set up for the throw. The fielder should step with the glove-hand foot directly toward the target (see figure 4.26c) and finish the throw using proper throwing mechanics, as discussed in "Throwing" on page 56.

Figure 4.26 **Moving into the throw when using the safety method.**

The run-through method is easier to throw from because the fielder already has momentum. After fielding the ball, as shown in figure 4.27*a*, the fielder takes the glove hand to the ear of the throwing-hand side (see figure 4.27*b*). The throwing hand gets to the ball as quickly as possible, preferably before it reaches the ear. While the glove and throwing hand are getting into position to throw, the throwing-hand foot plants with the instep facing the target (see figure 4.27*c*). The stride foot then moves forward in line with the throw, and the player finishes the throw using proper throwing mechanics.

Figure 4.27 **Moving into the throw when using the run-through method.**

(continued)

One additional element of the throw that outfielders need to focus on is making sure that the fingers are directly behind the ball on the release. Players often let the fingers slide to the side of the ball on release, creating a curve effect that can cause the throw to curve away from the target by several feet. Infielders may not see that result because their throws are generally shorter, but a curve thrown by an outfielder becomes exaggerated with distance.

USING THE CROW HOP

When outfielders are moving into a throw using either method, they commonly use a "crow hop" to help them achieve the momentum that they need for long throws. To execute the crow hop, as the fielder moves forward toward the target (see figure 4.28*a*) the throwing-hand foot actually lifts (see figure 4.28*b*) and crosses over in front of the glove-hand foot. The instep faces the target before it plants to begin the drive with the legs (see figure 4.28*c*). This crossover step helps the fielder gain more power and momentum because she is covering more ground with the legs.

a   b   c

Figure 4.28 **Outfielder using a crow hop to gain momentum into the throw.**

Common Errors

Following are several common errors that you might run into when teaching your athletes how to field ground balls in the outfield.

Error	Error Correction
The ball is bouncing off to the side when using the safety method.	Be sure that the player squares the shoulders and hips to the ball. The challenging shoulder is the glove-hand shoulder.
The ball is getting through the feet of the fielder when using the safety method.	Be sure that the fielder's knee is close enough to the foot so that the glove covers all remaining gaps.
The athlete is mishandling the run through the ball.	Be sure that the fielder is in line in time and then emphasize the length of the fingertip drag into contact.
The path of the fielder is not in line soon enough.	The fielder should angle back a little to get behind the ball and then round into its path.

Catching a Throw

KEY POINTS

The most important components of catching throws are

○ lining up with the ball,

○ catching the ball away from the body, and

○ making the catch with both hands.

Catching is one of the easiest skills for a good softball player and one of the most alarming for a beginning player. A ball thrown at you can be unnerving if you don't have confidence in your catching abilities. Learning how to catch doesn't take long, however, and players should learn good habits from the beginning. After players become confident in their ability to catch, they can become lazy with their body position and feet. Catching becomes so easy that players often cut back on their effort by reaching for the ball. But they should not use the glove as a butterfly net; it is a tool that is part of the body.

LINING UP WITH THE BALL

Centering the body on the ball puts the player in the best position not only to adjust to a ball that she has misread or that might curve slightly but also to see the ball well and catch it in front of the throwing-hand shoulder. As players advance in their skill level, they can learn to shift the catch to the throwing-hand side to enable a quicker transition into the throw. If your team can throw the ball with speed, players will need quick feet to center the ball in the infield, but it is important that they develop this quickness. Great players make centering the body on the ball look routine, and you hardly notice how quickly they do this.

CATCHING THE BALL AWAY FROM THE BODY

Figure 4.29 **Basic position when preparing to catch a throw.**

When preparing to make a catch, the player assumes a basic athletic position. The feet are shoulder-width apart, the knees flexed, the body slightly bent at the waist, the arms extended and the elbows slightly bent (see figure 4.29). The eyes are in line with the ball over the top of the glove so that they can track the ball into the glove. The player should reach out for the ball away from the body, let the arms absorb the impact (see figure 4.30a) and then quickly bring the ball to the throwing-hand side (see figure 4.30b).

a   b

Figure 4.30   **Catching a throw.**

Note that the height of the ball will alter the angle of the glove. If the ball is shoulder height or higher the fingers of the glove point upward (see figure 4.31a), if the ball is below the shoulders to waist height the fingers point sideways (see figure 4.31b), and if the ball is below the waist the fingers point down (see figure 4.31c).

a   b   c

Figure 4.31   **Angle of the glove for throws (a) at the shoulders or higher, (b) below the shoulders to the waist, and (c) below the waist.**

(continued)

MAKING THE CATCH WITH BOTH HANDS

When catching throws, the throwing hand should always stay close to the glove, as shown in figure 4.30, *a* and *b*. This positioning allows a quicker exchange into the throw for better players, provides some assistance in the catch for younger players and reinforces the centering up of the catch. Players often become lazy with this aspect of catching, so you should emphasize it in practice and warm-ups.

Common Errors

Following are several common errors that you might run into when teaching your athletes how to catch throws.

Error	Error Correction
The ball is bouncing out of the glove.	Check to see how well the glove is broken in. If it is stiff and difficult for a player to close, the ball will not stay in the pocket.
The athlete is not using two hands.	Some professional players tie a stretchy cord between the wrists. The cord is about the length of a shoulder-width. Because the hands are tied together, they must learn to work in concert. This technique also promotes proper throwing.
The athlete is not centering the catch.	This bad habit simply needs attention. Emphasize centering from the beginning of warm-ups into team throwing and fielding drills.
The athlete exhibits fear of the ball.	Start with a ball that is soft and use an easy throw to the player. As the player gains confidence with the correct hand movement, advance to a regulation softball and then pick up the speed of the throw.

Although catching a fly ball seems simple, great outfielders work hard to develop their skills. Although outfielders may become a little lazy and not react as quickly as they can, or may float to the ball and catch it just in time, the best outfielders are quick to react to a ball off the bat and move immediately to the ball, whether it is a fly or a grounder.

MOVING TO THE BALL

As stated earlier, many outfielders float to the ball, moving just quickly enough to time the catch with getting to the ball. They run only as fast as necessary to catch the ball. But that approach does not allow for last-second adjustments, misjudgments or the transition into the throw. To prepare to catch the ball properly, players must first learn to react to the ball off the bat and sprint to the path of the ball. You will often see a fielder misjudge the speed of a ball and not run as hard as she should when the ball is hit. But as the fly ball continues to travel, the fielder recognizes that she needs to cover more distance and increases her speed. A better approach for the outfielder is to move as quickly as possible as soon as she realizes that the ball is coming in the direction of the outfield, even if she needs to wait after she gets there.

An outfielder can move most quickly from an athletic stance similar to the one that a tennis player uses when receiving a serve. The outfielder should be moving slightly, standing upright and keeping the feet spread so that she can react to either side. Because an outfielder may have to go backward or forward, the feet should be slightly staggered, with the glove-hand foot forward of the throwing-hand foot (see figure 4.32). The player should focus directly on the strike zone to make the earliest judgment possible. An outfielder can see the angle of the bat on contact if she focuses well enough. Doing so will enable her to anticipate where the ball might go and get the best jump possible.

KEY POINTS

The most important components of catching fly balls are

- moving to the ball,
- approaching the ball,
- tracking the ball,
- setting up for the catch,
- making the catch, and
- preparing to throw.

Figure 4.32 Outfielder's ready position.

(continued)

APPROACHING THE BALL

Outfielders need to catch a fly ball by getting on line with its path. Taking the correct angle is the foundation of getting into position, making a good transition and having good balance. When approaching a fly ball, the fielder should get in the path of the

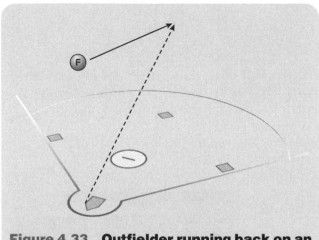

Figure 4.33 Outfielder running back on an angle to the ball.

ball, behind where the ball would drop if she didn't catch it. Doing this requires judging the depth and speed of the ball and running to get behind it. If the ball is hit too hard or too deep, making it impossible for the fielder, running full-speed, to intersect with the path of the ball, she should run back on an angle, allowing her more time to get to the line of the ball. She should run deep enough so that she can round into the path of the ball and still be behind it (see figure 4.33). Doing this requires the fielder to run back more than she would simply to catch the ball in passing.

Figure 4.34 Outfielder's body position when setting up for a catch.

TRACKING THE BALL

The better an outfielder sees the ball, the more accurate her judgments will be and the fewer errors she will commit. Outfielders should practice seeing the entire path of the ball from the bat to the glove to help improve how well they see the ball. Outfielders wants to move smoothly as they run toward the ball, keeping their eyes steady. To do this, they should learn to run on the balls of their feet more than on the heel to toe. A heel strike causes a slight jarring that makes the ball seem to bounce in the air.

SETTING UP FOR THE CATCH

To enable her to see the ball all the way into the glove, the outfielder should catch the ball out in front and above the head, as if she is going to volley a volleyball. The knees should be slightly bent, and the feet should be shoulder-width apart. The glove-hand foot should be forward of the throwing-hand foot (see figure 4.34). The outfielder should make the catch with two hands to center the catch and to put the throwing hand in position to get to the ball quickly. But as the skill level of your outfielders increases, they should learn to shift the catch to the throwing-hand side of the body, level with the head. In addition, a ball hit deep to either side of the outfielder that she has no chance of getting behind requires her to use a different method of catching. The fielder must learn to catch the ball over the shoulder or slightly to the side of the body while on the run.

MAKING THE CATCH

Footwork is the first step in a quick reaction and proper move to the ball. If the ball is hit to the left side, the left foot drops back and the foot opens to allow a smooth, easy crossover step with the right foot so that the fielder can run in a direct line back to the ball. Conversely, the right foot drops back on a ball hit to the right side. The outfielder should run on the balls of the feet so that she can see the ball better.

After the outfielder moves in one direction or the other, she will need to do one of two things depending on which hand is her glove hand and which is her throwing hand. If the ball is hit to the glove-hand side, the fielder turns and runs back while looking over the throwing-hand shoulder. She eventually catches the ball in front of her after it passes over that shoulder. In this case, tracking the ball into the glove is a challenge because the outfielder is looking over her shoulder. Catching the ball is easier on the glove-hand side because the glove is in a natural position and the hand and pocket are already turned correctly. The fielder simply needs to raise the glove to catch the ball.

If the ball is hit to the throwing-hand side, the outfielder turns that direction with the required drop step and runs to the ball, tracking it over the glove-hand shoulder. The challenge in this case is to catch the ball on the same side of the body as the glove while running backward. If the ball travels directly over the shoulder to the midline of the body, the glove-hand motion will be a simple lift to the ball because the pocket is already facing the ball. If the ball needs to be caught outside the shoulder and farther from the body, the glove hand turns so that the elbow is facing the oncoming ball, turning the pocket 180 degrees. This technique makes it easier for the fielder to reach for a ball hit farther away.

At a Glance

The following parts of the text offer additional information on catching fly balls.

Playing Second Base	108
Playing Shortstop	121
Playing Third Base	114
Playing First Base	102
Outfield Defensive Responsibilities	176

PREPARING TO THROW

An advanced outfielder prepares to throw before she catches the ball by lining up with the ball and staying behind it, allowing her to begin moving forward through the catch and immediately into the throw. The skilled outfielder gets momentum into her throw before she catches the ball, whereas a less-skilled outfielder tends to stay stationary when she catches the ball and moves into the throw only after securing the ball in her glove.

(continued)

When catching a fly ball, after the momentum takes the fielder through the catch and toward the target, the throwing-hand foot plants, turning the instep to face the target. Many fielders then use the crow hop in which the throwing-hand foot lifts and crosses over in front of the glove foot, going into the planting motion to help in covering the distance needed to generate power. The glove foot then strides directly toward the target, and the fielder releases the ball. To create more power for the long throws required, outfielders use a bigger arm circle than infielders do and throw more over the top of the head.

Common Errors

Following are several common errors that you might run into when teaching your athletes how to catch fly balls.

Error	Error Correction
The athlete is catching the ball behind the head.	When the outfielder sets up to catch the ball, make sure that she keeps moving her feet to stay behind the ball. Catching behind the head results from poor judgment or moving too early into the catch.
The athlete is running at the fly ball with the glove hand extended.	Ensure that the player has the glove hand tucked like a sprinter.
The athlete is taking too many steps to stop and throw after catching a routine fly ball.	Teach the player to be quicker to get behind the ball and to move through the catch toward the throw.
The athlete is not running back in a direct line to catch a ball hit over the head.	Be sure that the player's drop step is far enough back to clear a path for the crossover step to go back and not across the front of the body.

Pitching is the most important component of any softball game. Because good pitching can silence good hitting, pitching will often decide the outcome. As coaches we often feel comfortable teaching our athletes fielding and offensive skills, but we may shy away from teaching players about pitching because we don't know enough about it. But as in any other athletic movement, the body follows consistent and recognizable movement patterns. After you separate the skill into understandable parts, you will notice that pitching isn't as unique a movement as you may have believed.

GRIPPING THE BALL CORRECTLY

First, proper grip for a pitch is necessary. The ball should rest on the full length of the fingers, not in the palm, and the finger pads and thumb should be on a seam (see figure 4.35). The thumb should be on the opposite side of the ball from the fingers.

USING THE PROPER WINDUP

The windup—or premotion—is the movement to prepare to throw the ball. The windup should help the pitcher be relaxed and comfortable. The feet are apart, the throwing-hand foot is on the front of the rubber, and the glove-hand foot on the back. To begin the motion, the hands come together in front of the body, an action called the presentation (see figure 4.36a), the weight shifts to the back leg, and the pivot foot typically turns to allow the body to rotate (see figure 4.36b). As the weight begins to shift forward to initiate the pitch, the throwing arm either pushes down, drops back or reaches up to begin the arm circle (see figure 4.37, a–c). All these styles are correct. The key in choosing one is comfort.

The windup is an act of getting the stationary body moving into the pitch. The pitcher should not exert a lot of effort and waste energy during the windup. The more advanced pitchers will begin slowly and gather their energy as they go. Less experienced pitchers will often try to be too quick in the windup and lose that momentum at the release point, where they need it most. The goal is to stay smooth, comfortable and consistent.

KEY POINTS

The most important components of pitching are

- gripping the ball correctly,
- using the proper windup,
- striding and moving the body toward the target,
- achieving proper rotation and balance,
- using a full arm circle,
- snapping the wrist on the release, and
- using the proper follow-through.

Figure 4.35 Proper grip for a pitch.

(continued)

Figure 4.36   Pitcher's windup for a pitch.

Figure 4.37   Pitcher's throwing-arm movement before the arm circle: (*a*) push down, (*b*) drop back, or (*c*) reach up.

STRIDING AND MOVING TOWARD THE TARGET

Beginning pitchers often overlook the stride and body movement. Better pitchers focus on these elements. After the weight has transferred to the pivot foot, or throwing-hand foot, the plant foot strides forward toward the target (see figure 4.38). As the foot lands it should be turned. If the landing is incorrect, the toes will be pointing toward the catcher.

The body then moves in a linear fashion from the pivot foot toward the target. Also note that, as in the overhand throw on page 57, the line of force, which extends from the pivot foot to the target, is critical. The stride foot should reach forward and plant on that line. If the foot is off line, the pitcher will be unable to reach her potential.

ACHIEVING PROPER ROTATION AND BALANCE

As in the overhand throwing motion discussed on page 57, the body needs to open, or to rotate the shoulders and hips, to produce a natural and powerful pitch. You know this instinctively when swinging a heavy object in a circle. For example, picture swinging a bucket of water. We naturally open and let the arm swing in front of the body. Because this movement is the natural path of the arm, it is the most injury-free movement. Hip rotation is important to producing speed, but speed is not a direct result of it. All aspects of the pitch will be hampered if the pitcher fails to open or rotate correctly.

Figure 4.38 Pitcher's plant foot striding toward the target.

As the arm begins the circle going up and back (see figure 4.39), the stride is going forward at the same time. When the glove-hand foot reaches forward and the throwing arm reaches back, a natural rotation occurs. That rotation is maintained to some degree throughout the linear drive forward and the release of the ball. After the ball has passed the hip, the hips and shoulders continue forward until the body comes to a relatively closed position. Pitchers vary, however, in the amount of rotation that they use.

To achieve proper balance, accomplished pitchers lean forward to begin the drive toward the target, but they are always upright and balanced between their feet by the time the arm reaches the top of the circle. They maintain this balance through release. Just before release and at release, the throwing-hand shoulder, hip and knee are typically in alignment.

USING A FULL ARM CIRCLE

The arm circle that a pitcher uses is simple in theory. Pitchers can master it easily if they know a few points to focus on and commit to from the beginning. The arm circle generally starts with the arms pointing down toward the ground. The circle then travels down the line of force toward the target, up over the head, and then descends down and forward on the line of force. To be comfortable and prepare the arm and wrist for a dynamic release, the elbow is never locked and the hand and ball again lag behind the forearm. Check for correct hand position throughout the circle.

To begin the circle, the ball is pointing down to the ground or to the midline of the body. Note that the wrist is not cocked and that the hand is loose and allows the arm to move freely. The arm then circles back behind the body. Before descending, the hand rotates naturally until the ball is pointed away from the body. The little finger leads the hand on the descent. On its descent, the hand naturally lags behind the forearm into the release area. As the hand enters the release point, the arm is long and the hand will square up as it catapults the ball past the hip. See figure 4.39 for an example of the pitcher's arm circle.

(continued)

a

b

c

d

Figure 4.39   Arm circle for a pitch.

SNAPPING THE WRIST ON THE RELEASE

The wrist snap on the release should be the key focus for the pitcher. After the pitcher masters the wrist snap, the body can assist it, but the wrist snap is the key to speed, control and eventually the ability to throw moving pitches.

The wrist snap is a firm yet relaxed flick of the wrist. The fingers stay long and throw or push the ball, much like an inverted basketball shot. But the wrist snap for a pitch is a much more powerful and explosive move. As the pitcher releases the ball, the ball rolls down the fingers until it reaches the finger pads. With a very quick bend at the wrist, the full length of the fingers pushes, or flicks, the ball forward. This action occurs at the bottom of the arm circle, close to the thigh of the pivot foot. The hand often appears to roll over after release, which is a good sign of a quick and relaxed movement.

Two natural movement planes govern the action of the wrist. One is a front-to-back movement, and the other is a side-to-side movement. When a pitcher learns to snap the wrist, it will typically do a little of each but it usually develops more of one than the other. Both are correct as long as the movement isn't stiff or forced.

PROPER FOLLOW-THROUGH

The follow-through may include some variations, but there is always a release of tension in the arm, shoulder and body after release. The arm typically moves past the release point, and the elbow releases or relaxes. In most pitchers, the forearm and elbow continue past the hip or release point and float to a natural finish. A point that should be emphasized is that the follow-through is a natural result of the wrist snap; the follow-through doesn't create the wrist snap. The pitcher should focus on releasing the ball correctly and then letting the arm naturally relax.

At a Glance

The following parts of the text offer additional information on pitching.

Common Errors

Following are several common errors that you might run into when teaching your athletes how to pitch.

Error	Error Correction
The athlete has no wrist snap.	Work with the pitcher to isolate the wrist without the full motion, such as by having her throw the ball into the glove or flip it to the catcher with just the wrist.
The arm circle is off line or bent.	Teach the pitcher to focus on reaching down the line of force toward the target to begin the motion. The arm is easily controlled out front. With proper rotation, the arm will continue on a correct path if it begins on a correct path.
The athlete is striding off line.	Draw a line of force during practice and have the pitcher focus on striding down the line.
The athlete is leaning forward or bending at the waist on release.	Have the pitcher start from a stationary and open position. She should work on a full circle and release the ball while maintaining the correct posture. Her legs should be slightly bent.

KEY POINTS

The most important components of catching are

o using the proper stance when receiving the pitch,

o giving signals,

o receiving the pitch,

o framing a pitch,

o blocking pitches in the dirt,

o preparing to throw,

o catching pop-ups,

o making tag plays at home, and

o fielding bunts.

No player is more involved in the game than the catcher. She not only catches every pitch but also directs the defense and makes defensive plays. And she has the additional job of handling the pitchers! Great catchers are quick, durable, game smart and determined. They do for others on the team. They need to be level headed so that they make good decisions, and they must be able to communicate those decisions to the defense.

USING THE PROPER STANCE WHEN RECEIVING THE PITCH

When receiving the pitch, the catcher needs to use a stance that allows her to receive the pitch no matter where it might go and to be prepared to move to make a defensive play. The catcher should squat behind home plate with the feet a little more than shoulder-width apart, weight balanced and toes turned slightly outward (see figure 4.40). The catcher should be able to shift her weight from side to side by using her ankles, called an ankle sway, as shown in figure 4.41. In addition, the catcher wants to be as far forward as she can without risk of being hit by the batter.

Figure 4.40 Catcher's stance when receiving a pitch.

Figure 4.41 Ankle sway.

GIVING SIGNALS

To give a signal properly, the catcher waits until the pitcher is on the mound, places the glove hand outside her knee or shin to block the view of the opposing team and keeps her knees just far enough apart to let the defense see the signal. The throwing hand should be close to the body and between the legs.

RECEIVING THE PITCH

Receiving the pitch is an art. The catcher sets up not only to draw the pitcher's attention and, ideally, the pitch to a specific area but also to try to convince the umpire that the pitch was a strike. After giving the signal, the catcher may shift her stance in line with the side of the plate that she wants the ball to cross. If the pitcher doesn't have that kind of control or is exceptionally advanced and doesn't need a target, the catcher can stay in the center of the plate.

The catcher gives the pitcher a target by extending the glove arm with a relaxed elbow and the pocket open to the pitcher. The throwing hand should be out of the way of the ball and held down behind the ankle. After the pitcher has started her motion, the catcher should loosen for the catch and for the possibility of needing to move for the catch. The catcher should relax the wrist of the glove hand, allowing a slight rolling move of the glove. This action helps the hand release from a stiff target and be ready to move to the ball. The catcher may want to use a slight ankle sway to have a little movement so that she can move quickly from a difficult squat position. To make the catch, the catcher can give slightly with the ball and bring it into the body (see figure 4.42a), or she can catch the pitch with a strong arm and hand, not giving with it but rather sticking the pitch (see figure 4.42b).

Figure 4.42 Catching the pitch: (*a*) giving with the pitch or (*b*) sticking the pitch.

(continued)

FRAMING A PITCH

Framing is simply catching a borderline pitch in a way that helps an umpire see it as a strike. Framing is done by turning the wrist slightly on the catch so that the pocket faces the middle of the strike zone. The catcher will feel as if she is catching the outside of the ball. The action is a smooth wrist turn, not a jerky motion. Catchers should use this technique for borderline pitches only, not for obvious balls.

BLOCKING PITCHES IN THE DIRT

Blocking is a technique in which the catcher uses the body as a wall to keep a pitch that goes in the dirt from getting past her. To block, the catcher stays low and pushes with the ankles to move in front of the pitch. The catcher goes to her knees and spreads them far enough for good balance and to center the pitch, with her weight on the inside half of either knee. The throwing hand is behind the glove, and the catcher moves the glove in close to the body and between the knees to help create a wall. The shoulders round forward, the chin is tucked to the chest, and the elbows are outside the body. The catcher should think of her body as a satellite dish at this point. She wants to be sure to face forward so that if the ball hits her body and not the glove, it will drop right in front of her. If she is turned on an angle, the ball will hit her and glance off, going to the backstop. The catcher should be soft to absorb the ball.

If the ball is directly at the catcher in the dirt, the body position is the same, but the catcher simply drops to her knees right where she is. The knees should replace the feet so that the catcher isn't going forward when moving to her knees.

PREPARING TO THROW

A catcher's throw needs to be the quickest on the team. When a runner is on base and the catcher anticipates a throw, she adjusts her stance to be ready by dropping the throwing-hand foot back slightly and opening the toe. By lifting the hips slightly (the catcher must be sure not to rise too high and block the umpire's view), the catcher will be able to move forward more quickly. After receiving the pitch, the throwing hand meets the glove hand on its way back to the throwing-side ear (see figure 4.43a). At the same time, the catcher comes out of her squat far enough to use her legs but not stand completely straight. As the hands come to the ear, the elbows lift and the shoulders and hips rotate in line with the target (see figure 4.43b). The throwing-hand foot slides directly under the body to help drive the body in a direct line to the target. The instep is facing the target. To shorten and quicken the throw, the catcher takes the ball straight back from the ear to a position behind the body at head level and strides toward the target, using correct mechanics to release the ball.

a　　　　　　　　b

Figure 4.43　Catcher making a throw after catching a pitch.

CATCHING POP-UPS

When a hitter pops up a ball to the catcher, the catcher should remove her mask and hold it in her hand as she locates the ball. After she spots the ball, she tosses the mask in the opposite direction to get it away from her feet. She should then turn her back to the infield and move so that the ball appears to be directly over her forehead. The catcher should keep her feet moving because the ball will appear to move as it comes down. She catches the ball by reaching up above the head with both hands.

MAKING TAG PLAYS AT HOME

When making a tag play at home, the proper sequence should be to discard the mask, set up in a correct stance, catch the ball and then place the tag. But catchers often become anxious, lose focus and make the mistake of trying to place the tag before they catch the ball. They must focus on the ball, not the runner.

First, taking the proper stance to receive the ball and place the tag will help the catcher be confident about controlling the situation and will help her avoid getting hurt on contact. The catcher should set up in front of the plate, within one step of

(continued)

Figure 4.44 Catcher setting up to make a tag play at home.

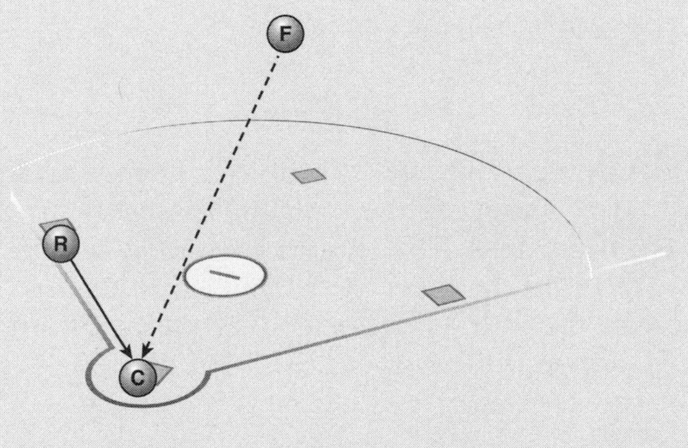

Figure 4.45 Catcher positioning in a triangle with the ball and the runner.

the plate and with the toe of the left foot pointing at the runner (see figure 4.44). If the catcher sets up completely blocking the plate, she has no idea where the runner will go, whereas if she is in front of the plate, she gives the back corner to the runner and knows where the runner will go. This setup allows the catcher to plan for a slide that she knows will take place to her side.

The catcher then forms a triangle with the ball and the runner (see figure 4.45). If the throw is easy to catch (in the air or a long hop) the catcher can have her shoulders and feet turned more toward the runner. If the throw will be difficult to handle, the catcher should square to the ball and use the body to block it. The catcher should also remember to let the ball come to her because the ball travels much faster than the body does. If a catcher reaches out to catch the ball, she will be much slower than she would be by letting the ball travel the full distance.

After the catcher has caught the ball, the left foot, which is pointing at the runner, can shift more to the foul line and help the catcher take away the back corner of the plate, in essence blocking the entire plate. By having the toe of the left foot pointing toward the runner, the shinguard is facing the runner and the knee is at an angle to give properly should a collision occur. A runner's slide into the side of the catcher's leg may cause serious injury.

To place the tag, the catcher should hold the ball with the bare hand and cover it with the mitt. The back of the mitt should be facing the runner. In this position the catcher can safely secure the ball, and the body can move normally if a collision occurs. If possible the catcher should hold the ball and glove close to the body to keep the ball from being knocked out of the glove. If a collision is certain, the catcher can absorb the impact by staying low, keeping the ball in the glove and against the body and tucking the head. She doesn't need to worry about placing a tag during a collision; she can just keep the arms and hands against the body and let the runner come into her. A good umpire will call the runner out if the play is close and the catcher holds on to the ball.

FIELDING BUNTS

On a bunted ball that is close to the catcher, the catcher comes up out of her squat as quickly as possible while taking off the mask and tossing it to the side. The approach to the ball depends on where the ball is and where the throw needs to go. In every case, the catcher should step past the ball with the glove foot to be sure that the ball is centered between her feet, which are in line with the throwing target. If the ball is still moving, she uses both hands to field it, using the glove like a backstop for the throwing hand to push the ball against and secure a firm grip. If the ball is stationary, the catcher can barehand the ball by pushing it into the ground with the throwing hand to obtain a secure grip.

By fielding the bunt toward the target, the catcher uses controlled momentum to be quick and to throw the ball with more force. The key is proper setup. If the ball is bunted toward third base and the throw needs to go to first base, a right-handed catcher needs to get around the ball quickly to get her feet and shoulders in line with the target. When the ball is bunted toward first base and the throw is going to first, the footwork is easy because proper setup takes the catcher in line to the target.

Common Errors

Following are several common errors that you might run into when teaching your athletes how to play the catching position.

Error	Error Correction
The athlete is falling to the side when moving to block.	The catcher's weight has probably shifted to the outside of the knee. Teach the catcher to control her body weight by keeping it in between the knees.
The athlete is taking a long time to throw the ball.	Teach the catcher to keep her body weight forward of the back leg as she comes out of her squat and to move the throwing hand quickly to the glove to get the ball.
The athlete is dropping pop-ups.	Ensure that the catcher gets under the ball quickly. The ball will keep moving, and the catcher will be able to adjust only if she starts from under the ball. In addition, the catcher should catch the ball above her head if possible.
The athlete is throwing off line after fielding bunts.	Poor throws usually occur because the feet aren't lined up to the target. The catcher should have the ball under the nose and between the feet when fielding it, and the feet should already be lined up with the throw.
Runners are backdoor sliding around the catcher at home.	The catcher is setting up too far away from the plate in the infield. She should be one drop step away from completely covering the back edge of the plate.
The ball is popping out of the glove after the catcher catches it.	Check the glove. Catchers' mitts are stiff and sometimes too heavy to control. Help your catcher break in her mitt.

KEY POINTS

The most important components of playing first base are

- being in the ready position,
- fielding bunts,
- receiving throws for force-outs,
- making cutoffs to home, and
- receiving a dropped third strike.

The greatest assets for a first-base player are quick feet and strong catching ability.

A tall player who is quick enough to catch balls in the dirt has an advantage because she has additional reach for throws that aren't right on target. First-base players will have more putouts than anyone else, so every minute of practice time that they spend in developing their catching skills is worthwhile. In addition, note that a left-handed player at the first-base position has an advantage over a right-handed player because she doesn't have to pivot to throw to other bases and her glove hand is closer to the infield, allowing her to cover more area.

BEING IN THE READY POSITION

The ready position for the first-base player is closer to the plate than the position for a middle infielder because the first-base player needs to field both batted balls and bunts

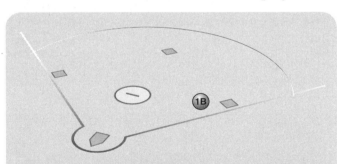

Figure 4.46   First-base player's positioning for a normal hitting situation.

Figure 4.47   Ready position for the first-base player.

(see "Fielding a Bunt" later in this skill). In a normal hitting situation, the first-base player should be positioned 4 to 5 feet in front of first base and close enough to the foul line to be able to field a ball hit directly down the line with one crossover step (see figure 4.46).

In the ready position, the first-base player's feet are spread slightly wider than shoulder-width apart. The glove-hand foot is positioned slightly forward of the throwing-hand foot so that the player can move quickly in any direction (see figure 4.47). The first-base player's ready position is low because she is close to the hitter and may not have time to get lower when the ball is hit. The player's knees and waist are bent, and the back is flattened enough so that she can field a ball hit at her feet. Both hands are held out in front of the body, and the pocket is open with the palm up so that the player can see the glove. The head is lifted, and the player should focus on the contact area of the strike zone.

FIELDING A BUNT

If the situation at the plate calls for a possible bunt, the first-base player will begin to move in the ready position to a point about halfway to the plate after the batter has squared to bunt (see figure 4.48). Note, however, that if the batter is left-handed, the first-base player may not want to move quite so close. She needs to make sure that she times her move appropriately because if she waits too long, she may not get there in time or may have to sprint forward, leaving her vulnerable to a hard bunt or push. See Defending the Bunt in chapter 6 for more information on this topic.

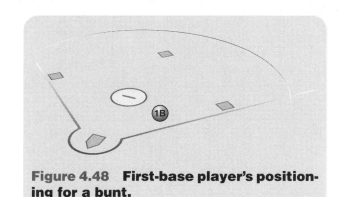

Figure 4.48   First-base player's positioning for a bunt.

The approach to the ball depends on where the ball goes and where the throw needs to be made. In every case, the first-base player should step past the ball with the glove-hand foot to be sure that the ball is centered between her feet, and the feet should be positioned in line with the throwing target (see figure 4.49). Her knees and waist should be bent and her back flat so that she can get

Figure 4.49   First-base player setting up to field a bunt.

low to the ball. If the ball is still moving, the player uses both hands to field it and uses the glove like a backstop for the throwing hand to push the ball against and secure a firm grip (see figure 4.50a). If the ball is stationary, the player should barehand the ball by pushing it into the ground with the throwing hand to obtain a secure grip (see figure 4.50b).

As the first-base player fields the ball, she should stay low and stride directly at the target to throw the ball, letting her weight shift almost entirely to the throwing-hand foot (see figure 4.51). As she throws the ball, the weight drives off the back foot to the front, making the only momentum into the throw from the weight shift. A first-base player's throws are usually back to first or to second, so she generally has no momentum and typically does not move through fielding a bunt into a throw. Therefore, to speed up the throw, the throw should start with an arm circle that goes directly back instead of looping down and around, as shown in figure 4.51.

(continued)

Figure 4.50 **Securing the ball with (*a*) two hands and (*b*) one hand.**

Figure 4.51 **First-base player making a throw.**

RECEIVING THROWS FOR FORCE-OUTS

When a ball is hit to the infield, the first-base player sprints to first base in anticipation of a throw to first. She drops the right foot back directly toward first base to allow a direct line to first and turn herself in a direction that allows her to stay open to the infield (see figure 4.52a). After the drop step, the player faces first base (see figure 4.52b) and sprints to a position directly between the base and the fielder with the ball, placing the ball of the throwing-hand foot on the edge of the base, facing the direction of the throw and giving the fielder a target using both hands (see figure 4.52c). After the throw is on its way, the player should stride toward it with the glove-hand foot, which allows the greatest reach. Note that the timing of the step is important. If the player is too early and the ball does not go where she expects it to, she won't be in position to adjust to it. In addition, if a runner is on any of the other bases, the first-base player should make the catch with two hands so that she can be quick to transition into making a throw if other runners continue to run.

a b c

Figure 4.52 **First-base player setting up to receive a throw at first base.**

If a ball is thrown short of the first-base player, she will need to adjust her stride to reach it. For long hops, the player does not step forward to catch the ball. Instead, she stays back and lets the ball come to her. For short hops, the player takes a long stride so that she can reach the ball before it bounces or a short stride close to the spot where the ball will bounce. In the latter case, she uses a wrist snap on the catch to control the catch because she is catching it right after it bounces. The key is getting the glove extremely close to and directly behind the bounce, and executing a forward snap of the glove pocket through the ball. If the throw happens to result in the dreaded medium hop, the best way to handle it is to take an aggressive stride and reach out in an attempt to make it a short hop. The last rule about receiving throws at first is that if the ball is thrown too wide for the first-base player to catch it, she should leave the base and go to the ball in an attempt to stop it.

(continued)

When a ground ball is hit hard to right field, the right fielder may be able to throw out the runner at first base. A right-handed first-base player again sprints to the bag, faces the right fielder and puts her throwing-hand foot against the bag. A left-handed first-base player needs to place the throwing-hand foot on the corner of the base closer to the right fielder, still inside the base path. Then, as the ball approaches, the first-base player stretches with the glove-hand foot to catch the ball. With no runners on, the catcher should back up the play because a throw wide to the foul line won't be safe for the first-base player to retrieve. To do that, the first-base player would need to cross over the base path, possibly colliding with the runner.

MAKING CUTOFFS TO HOME

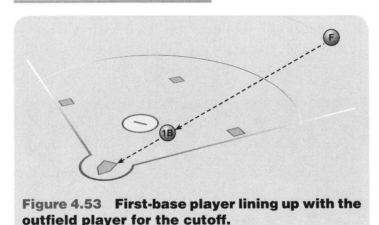

Figure 4.53 **First-base player lining up with the outfield player for the cutoff.**

The most common defense used to attempt to throw out runners at home and still be able to stop the ball and redirect it to another base has the first-base player as the cutoff. This defense is used only when the ball is hit deep enough to the outfield to warrant a throw home and when the first-base player has no immediate play at first on the hit.

For a cutoff, after the ball goes past the infield, the first-base player moves to the middle of the field about pitching distance from home plate, and the pitcher leaves the mound to back up the throw to home (see figure 4.53). The first-base player lines up with the outfielder who fields the ball to act as a cutoff and intercept the throw, if necessary.

RECEIVING A DROPPED THIRD STRIKE

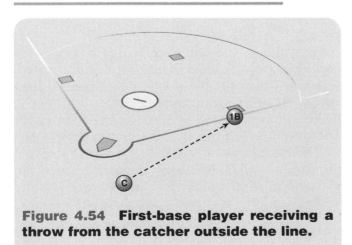

Figure 4.54 **First-base player receiving a throw from the catcher outside the line.**

The rules of softball allow the runner to run to first if it isn't occupied and there are less than two outs when the catcher drops a third strike. If the batter reaches the base before the catcher can either tag her or throw the ball to first, the runner is considered safe. A dropped third strike will most likely go behind the catcher, so to help the catcher make a good throw, the first-base player should assume a position outside the foul line next to first base (see figure 4.54). By being in that position, the first-base player creates a clear path between the catcher and herself. Because the catcher is concerned with getting the ball and is not looking at the runner, the first-base player is responsible for recognizing the clear path, moving to it while still being able to touch first base and communicating calmly to the catcher her position by loudly saying "Outside." The catcher then knows the general area to throw to and that the fielder is there waiting.

Common Errors

Following are several common errors that you might run into when teaching your athletes how to play first base.

Error	Error Correction
The athlete is missing balls from the infield that are thrown a little wide of first.	Make sure that the player's stride into the catch occurs after the throw is on its way. Remind the first-base player that if a throw is too wide for her to catch, she should leave the base.
The athlete is mishandling bunts.	The first-base player should call loudly and then center the ball with her feet. She should be sure to push the ball either into the glove or into the ground to secure it.
The athlete is bobbling balls thrown to first for force-outs.	The player should be more aggressive in sticking the catch (holding the glove hand still after the catch) and in pushing through the catch of a ball in the dirt.

Playing Second Base

KEY POINTS

The most important components of playing second base are

- being in the ready position,
- fielding ground balls,
- receiving bunt throws at first base,
- relaying throws from the outfield,
- using proper footwork for force-outs and double plays, and
- using the proper throws for double plays.

The second-base player is often referred to as the quarterback of the infield because she is involved in most defensive plays. In turn, infield defense is much more cohesive and solid when the second-base player is vocal and stays one step ahead of the offense. A good second-base player needs to have great range, quick feet, good game sense to anticipate what is coming, leadership ability, good fielding skills, ability to catch throws to bases and ability to move back quickly on hits to the outfield. The second-base player doesn't need to have a strong arm, just an accurate and quick one.

READY POSITION

The ready position for middle infielders is more upright than the position that corner players use. Because the distance from home to second is longer than the distance from home to first or third, the player has more time to drop down to the ball so she doesn't need to have the glove close to the ground. The most important aspect of the ready position for the second-base player is to make possible a quick first step so that the player can cover a lot of ground. To take the ready position, the feet should be spread slightly wider than shoulder-width and the glove foot should be slightly in front of the throwing-hand foot. The player can then move quickly in all directions. The glove hand should be held out with a relaxed elbow (see figure 4.55). The knees and waist are bent enough to keep the balance on the balls of the feet, and the shoulders are positioned over the knees. The second-base player doesn't have her back as flat as the corner players do because she doesn't need to be as low.

The players in the middle infield set up according to the situation. The second-base player sets up deep if no runners are on base (see figure 4.56a) and more shallow when runners are on and she needs to cover first or second on a throw or throw home (see figure 4.56b). She also adjusts more toward second if the defensive play calls for her to take the throws at second, and she moves more toward first if she needs to cover throws at first. Before the ball is hit, the second-base player needs to think about what the situation is and where she will need to go. She then adjusts her starting position so that she can get there in time. Note that a second-base player should be right-handed. The most common play for a second-base player is a throw to first base. A left-handed second-base player must turn 180 degrees, a maneuver that requires too much time and coordination.

Figure 4.55 Ready position for the second-base player.

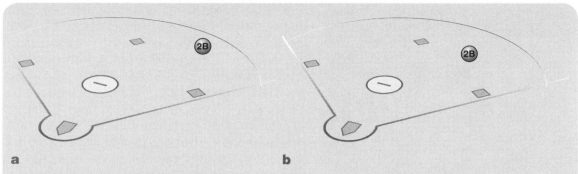

Figure 4.56 Second-base player's positioning (*a*) with no runners on base and (*b*) with runners on base.

FIELDING GROUND BALLS

Middle infielders have more time than corner infielders to center the ball and move through it using the correct angles (see "Fielding Ground Balls in the Infield" on page 72 for more information). The second-base player has a greater challenge than the corners do in controlling momentum in the forehands and backhands and transitioning into throws because she is often sprinting through the ball (see "Fielding Balls on the Forehand or Backhand Side" on page 67 for more information).

One of the most challenging plays for the second-base player is the slow-rolling ground ball hit in her direction. In this situation, she must determine whether the first-base player will cut off the grounder. If that happens, she will need to cover the throw at first. She may decide to call off the first-base player and take the grounder herself. She must make an immediate decision and may need to be somewhere else very quickly. If she hesitates, the runner will be safe. The second-base player must charge the slow roller hard and then control her weight as she moves through the ball. If she charges the slow roller and then begins to back up before the ball is in the glove in preparation to make the throw, she will have her weight on her heels and will likely mishandle the ball.

RECEIVING BUNT THROWS AT FIRST BASE

Because fast-pitch softball teams often use the bunt as an offensive strategy, the second-base player must learn the skill of covering the throw at first base. In baseball, the middle infielders turn many more double plays than their counterparts do in softball, but in softball bunting is much more common. In a bunt situation the second-base player adjusts to a shallower position and moves closer to first base before the ball is hit (see figure 4.57). If she

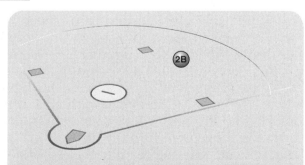

Figure 4.57 Second-base player's positioning for a bunt.

(continued)

Figure 4.58 Second-base player receiving a throw on a bunt.

is too far from first, she will need to leave her position too early to get there in time. Because she should hold her position until the ball has crossed the plate, she needs to be close enough to first to do both—hold her position yet be able to reach first in time for a throw.

After the ball has been bunted, the second-base player approaches first at a sprint. When she is close to the base, she plants the left foot against the side of the bag to stop forward momentum. Because the runner is close to the line of the throw on most bunts, the second-base player should always set up inside the base path to avoid collision (see figure 4.58). The second-base player won't have time to set her feet to stretch for the catch as a first-base player does, so after planting the left foot against the base she needs to face the fielder making the throw and assume the best athletic position possible, providing a two-hand target for the thrower. A two-handed catch is recommended because another runner will be on base and an additional quick throw may be necessary.

RELAYING THROWS FROM THE OUTFIELD

When an outfielder is required to make a long throw to the infield or to home, the middle infielders act as a relay to help cover the distance and aid in accuracy. Although relaying the throw home from the outfield isn't a difficult skill, there are a few points that will help the second-base player be more effective. The second-base player should go out as deep in the outfield as necessary, according to her skill level and the outfielder's, to be in a position to receive a good throw from the outfielder. She lines up directly between home plate and the outfielder. The second-base player should then communicate to the outfielder her position to help the outfielder identify the direction in which she will throw before she turns to release the ball.

To receive the throw, the second-base player faces the outfielder and raises both arms to provide a big target. She stays mobile by keeping her feet moving. After the ball is on its way, the second-base player will likely have to adjust to one side or the other and either forward or backward to catch the ball and still be able to move into her throw. When the ball approaches, the fielder turns toward the glove-hand side and opens sideways to the ball, in line with the direction in which she wishes to throw. At the same time, she wants to start moving backward toward the infield. She should actually catch the ball after she has turned and is moving back, which helps her transition quickly and gives her more momentum into her throw. Because the throw may be a long one, movement into the throw is critical for making a strong throw. She should be sure to listen to her teammates in the field so that she knows where the throw needs to go. Adjustments often happen on the fly, and the relay may have to go to a different spot than originally thought.

PROPER FOOTWORK FOR FORCE-OUTS AND DOUBLE PLAYS

Although the double play doesn't happen as often in softball as it does in baseball, middle infielders still need to master the skill of turning the double play. When the ball is hit to the left side of the infield with a runner on base, the second-base player takes the throw at second. Depending on how quickly the ball gets to second in relation to the runner and the accuracy of the throw, the play may be a force-out or turn into a double play. In either case, the second-base player should sprint to second and set up with the base between her and the fielder making the throw. If the play is going to be close at second, the second-base player crosses over the base and receives the throw like a first-base player. The throwing-hand foot stays on the edge of the base, and as the throw gets closer the player strides with the glove-hand foot to catch the ball. In this situation, there is no chance for a double play because the second-base player will have stretched to make the catch and won't be able to recover her feet to make another throw in time.

If there is time for a double play, two options are available for catching and throwing the ball. Assuming that the second-base player is right-handed, her footwork to touch the bag and then make the throw will be a left, right, left combination. When the second-base player has set up with second base between her and the fielder throwing the ball, she can either catch and throw on that same side of the base or cross over the base in the process of catching the ball.

If the second-base player gets to the base just in time to catch the thrown ball, she does not want to cross over the bag because doing so will take too much time. She steps with the left foot on the base (see figure 4.59a) and may have already caught the ball or will catch it at the same time that she touches the bag. The player then pushes off the base, steps back with the right foot (see figure 4.59b) and then steps toward first with the left again to throw the ball to first (see figure 4.59c). The footwork is left, right, left. If she steps on the bag with the right foot, she will have to take a couple of extra steps to get away from the runner and still get her feet lined up for the throw.

Figure 4.59 **Second-base player receiving a throw for a double play when reaching the base just in time.**

(continued)

If the second-base player gets to the base in plenty of time to receive the throw, she may want to cross over to catch the ball because that is a quicker way to the ball. For the crossover, the player steps on the bag with the left foot, strides over the base while catching the ball, plants with the right foot to stop momentum and redirects her motion with a left-foot stride to first as she throws. The footwork is again left, right, left. The key to a correct start is getting the left foot on the base and controlling balance to be able to move from the catch into the throw.

PROPER THROWS FOR DOUBLE PLAYS

Although most middle infielders want to practice their footwork more often than their feeds, if the feed isn't good, the footwork won't matter. If the ball is hit to the second-base player, her first decision is whether to make the double play unassisted or to make a throw. As a rule, if the second-base player can field the ball and get to second as quickly as a throw to the shortstop would, she should make the play herself. But when a throw is necessary, the second-base player should know the different variations—the scoop throw, the three-quarter throw with a half pivot (sometimes called a dropped-knee feed) and the full throw to cover a long distance.

The scoop throw, or underhand toss, as shown in figure 4.8 on page 64 of "Infield Throws," is used when the second-base player's momentum takes her close to second. The scoop throw is the easiest and generally the most accurate. The key is making sure to face the shortstop with squared shoulders and then moving through the toss.

The three-quarter throw with a half pivot is used when the ball is hit directly at the second-base player and she is a little too far from the base to use an underhand toss. After the ball is in the glove, the second-base player drops to the glove-hand knee while rotating her shoulders so that the glove shoulder points to second base (see figure 4.60*a*). From that position, the fielder uses only the upper body to throw the ball (see figure 4.60*b*). The throw is quick but not hard.

The full throw is necessary when the ball is hit closer to first base and a longer throw is necessary. The second-base player fields the ball using a forehand and moving through the ball. She plants the throwing-hand foot to stop forward movement and redirects her motion into the throw to second. She turns her back to the infield as she plants the throwing-hand foot and then strides at second with the glove-hand foot to make the throw.

a   b

Figure 4.60   Three-quarter throw with half pivot.

Common Errors

Following are several common errors that you might run into when teaching your athletes how to play second base.

Error	Error Correction
This athlete is making errors when fielding ground balls.	Teach players to make it a habit to move through the ball with quiet hands to eliminate errors.
This athlete is colliding with runners at first when taking bunt throws.	The thrower most likely causes this kind of error. The thrower must make every effort to throw down the line, not across it.
The outfielder's relay throw is landing at the feet of the second-base player.	Teach players to move far enough out so that they can receive a good throw from the outfielder. They usually need to move farther out than they suspect because they also want to back up as they catch the ball.
This athlete is making poor underhand tosses.	Almost without exception, poor underhand tosses occur because the fielder is not following her toss. Have the thrower move with the toss.

Figure 4.64 Third-base player fielding a ball using a forehand.

The third-base player is responsible for cutting off slow-rolling ground balls hit in the direction of the short-stop. If the third-base player can reach the ball and field it with a forehand (see figure 4.64), she will be able to make a quicker play and have a better chance to get the out. On this play she must be able to adjust her momentum into the direction of the throw. When fielding any ball to the left with a forehand, she moves quickly across the path of the ball to intercept it. Her momentum will have her facing the second-base area. If she simply stops, her body will be lined up to throw to left field.

When making the throw to first, although it isn't a long one, the third-base player must line up the feet, hips and shoulders with the target. This technique will not only ensure a better throw but also protect the throwing arm from injury. After the ball is in the glove, the third-base player should have time to take a couple of quick shuffle steps to adjust her angle, regain proper balance and control her momentum. When taking these steps, the player should keep the knees bent and move quickly to get the instep of the throwing-hand foot and the glove-hand shoulder turned to the target. A good practice is to take one more shuffle step to the target after lining up to help ensure the proper angle and control the pace. See figure 4.65, *a* and *b* for an example of the shuffle steps.

a

b

Figure 4.65 Third-base player using shuffle steps to adjust her angle.

Lining up to make a throw after fielding a backhand (on balls hit to the foul line) is much more natural because the body will already be turned in the correct direction. The key is to take one step past the backhand (see figure 4.66). After the ball is in the glove, the third-base player takes one more step with the throwing-hand foot in the direction (toward the foul line) that the ground ball took her. This second step is a planting motion that stops the forward momentum and reverses the body to throw back across the infield. Stepping with the glove-hand foot in the direction of the target will help with accuracy.

Figure 4.66 **Third-base player fielding a ball using a backhand.**

FIELDING BUNTS

The third-base player will likely field most bunts because she can use her momentum into the throw. The third-base player is generally more aggressive coming forward toward the ball than the pitcher or first-base player can be. Therefore, third-base players should work to become proficient at this skill.

When the situation calls for a possible bunt, the first- and third-base players want to be just close enough to be able to make an out, typically a position halfway up the line. After the batter has squared to bunt, the corners begin to creep as close to the plate as they can. If the fielder is nervous about getting close to the hitter and stays back, she is susceptible to not getting there in time or having to sprint forward, which leaves her vulnerable to a hard bunt or push. After the ball is bunted, communication between the corners, pitcher and catcher is necessary. If the third-base player is going to field the ball, she yells, "Mine" loudly and repeats it so that the others know to move out of the way.

The approach to the ball depends on where it is and where the throw needs to go. In every case, the fielder should step past the ball with the glove foot so that she can center the ball between her feet and place the feet in line with the throwing target. If the ball is still moving, she should use both hands to field it, using the glove as a backstop for the throwing hand to push the ball against and secure a firm grip. If the ball is stationary, she barehands the ball by pushing it into the ground with the throwing hand to obtain a secure grip.

As mentioned previously, the third-base player has an advantage in fielding bunts because her momentum takes her through the ball and into the throw. Because she has this momentum, she is usually the quickest in getting the bunt and making the throw. If the throw is going back to third, however, the third-base player will need to shift her weight almost entirely to the throwing-hand foot. As she is throwing the ball, the weight drives off the back foot to the front. The momentum into the throw is from the weight shift only. Additionally, if the third-base player does not field the ball, she should return quickly to third base to keep the runner who has been advanced to second from running to third.

(continued)

MAKING TAG PLAYS

Figure 4.67 Third-base player setting up for a tag play by straddling the base.

Receiving a throw immediately before having to place a tag takes discipline and focus because it is all too easy to be distracted by the runner or to attempt the tag before catching the ball. The third-base player has two options to set up and receive the throw. First, she can straddle the base, placing her feet toward the back of the bag so that most of it is in front of her. This position makes it easier to adjust to either side if the throw is wide (see figure 4.67). She can then place the tag directly in front of her.

Second, the third-base player can set up on the side of the base that the ball is coming from. For example, if the throw is from the right side of the bag, the third-base player places the side of the left foot against the inside of the bag. If the throw is from the left side of the bag, the player sets up with the side of the right foot on the outside of the bag. The advantage to this method is that the fielder is generally out of the running lane, reducing the chance that the throw will hit the runner. The disadvantage is that placing the tag may require more time.

As with any tag placed by a defensive player, the third-base player should let the ball travel all the way to the base, when possible, because reaching out for it and bringing it back is much slower. The player should catch the ball at the base and let the runner slide into the glove and tag herself out. After catching the ball, the player should turn the glove so that the back of the glove is against the runner, protecting the ball from being knocked loose. This technique is also the safest way for the wrist to bend if the runner slides hard.

If the throw is wide of the base the fielder will have to reach for the ball and pull it back to the bag in a sweeping motion, using a sweep tag (see figure 4.68, *a* and *b*). If the ball is high but right above the base, the fielder catches the ball and quickly snaps the glove straight down to place the tag, using what is called a pop tag (see figure 4.69, *a* and *b*). The third-base player should be able to use all these types of tags and know which one to use according to where the ball is.

It would be great to think that all throws a fielder receives would be close enough to the base to allow the fielder to stay in her initial setup. However, it's more often not the case. At third base in particular, it's critical that players learn to leave the base and go to the ball if the throw is off line. The tag is secondary to catching or stopping the ball. "Ball first, tag second" is a good mantra for all fielders. If a third-base player stays rooted to the ground and doesn't move to get a ball thrown off line, the chances are that the ball will get by her, and the runner then has an excellent opportunity to score. The more difficult the throw is to handle, the more important it is that the fielder move to get in front of the ball that might take her away from an easy tag. Keep the feet light on the ground and adjust to the ball.

a

b

Figure 4.68 Sweep tag.

a

b

Figure 4.69 Pop tag.

(continued)

DEFENDING THE SQUEEZE BUNT

The third-base player should position a little farther back from home on a squeeze bunt than she might on a sacrifice bunt because the hitter could also hit away to score the runner at third. Therefore, the third-base player must be alert to the movements of the hitter. After the hitter squares to bunt, the third-base player needs to charge hard to the ball, approaching it so that she fields it on the throwing-hand side. If possible, the player should not field it on the glove side because she will then have to use a backhand flip, which is less dependable. As the third-base player gets to the ball, she should be low and in control. She should field the ball with the throwing hand by using the glove as a backstop or the ground to push against. The toss to the catcher should be an underhand toss or flip. Keys to a successful toss are showing the ball to the catcher for a split second before tossing it, continuing to move while fielding the ball, tossing the ball while maintaining forward movement and not allowing anxiety to cause her to throw too hard. After the tag play at home, the third-base player should remind the catcher that another runner is on base and then return quickly to third to cover and prevent that runner from advancing.

Common Errors

Following are several common errors that you might run into when teaching your athletes how to play third base.

Error	Error Correction
The athlete is making bad throws after fielding grounders.	Teach the player to take more time to line up for the throw. Some player rush the throw before they line up their feet and shoulders with the target.
The athlete is using a high underhand toss to the catcher on a squeeze.	Ensure that the player moves through the toss and doesn't stop. Teach the player to follow the toss.
The athlete is bobbling back-hands.	Teach the player to keep the shoulders low, slide the glove across the ground to the ball and leave the glove down for a split second after the ball is in the glove. Check to be sure that the arm is completely rotated so that the glove faces the ball. The elbow should point at the ball.

In softball, the shortstop should be one of the best athletes on the team. She needs to be quick to cover a lot of ground, have a strong and accurate arm and be skilled at fielding ground balls. She should also have a quick first step going in any direction so that she can get to ground balls and run down as many pop-ups as possible. The shortstop should be vocal because many plays happen quickly and the infield must be able to communicate on the fly. Game sense is a must for a shortstop. Because the shortstop must react almost instantly, she must think ahead of the play and know what the situation requires. A calm, confident shortstop is the pitcher's greatest tool. A right-handed player will be more successful as a shortstop because left-handers have a difficult angle in making quick throws to first and second.

KEY POINTS

The most important components of playing shortstop are

- being in the ready position,
- relaying throws from the outfield,
- receiving throws for force-outs,
- using proper footwork on double plays,
- making proper feeds for double plays, and
- covering second on a steal.

BEING IN THE READY POSITION

The ready position for middle infielders is more upright than the position that corner players use. Because the shortstop is farther from the hitter than the corner players are, she has more time to get into position and doesn't need to have the glove close to the ground. The most important aspect of the ready position for the shortstop is to make possible a quick first step so that the player can cover a lot of ground in any direction. To take the ready position, the feet should be spread slightly wider than shoulder-width apart and the glove foot should be slightly in front of the throwing-hand foot (see figure 4.70). The knees and waist are bent enough to keep the balance on the balls of the feet, and the shoulders are over the knees. The shortstop doesn't have her back as flat as the corner players do because she doesn't need to be as low. A good practice is to keep the glove hand out toward the hitter with a relaxed elbow.

The middle infielders set up according to the situation. To maximize her range, the shortstop typically sets up as deep as possible while still being able to throw out the runner. The slower the runner and the stronger the shortstop's arm, the deeper she can set up. But when a lefty slap hitter is up or when the shortstop may need to throw home, she should set up shallower. She should adjust more toward second in a steal situation and more toward third in a bunt situation with a runner at second. The shortstop must think about where she will need to go in every situation before it happens and then adjust her starting position so that she can get there in time. She should never play the game from the same spot.

Figure 4.70 Ready position for the shortstop.

(continued)

RELAYING THROWS FROM THE OUTFIELD

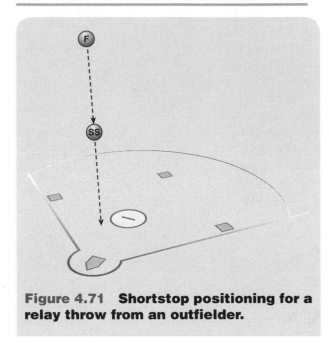

Figure 4.71   Shortstop positioning for a relay throw from an outfielder.

Although relaying the throw home from the outfield isn't a difficult skill, there are a few points that will help the shortstop be more effective. The shortstop should go out as deep in the outfield as necessary so that she can receive a good throw from the outfielder. As we mentioned previously, how far she goes out varies with the arm strength and accuracy of the outfielder's arm. The shortstop should line up directly between home plate and the fielder who fields the ball (see figure 4.71). She then communicates to the outfielder her position so that the outfielder hears the direction in which she will throw before she turns to release the ball. The shortstop should face the outfielder, stay mobile and raise her arms to give the outfielder a big target to throw to.

After the ball is on its way, the shortstop will likely have to adjust to one side or the other and either forward or backward to catch it and still be able to move into her throw. When the ball approaches, the fielder turns toward the glove-hand side and opens sideways to the ball in line with the direction in which she wishes to throw. At the same time, she wants to start moving backward toward the infield. She should actually catch the ball after she has turned and is moving back. This movement helps her transition quickly and gives her more momentum into her throw. Because the throw may be a long one, movement into the throw is critical for making a strong throw. The shortstop should be sure to listen to her teammates in the field so that she knows where the throw needs to go. Adjustments often happen on the fly, and the relay may have to go to a different spot than originally thought.

RECEIVING THROWS FOR FORCE-OUTS

If the timing of the play is too close at second or third for a double play, as discussed later in this skill, the shortstop should not attempt the double play. Instead, she should prepare for a force-out and set up to receive the throw if necessary. Note that the shortstop typically covers third on a force play only if the ball is bunted or hit slowly to the third-base player. Usually the ball is hit hard enough for the third-base player to make the play unassisted.

The shortstop takes the throws at second when the ball is hit to the pitcher or to the right side of the infield. The shortstop should catch the ball and continue across the bag to get out of the way of the runner. If the play is not going to end with a double-play attempt, the shortstop steps on second with the throwing-hand foot and faces the fielder. After the throw is on its way, the shortstop strides toward the ball with the glove-hand foot to stretch out and make the catch. The most common defensive play that requires the shortstop to stretch is a bunt play.

In almost every other ground-ball situation that requires the shortstop to cover second, she uses double-play footwork and then decides either to continue with the throw if she has a chance for two or to settle for just the out at second, as discussed in the next section.

USING PROPER FOOTWORK FOR DOUBLE PLAYS

For a right-handed shortstop, the footwork at second is similar to the second-base player's left, right, left combination. The footwork depends on the throw location, not just where the shortstop feels most comfortable. When the ball is hit, the shortstop moves close to second to receive the throw.

If the ball is hit to the pitcher or second-base player, the shortstop will most likely take the throw on the outside of the base, meaning that the left foot plants just past it on the right-field side but still close to the base. The throw should reach the shortstop sometime just before she plants or at the same time. After she has the ball, her motion continues. The right foot crosses over in front of the left foot and plants with the instep facing first base. The right foot also drags, or brushes, over second base as it crosses over. After planting the right foot, the shortstop strides with the left toward first to complete the throw.

If the ball is hit to the first-base player, the throw will likely need to stay on the inside of the base to limit its potential to hit the runner. In this case, the shortstop again moves close to second base. This time she steps on the inside of the bag with the left foot, steps forward and more toward the infield with the right foot and then steps directly toward first with the left foot to make the throw. If she receives the ball early, she should approach second, stay behind the base and not take time to cross over. She then plants the throwing-hand foot with the instep turned and with the glove-hand foot strides directly at first, planting the foot on second base. Note that in all these variations, the shortstop must be sure to stay out of the base path to avoid collisions with the runner.

MAKING PROPER FEEDS FOR DOUBLE PLAYS

If the ball is hit to the shortstop, her first decision is whether to make the double play unassisted or to use a throw. If she can field the ball and get to second as quickly as a throw to the second-base player would, she should make the play herself. If a throw is necessary, she can use several variations—the underhand toss, the three-quarter throw or the full throw.

The underhand toss, also called the scoop throw, is used when the shortstop's momentum takes her close to second. This underhand toss is the easiest and generally the most accurate. The key is making sure to face the second-base player with squared shoulders (see figure 4.72a) and then moving through the toss (see figure 4.72b).

(continued)

a   b

Figure 4.72   Underhand toss.

The shortstop uses the three-quarter feed when has the ball is hit directly at her and she is a little too far from the base to use an underhand toss. After the ball is in the glove, the shortstop drops to the throwing-hand knee while keeping her shoulders lined up to second base (see figure 4.73a). From that position, the fielder uses only the upper body to throw the ball (see figure 4.73b). The throw is quick but not hard.

a   b

Figure 4.73   Three-quarter throw.

The full throw is necessary when the ball is hit closer to third base and a longer throw is necessary. The shortstop fields the ball using a backhand. After moving through the ball, she plants the throwing-hand foot to stop forward movement and redirects her motion into the throw to second.

COVERING SECOND ON A STEAL

Receiving a throw immediately before having to place a tag takes discipline and focus because it is all too easy to be distracted by the runner or to attempt the tag before catching the ball. If the shortstop anticipates a steal at second, she should set up closer to second before the ball is pitched. Chances are greater that the runner will attempt a steal than that the ball will be hit to the far right of the shortstop, so good shortstops cheat a little toward second to be sure that they can get there in time. When the runner breaks for second, the shortstop needs to hold her position until the ball crosses the plate. After this happens she sprints to the base and straddles it to receive the throw, placing her feet toward the back of the bag so that most of it is in front of her. If the shortstop sets up in front of the base closer to home plate, she may be out of the way of the runner, but the backdoor slide becomes difficult to protect against. From the bag, the shortstop can then place the tag directly in front of her. She should let the ball travel all the way to the base, if possible, because reaching out for it and bringing it back is much slower. The shortstop should catch the ball at the base and let the runner slide into the glove and tag herself out. In addition, if the runner slides past the base, the shortstop shouldn't follow her. Instead, she should keep the glove close to the base and tag the runner when she tries to reach back for it.

Common Errors

Following are several common errors that you might run into when teaching your athletes how to play shortstop.

Error	Error Correction
The athlete is bobbling throws at bases.	Make sure that the shortstop gets to the base early enough to set up to receive. She needs to anticipate the play and adjust her starting position accordingly.
The athlete is mishandling ground balls.	The shortstop must learn to get low enough, move through the ball and keep the hands quiet.
The athlete is bobbling a good throw on a steal attempt.	The player may bobble the ball by reaching for it and trying to pull it to the base. In most cases the player anticipates the tag and moves before she catches the ball. The player should learn to catch and then tag.

PART III

Teaching Tactical Skills

Tactical skills get at the heart of softball. Without proper understanding and execution of this type of skill, your players will often commit basic errors in game situations. You can empower your athletes by teaching them how to read situations, apply the appropriate knowledge and make the correct decisions.

This part focuses on the basic and intermediate tactical skills in softball, showing you how to teach your athletes to make good decisions on the field. These skills include offensive tactical skills such as the first-and-third play, hit and run, getting out of a rundown and stealing second and defensive skills such as defending the first-and-third double steal, defending against the bunt and double-play defenses. Like the technical skills chapters, these chapters have been designed so that you can immediately incorporate the information into your teaching.

THINKING TACTICALLY

Throughout the presentation of tactical skills you will see references to the need for athletes to know what is called the game situation. As described in Rainer Martens' *Successful Coaching, Third Edition*, the game situation includes "the count on the batter, the number of outs, the inning and the score." In other words, your players need to know specific information when your team faces a specific situation. For example, when you need to get a runner to second base in position to score, you may ask yourself, How important is the run at second? Is it the tying or winning run? Is it an insurance run?

You and your team must know what key information you need to make the best decision. Following are a few questions that you and your team must keep in mind when facing tactical situations during a game:

- What is your strategy?
- How does your game plan affect your strategy?
- How does the game situation (the score, the strengths and weaknesses of the players involved, the physical playing conditions and so on) affect your game plan?

For each skill you are first presented with an overview that paints a picture or puts you and your athletes into a specific scenario in which you would be likely to use that particular tactical skill. The "Watch Out!" element highlights the distractions that may affect your athletes' ability to make appropriate decisions and provides insight on what to look for. The "Reading the Situation" element offers important cues that your athletes need to be able to read so that they can make the appropriate decisions for the situation. Next, you will find an element called "Acquiring the Appropriate Knowledge," which provides the information that your athletes need to understand so that they can make the proper decision and successfully execute the skill, as presented in the overview. Finally, as in the technical skill chapters, the "At a Glance" element refers you to the other important tools in this book that will help you teach the skill.

chapter 5

Offensive Tactical Skills

This chapter will cover the offensive tactical skills that you and your players must know in order to be successful. In this chapter, you will find:

In softball, the short game refers to offensive skills other than hitting, such as bunting or slap hitting, employed to get on base or advance runners. Coaches can combine short-game skills and baserunning skills in many ways to begin creating an offensive strategy.

Generally, we will look at using the short game with a runner on first base. This situation presents the most common opportunity to incorporate short-game skills, but you can use short-game skills with runners on any base. The only time when short-game skills are rarely used because of decreased success in execution is when the bases are loaded, which makes the force play at home available to the defense. Short-game skills are best used when the benefit of moving runners into scoring position outweighs the disadvantage that the batter may make an out. Of course, an out on the batter will not always be the outcome with the short game, but generally coaches will not risk using short-game skills with two outs. The element of surprise can work with short-game skills with the bases loaded or possibly with two outs, but coaches will have to make hard decisions to use such tactics as they evaluate their offensive strategy during the game situations that come up.

READING THE SITUATION

How can you and your players know when to play the short game? Teach your players to do the following:

- Be aware of the count on the batter. If the pitcher is behind in the count she will likely be throwing a good pitch in the strike zone.
- Know that bunts to advance runners to third base are best bunted to the third-base player or pitcher.
- Know that bunts to advance runners to second base are best bunted to the first-base player or pitcher.
- Read the defensive movement of the corners as the pitch is being released and be ready to switch from a bunt to a slap or vice versa.
- Take advantage of placing bunts to one side of the field or the other if the defense decides to keep one of the corners back.
- Read the movement of the outfielders. Sometimes the outfielders will move toward one of the foul lines.

 WATCH OUT!

The following circumstances might distract your athletes:

- Pitches out of the strike zone make it harder for the batter to use a bunt.
- Pitchers throw away from the batter or high and in toward the batter to force a pop-up.
- The defense moves aggressively. If defensive players shift their positions to defend the bunt, advancing the runners will be more difficult because the corners will have moved in close to the batter where they can throw out the lead runner instead of taking the out with the batter.

REMINDER!

When playing the short game, your players must know your team strategy and game plan. Don't forget to consider the questions on page 128.

- Pitchouts used to catch the offense off-guard. If a defense chooses to use a pitchout in a short-game situation, they may catch a runner taking too large a leadoff or even throw out the runner on a steal attempt. Batters have a difficult time protecting runners when the pitcher throws a pitchout.
- Batters who interfere with a defensive player who is attempting to field a bunt, including the catcher. If the batter interferes, a dead-ball out is called and runners return to the bases where they started.

ACQUIRING THE APPROPRIATE KNOWLEDGE

To play the short game successfully, you and your athletes must understand the following:

Rules

You and your athletes need to know several main rules when you are playing the short game:

- Rules about foul bunt attempts
- Rules about the running lane
- Rules about dead balls

Physical Playing Conditions

The physical playing conditions will significantly affect the game. Thus, you and your players must pay attention to the following physical conditions when playing the short game:

- The condition of the infield. A hard infield will be tougher to bunt on because the ball will roll quicker to the corners. A push bunt or slap will get past the infielders more quickly because the hard ground will not slow down the ball, so a drag bunt or bunt for a base hit might work better to advance the runners by trying to make the defense move farther to get to the ball.
- The condition of the outfield. If the outfield is wet, when attempting to move the runners and create offense the coach may opt to use the slap or push bunt to get the ball to the outfield where it can pick up moisture and be difficult to throw or handle.
- The condition of the base paths. Muddy or extremely soft base paths will slow down runners and make it more difficult for batters to advance them.
- The field conditions near home plate. The field conditions near home plate are important because a soft field will deaden the ball and could allow the catcher to field the ball more easily and tag the runner.

Strengths and Weaknesses of Opponents

You and your players must account for your opponent's strengths and weaknesses when playing the short game. Teach your players to consider the following about your opponents:

- How aggressive and agile are the corners? If the corners are extremely aggressive then you may need to attempt to keep the bunts from going to them or use hard or slap bunts to take advantage of their aggressiveness. If the corners get to bunts put down in front of them, then you may want to incorporate bunts or short-game skills that will go toward the gaps between the corners to keep the ball farther from them.

(continued)

POSITIONING IN THE BOX FOR A BUNT

There are several schools of thought on the advantages of bunting from different locations in the batter's box. Here are some thoughts:

- Bunting in the back of the box moves the catcher farther from the pitcher, which increases the chance of a wild pitch or passed ball. The catcher also has to make a longer throw to get a runner attempting to steal second.
- Bunting from the back of the box gives the bunter a better chance to keep a bunt along the foul line as a fair ball.
- The front part of the batter's box is considered fair territory. Bunts in this area are close to the catcher and less likely to advance the runner if the catcher can make a play to second base.
- Moving to the back of the batter's box on a sacrifice moves the play farther from second base when the corners pick up the bunt.
- Bunting from the front of the box gives the hitter more fair territory below her and to the sides.
- Bunting from the front of the batter's box can be advantageous if the pitcher has a lot of movement on her pitches but doesn't throw extremely fast.
- Bunting from the front of the box may be better for weaker bunters because they have a greater chance of getting the bunt down in fair territory.

○ How strong are the corners? If a particular corner player has a strong arm, you will want to avoid bunting in her direction. Bunting toward corners with exceptionally strong arms will likely allow the defense to go after the lead runner and therefore reduce the effectiveness of the short game.

○ How quickly can the pitcher move to field bunts? The pitcher is sometimes the best fielder in the bunting area and thus you would want to keep your bunts away from her. The pitcher may be physically one of the strongest defensive players with the strongest arm. Keeping the ball away from this player may be the best strategy to advance the runners.

○ Do the middle infielders have good range? If they have good range and can cover a lot of ground from side to side, then the slap may not be as effective unless the batter puts it in a gap outside their range.

○ Do the middle infielders vacate their positions early when the batter squares up? If they do, large gaps could open up in the defense, offering great potential for using the hard bunt or the slap. A well-placed hit could allow both the batter and runner to be safe because the ball will likely travel all the way to the outfield.

○ Does the opponent have a strong defensive strategy to defend certain parts of the short game? Some teams use specific defensive alignments in short-game situations. One of the corners may stay back, or the opponent could use dramatic shifts in the starting positions for every infielder. Evaluate the defensive setup and use short-game skills that will have higher odds of success in those situations.

Self-Knowledge

Besides being aware of your opponent's strengths and weaknesses, you and your players need to have knowledge about your own team's ability. When playing the short game, you and your players must be aware of the following:

- How strong are the batter's bunting skills? Bunting skills are important to maximizing your team's offensive threat. Generally, batters who are less competent or not committed to team strategy will begin to run in an attempt to reach first base safely instead of executing the skill correctly. Teach your players that being safe at first is not the goal in short-game situations but that it is a huge bonus as long as the runners are advanced.

- How quick is the runner on first base? If your runner is not quick you may need to use a drag bunt, push or hard bunt, or slap to keep the corners from getting the lead runner on the sacrifice. With a slower runner on first base, a better bunt will be needed to advance her safely; using one of these bunts may keep the ball from going to the corner defenders.

- How strong is the on-deck hitter if runners are in scoring position? If the on-deck hitter is exceptional, the opponent could choose to walk her intentionally when she comes to the plate. The sacrifice bunt may just create an open base for the opposing team to walk your biggest threat. Plan two to three batters ahead so that you will be prepared for situations that come up.

- How quick is the runner on third? When a squeeze bunt is used this runner's speed is important to increasing the odds of success because she will be running toward home on the pitch and trying to beat the defense's attempt to throw her out at home.

- Can your batter disguise or decoy her short-game skills? A batter who can show the defense that she is going to sacrifice bunt and then be able to pull the bat back and slap will be more effective than a player who cannot disguise her short-game skills. Additionally, can the batter delay her movement on the drag bunt or bunt for a base hit so that the defense cannot anticipate the bunt?

- What short-game skills were effective earlier in the game? Is the defense expecting a specific short-game skill? The element of surprise can prevent the defense from making a play on the lead runner.

Decision-Making Guidelines

When playing the short game, you and your players should be sure to consider the previous information. Also consider the following guidelines:

- With a runner on first in the late innings of a low-scoring game, you may consider a more conservative approach and use a sacrifice rather than a slap, push bunt or drag bunt. The sacrifice bunt is easier to execute and has less risk of failure. Although the hard bunt, push bunt, drag bunt and slap can be effective and successful, they also come with greater risk if they don't succeed. The lead runner may be thrown out, and a double play may even result.

- If a runner is on first, pay attention to the shortstop, who may vacate early to cover second base and thus be vulnerable to the slap. Likewise, the second-base player may vacate early to cover first base and thus be vulnerable to the push bunt.

- If a runner is on second in a close game, the coach needs to determine whether the batter and the on-deck batter have a good chance of getting a hit against the pitcher. This judgment may determine whether the coach will resort to short-game strategies or allow the hitters a chance to bring the run in by swinging the bat.

(continued)

ADVANTAGES AND DISADVANTAGES OF THE SHORT GAME

Each element of the short game carries advantages and disadvantages. If the batter executes them successfully, all short-game elements should be effective. The challenge arises in considering the odds of successfully executing each of the short-game skills in different situations. Here, the coach must apply a decision-making process. Some basic thoughts on each type of short-game skill follow:

- The sacrifice bunt is the most basic and least risky to execute. Successful execution is not difficult, and the sacrifice is considered conservative in the short-game strategy. The risk comes only when the defense reads the play early and plays an extremely aggressive style that allows them to go after the lead runner. Placing this bunt toward the center of the field usually causes the greatest challenge for the defense.

- Hard bunts or push bunts are effective, but they can be risky if the angle of the bat does not place the ball in the gap between the pitcher and the first-base player or between the pitcher and the third-base player. If done correctly, hard bunts or push bunts are incredibly difficult to defend, and they often both advance the runner and allow the batter to reach first base safely.

- The slap is another effective way of taking advantage of corners who play in close or aggressively charge on the sacrifice bunt. The slap is more of a half swing or punch, whereas the hard bunt just firmly pushes the bunt past the corners. The risk with the slap is that the batter may overswing, resulting in a ground ball right to the third-base player and thus an easy play to get the lead runner.

- The drag bunt can be deceptive and catch the corners sleeping. If the second-base player is playing extremely deep or up the middle, the drag bunt can also be effective. The downside with the drag or bunt for the base hit is that some bunters step out of the box or on the plate when trying to move toward first base too soon. Execution may be more difficult because the bunter squares late.

- The squeeze bunt, or suicide bunt, can be an effective and exciting way to score in a close ball game. This play always presents the risk that the runner on third base will be thrown out at home, doubled off if the batter pops up or tagged out if the batter misses the ball on the attempt. If done at the right time in the at bat, the squeeze is the ultimate short-game strategy for scoring a run without getting a hit.

- You may decide to combine the hard bunt, slap bunt or running slap with having the runner on third base going on the pitch. This play is similar to the suicide, but it uses one of the other short-game skills instead of the standard bunt. This play still carries high risk because the runner is going on the pitch, but it may offer some batters greater opportunity for success.

- If a runner is on second, sacrificing an out to move her to third base is more valuable with no outs than with one out. A runner on third base with one out or no outs can score in many ways, including ground balls or fly balls that result in an out on the batter. With two outs and a runner on third, the fly-ball out or ground-ball out will not score the runner.

- If a slow runner is on second, she may be unable to score on a base hit. A slower runner on second will require two hits or a ball hit in the gap to score. In this situation the coach may want to advance the runner to third using the short game or use a pinch runner who can score on a routine single to the outfield.

- With a runner on second the push bunt can still be effective, but the slap is difficult to execute successfully because the shortstop is moving toward the 5-6 hole. One of the primary goals of the slap is to draw the third-base player in toward home for the sacrifice and then slap or hit the ball past her into the gap between her and the shortstop, also known as the 5-6 hole. Because the shortstop is breaking or cheating toward third base to cover the base, the 5-6 hole is smaller and the shortstop is prepared to move aggressively in that direction. Another difficulty in executing the slap to the third-base side of the field is that in attempting to move to third base, where the defenders and the ball are converging, the runner on second cannot break until she sees the ball get past the defense into the outfield.

- If a runner is at third base with less than two outs, the batter wants to hit the ball deep enough to score the runner from third.

- If a runner is at third base with less than two outs, a squeeze play or safety squeeze is an option. The safety squeeze is simply a bunt by the batter with the runner at third holding there until the defense makes a play on the batter. The runner on third then attempts to score.

The regular squeeze play works best when it surprises the defense or when the corners are playing back. If the opportunity presents itself in a count that increases the likelihood that the batter will get a good pitch in the strike zone, the odds of success are better.

At a Glance

The following parts of the text offer additional information on playing the short game.

Stealing a Base

Stealing bases is a useful component of fast-pitch softball because the speed of play is dramatic with the bases just 60 feet apart. A successful steal can build offensive momentum and increase the pressure on the pitcher and defense by moving a runner into scoring position without sacrificing an out. In fast-pitch softball, however, the playing rules largely control the timing of the steal. Runners must remain in contact with the bag until the pitch is released when attempting a steal, so they cannot take an aggressive lead or try to read the pitcher to get a more aggressive jump. Thus when stealing, the key factors to consider are the runner's foot speed, the catcher's arm strength, or glove-to-glove time, and the speed of the pitch.

 WATCH OUT!

The following circumstances might distract your athletes:

- A first-base player plays back and blocks the view of the pitcher.
- Pitchers change their motion or arm speed on different pitches.
- The athlete has a poor jump or leadoff because of starting late and not anticipating the release.
- A second-base player decoys a pickoff.

READING THE SITUATION

How can you and your players know when to steal a base? Teach your players to do the following:

- Keep an eye on the coach for the steal signal. Many coaches give a steal signal late and only to the runner after the batter has taken her position in the box.
- Study the pitcher's motion at every opportunity to become familiar with the tempo and speed of the arm circle and thus get a good jump off the base on release.
- Be aware of the first-base player so she does not hamper the view of the pitcher when timing the leadoff.
- Be aware of the middle infielders and who has coverage responsibility on the steal. Defenses will sometimes use the second-base player to cover on the steal.
- Sneak a peak at home after a couple of steps to see whether the hitter made contact.
- Read the middle infielder as she is covering to see whether the throw is pulling her off the base.

ACQUIRING THE APPROPRIATE KNOWLEDGE

To steal bases successfully, you and your athletes must understand the following:

REMINDER!

When stealing a base, your players must know your team strategy and game plan. Don't forget to consider the questions on page 128.

Rules

You and your athletes need to know several main rules when you are deciding whether to steal bases:

- Rules regarding leadoffs and when a runner may leave the base (some leagues or levels of play may vary from the release of the pitch).

- Rules about making contact or being hit by the ball after it is hit.
- Rules about making contact or interfering with a defensive player attempting to make a play.
- Rules about a defensive player obstructing the base runner.
- Rules about the defensive player blocking a base when receiving the throw.
- Rules about foul tips and live balls.
- Rules about the pitching circle and what the runner can and cannot do.

Physical Playing Conditions

The physical playing conditions will significantly affect the game. Thus, you and your players must pay attention to the following physical conditions when contemplating whether to steal a base:

- The quality of the base-path surface. If the field is wet or soft, runners may have poor footing and traction. In addition, a wet field usually makes it difficult to accelerate and pick up foot speed. Players should also be aware of the surface quality near second base to help them determine what type of slide they should use. For example, on a muddy or damp surface the runner will slide much slower after she leaves her feet. Therefore, she will need to slide a little later to make sure that she gets all the way into the base. If the surface is extremely torn up, the runner may want to consider sliding later and using a pop-up slide so that she can avoid the poor sliding surface.

- The weather. Rainy or wet conditions may cause the catcher's throws to be less accurate and slow the speed of the runner because of poor footing. The ball may be damp as the catcher receives the pitch. When the catcher has to hurry or rush a throw on a steal, she will not have much time to adjust her release to compensate for the slick ball. On the negative side for the offense, damp conditions will slow the runner because the wet dirt or soft ground will not allow for rapid acceleration on each leg drive.

Strengths and Weaknesses of Opponents

You and your players must account for your opponent's strengths and weaknesses when deciding whether to steal a base. Teach your players to consider the following about your opponents:

- How fast is the pitcher's delivery? The speed of the pitch will affect the timing of the leadoff as well as the amount of time that the runner has to get away from first base before the catcher receives the pitch. The runner's timing of the leadoff may be challenging if she is not able to get into a correct rhythm and leave the base on time with the release.

- What is the arm strength of the catcher? The speed of the catcher's release and strength of her arm are important factors to consider because the runner cannot leave first base until the pitcher releases the ball. The maximum amount of time that a runner has can be calculated from the time that she can leave the base until the catcher can get the ball to second base. The time required for the pitch to travel from release to the catcher's glove plus the time that it takes for the catcher to throw to second base is the time that the runner needs to beat. The strength of the catcher's arm is a factor in glove-to-glove time, but so is the quickness of her release. For that reason, a catcher should not be judged by arm strength alone. A catcher may have average arm strength but excellent glove-to-glove time if she can quickly get the ball out of her glove and on its way to second base.

- What is the speed of the shortstop and second-base player? If these players are quick, your runners should expect that the middle infielders will be able to cover bases from any position on the field where they might be playing. If they are slower, your runner's speed may be enough to steal a base if the middle infielders do not cheat enough toward second to beat the runner to the base.

(continued)

○ How consistent is the pitcher? If a pitcher throws many pitches outside the strike zone, the catcher may have more difficulty making a good throw. When the catcher has to move from her squatted position or stand up to catch a pitch, she will have difficulty keeping her legs loaded and prepared for the release to second. A catcher's legs have a tremendous effect on her glove-to-glove time, and an inconsistent pitcher can disrupt the catcher's rhythm.

○ What is the skill level of the catcher? As a rule, your runners can steal more often on catchers who have a hard time handling the pitches or are less skilled with the glove.

DELAYED LIVE BALL STEAL

After the pitch as the catcher is returning the ball to the pitcher, the defense sometimes fails to focus. The middle infielders may not fully cover second base, or the catcher may not look to make sure that the runner is returning to first base. Some pitchers direct all their attention to the pitch and the call from the umpire, and they forget about the runners on base. In this situation, a delayed live ball steal can be effective. For example, a runner can set up a delayed steal by using an aggressive lead to draw a throw from the catcher. If the catcher becomes predictable on her throw back, a quick runner can attempt to take the next base when the catcher throws behind the runner to pick her off.

Nonetheless, a delayed live ball steal requires your runner to read the defense, in particular the catcher and the pitcher. You and your players should be aware of several points about the delayed steal:

- An aggressive lead on previous pitches can entice the catcher to throw behind the runner to attempt a pickoff. The runner can then set up a delayed steal on the catcher. If the catcher is predictable with her throw behind the runner, the runner can set her up to attempt a delayed steal on her throw to the base behind her.

- An average lead with low-level intensity can lull a catcher and pitcher into not paying close attention to the runner. The defense may stop focusing on the runner and become lazy about making sure that the runner is returning to the base before the catcher releases the ball back to the pitcher.

- Patience is important. If the runner breaks too soon, she will be hung up between bases. The runner must wait until the catcher releases the ball. If the runner becomes anxious or breaks slightly early, before the catcher releases the ball, the catcher may be able to readjust midthrow and make a full throw to second base or perhaps hold on to the ball and catch the runner between the bases.

- The runner should watch the defensive coverage at second base on previous pitches. When the middle infield fails to cover or fails to remain in covered position, the defense is vulnerable to the delayed steal.

- A delayed steal can also occur following a single or error. When the runner is returning to first she should check the defensive coverage at second base. Many times infielders return to their positions early, and the pitcher may not be alert as the ball is being returned to her in the circle. Timing is important because the runner cannot take second base if she has returned to first base when the ball is back in the circle.

- A single to the outfield can also set up a delayed steal if the throw from the outfielder is lofted and is cut off short of the base. After rounding the base, the runner should watch the defense. If they relax and toss the ball to an infielder, the runner can take off for the next base. Although this tactic can be risky, a good base runner who reads the defense well can execute it successfully.

Self-Knowledge

Besides being aware of your opponent's strengths and weaknesses, you and your players need to have knowledge about your own team's ability. When deciding whether to steal a base, you and your players must be aware of the following:

○ How fast is the runner at first base? Giving the steal sign to the runner at first base makes sense if that runner's base-to-base time is less than the catcher's glove-to-glove time.

○ How well can the runner read the release so that she can get a good jump? Some runners maximize their leadoff at first base by always getting a good jump. The speed of the runner has no bearing on how well she times the release of the pitch. Some fast runners consistently get extremely poor jumps, which can frustrate their coach's effort to employ the steal.

○ How well can the runner slide? A runner who has excellent sliding ability and can use various slides at second base to avoid the tag has a better chance of being safe even if her foot speed is average.

○ How well does the batter protect the runner? If your batter has strong ability to fake a slap or swing, the middle infielders must hold their positions longer and the catcher must stay back until the hitter completes her swing. These two factors can cause the defense to become anxious, which may force an inaccurate throw or poor coverage at second base.

Decision-Making Guidelines

When deciding whether to steal a base, you and your players should be sure to consider the previous information. Also consider the following guidelines:

○ Take more risks early in the game or after you have a lead. When you have a lead, your opponent is already feeling pressure to catch up and thus will feel greater pressure on defense. Early in a ball game, taking greater risks with steals can give you a better evaluation of your opponent's ability, which you can use later in the game when pressure increases.

○ Use the speed of your team to create holes in the defense. Getting your fast runners started even without the batter's knowledge can cause the middle infielders to vacate their positions a split second early or get them leaning in one direction. This tactic can open up gaps between the third-base player and the shortstop or between the first-base player and the second-base player. Making decisions about when to have the runners steal without the batter's knowledge may depend on the count as well. If you believe that the pitcher will likely throw a good hitter's pitch and that your hitter is generally aggressive about hitting strikes, then getting the runner started makes good sense. There is a risk of being thrown out, as well as a risk of being doubled off on a line drive, but the rewards will be great if the ball is hit sharply or in a gap.

○ With a fast runner on first base and your best hitter at the plate, attempting a steal and risking giving away an out may not be a good idea. Even if the risk that the runner will be thrown out is low, you should consider whether moving the runner to second base will result in an intentional walk of your best hitter after first base becomes open.

○ With two outs, an average runner on first base and an outstanding hitter up, attempting a steal to get the runner into scoring position may be in your best interest. If the steal attempt fails and ends the inning, you may start the next inning with a better combination of hitters coming up. For example, suppose that your number 8 batter is on base and your number 9 batter is up. Your number 9 batter does not hit for a lot of power,

(continued)

but she has a good on-base average. You may choose to attempt to start the following inning with your number 9 hitter up so that she can be on base with no outs and the top of your order coming up. If the steal works, you have a greater chance to score. In this win–win situation little risk is involved.

○ Steal in counts when the pitcher is likely to throw a pitch that might be moving out of the strike zone or when she is likely to throw an off-speed pitch. Both situations put the catcher in poor position to get the ball to second base quickly.

○ As a rule, your players should slide directly into second base to beat the throw. Most of the time a runner's feet will get in and touch second base before the ball is there, but when the runner slides to the outside of the base, she gives the fielder more time to apply a tag before she gets her hands on the base.

○ The runner should slide away to the outside of the base to avoid the tag only when the throw will beat her to the base. Runners need to read the defenders. If the runner reads the throw and judges that it is going to beat her, she may want to use a different technique in an attempt to be safe.

In fast-pitch softball a runner cannot leave the base until the release of the pitch. To protect the runner, the batter can keep the catcher in her set position and delay the defense's break to cover the base. By protecting the runner, the batter can give the runner valuable extra time and cause the defense to rush when they attempt to get a runner who is stealing.

Exactly how the batter can aid the runner depends on the game situation and the location of the runner. The infielders' coverage scheme for the base that the runner is attempting to steal will determine how the batter can best disrupt or delay the infielder's break to the base. For example, if the shortstop is covering second base on the steal attempt with a runner on first base, a late swing or a fake slap bunt can force the shortstop to hold until after the batter misses the ball. These extra seconds of delay for the infield can make it more challenging for the defense to cover the base. If the third-base player is covering the steal at third base, the batter can show a fake bunt, which will cause the third-base player to move or take a few steps in toward home while the runner is on the move.

 WATCH OUT!

The following circumstances might distract your athletes:

- A pitchout could make the protection ineffective.
- Inadvertently fouling off the pitch negates the stolen base and returns the runner to the original base. The batter must stay focused on missing the pitch and fake the defense into believing that she is going to make contact.
- Players making a realistic attempt at freezing the defense. The attempt must have gamelike intensity and look realistic to the defense.
- Leaning over the plate on a steal of second can be interpreted as interference, which would result in the batter being called out and the runner being required to return to first base. The batter should not move into the sight lines of the catcher, but she is not required to move out of the batter's box.

ACQUIRING THE APPROPRIATE KNOWLEDGE

To protect the runner on a steal, you and your athletes must understand the following:

Rules

You and your athletes need to know several main rules when you are deciding whether to protect the runner on a steal:

- Rules about interfering with the catcher's throw

READING THE SITUATION

How can you and your players know when to protect the runner on a steal? Teach your players to do the following:

- Know where the runner is and which defensive players have coverage responsibility. Depending on the defensive coverage of the steal, your batter will need to attempt to get the covering defender to freeze or move in the opposite direction while the runner is on the move.
- Know how many outs there are. With less than two outs the fake bunt and fake slap can be effective at freezing the defense. With two outs, the fake bunt is often less effective.

REMINDER!

When determining whether to protect the runner on a steal, your players must know your team strategy and game plan. Don't forget to consider the questions on page 128.

(continued)

- Rules about what constitutes an attempt on a swing or bunt
- Rules about defensive obstruction of the runners
- Rules about the pitcher's circle

Physical Playing Conditions

The physical playing conditions will significantly affect the game. Thus, you and your players must pay attention to the following physical conditions when contemplating whether to protect the runner on a steal:

- The condition of the infield. A muddy or wet infield surface can affect the footing for both the runner and the infielders. Although the infielders do not have to travel as far to reach the base as the runner does, they are sometimes more negatively affected by a wet or muddy playing surface. They must delay their move until the hitter misses the ball, and therefore they need to accelerate quickly to catch up to the speed of the runner.
- The position of the sun. The sun can create a glare that may make it challenging for the defense to read the hitter or see the throw from the catcher.

Strengths and Weaknesses of Opponents

You and your players must account for your opponent's strengths and weaknesses when deciding whether to protect the runner on a steal. Teach your players to consider the following about your opponents:

- How strong is the catcher? In fast-pitch softball a runner cannot leave a base until the pitch has left the pitcher's hand. Therefore, the speed of the pitch and the catcher's arm are factors that could affect a runner's chance at a successful steal.
- How well does the catcher handle distractions? If the batter is swinging to protect the runner, the bat traveling through the strike zone at the same time as the ball can cause a visual distraction. Of course, the catcher must stay back in her receiving position until the hitter has completed her swing.
- How quick are the middle infielders? A batter's late swing to protect the runner can hold the defense longer in their positions. The batter's swing will keep them from being able to leave their fielding position until the swing is complete, even when they know that the runner is stealing.
- Is the defense easily distracted? A swing or an attempted bunt can distract some infielders and slow their reaction to the steal.
- How well does the defense communicate? A defense that has trouble communicating may react poorly to the batter's protection of the runner. They may panic when responsibilities increase, so raising the amount of visual distraction with the fake swing or bunt may put them outside their comfort level. In addition, some defenses become confused when runners are on base. By observing the communication by the defense, you may be able to read that they are somewhat uncertain about their responsibilities. You may hear the shortstop say to the second-base player, "Do you have the steal or do I?" or you may notice poor communication between the catcher and the infielders. Body language and oral cues can give away a lot of information if you take the time to watch and listen to the defense's communication or lack thereof. Stealing with protection may be effective in these circumstances because the added decision-making responsibility caused by the batter's protection will increase the pressure on the defense.
- Which action will freeze the defense better—a fake bunt or a swing? By reading the defensive positioning, you will be able to decide how best to protect the runner.

Self-Knowledge

Besides being aware of your opponent's strengths and weaknesses, you and your players need to have knowledge about your own team's ability. When protecting the runner, you and your players must be aware of the following:

- How quick is the runner who is attempting the steal? The speed of the runner will determine the need to protect her with a full swing or just a fake slap. If the runner is extremely quick and you do not want to give away the strike on the batter, you may choose to have the batter just hold the defense by showing the slap.

- How confident are you that the batter understands the signal and her responsibility? Before you put on the steal in which the batter needs to protect the runner, you want to make sure that your batter is confident about her role and her job; otherwise, she may not fully protect the runner and you will end up with a strike on the batter and the runner being thrown out.

- How well does the batter fake a bunt attempt? When the runner is attempting to steal third and the third-base player is covering the play, a fake bunt can be just as effective as showing bunt and taking the strike. Some batters are less convincing with their fake bunt so you may choose to have the batter square around fully and take the strike with the bat in the strike zone to ensure that the corner players are charging toward home.

- How realistic is the bunt attempt for the batter? Is she a player who would normally be a threat to bunt in that situation in the game? Batters who have decent foot speed and use the short game to get on base at times are generally good decoys for the fake bunt. If the batter is not normally a threat to put down a bunt because of lack of foot speed or bunting skill, the defense will probably not be fooled in the game situation.

- How well does the batter swing through the plane of the pitch without making contact? Remember that the batter's job is to hold the catcher back in her position and ideally create a visual diversion with the bat. If the batter's protection swing is slow, very early, very late or nowhere near the pitch, then it will do little to protect the runner.

Decision-Making Guidelines

When deciding whether to protect the runner on a steal, you and your players should be sure to consider the previous information. Also consider the following guidelines:

- The batter should move the catcher farther from the pitcher if possible by taking a position in the batter's box slightly deeper than normal. She should be careful not to give away the play by moving to the extreme back of the box unless that is where she would normally stand.

- A runner on first base who is stealing second is better protected with a late swing or fake slap to freeze the middle infielders until after the swing is finished. This action will give the runner a slight head start while the infielders wait for the swing to be completed.

- A runner on second base who is stealing third is better protected with a swing or fake slap if the shortstop is covering on the steal because she will have to wait until the batter misses the ball. But in the same scenario with the third-base player covering the steal, a fake bunt or

At a Glance

The following parts of the text offer additional information on protecting the runner on a steal.

Sacrifice Bunt	28
Slap Hit and Hard Bunt	32
Squeeze Bunt	35
Running Slap	37
Baserunning	42
Playing the Short Game	130
Stealing a Base	136

(continued)

late bunt attempt will better protect the runner because the bunt attempt will draw the corners in toward home and away from third base.

○ To distract the catcher, the batter should swing late as close as possible to the plane of the pitch and on the correct timing with the pitch. An early swing or an extremely late swing does not distract the catcher's vision as she is receiving the pitch.

○ A batter who stays in the batter's box and makes herself as large as possible can hinder the catcher visually without interfering.

○ The call for a steal with protection is usually done early in the count to keep the hitter from moving into a two-strike hitting situation.

○ Sacrificing the hitter with a fake swing with two strikes can be done as well to move the runner into scoring position for the on-deck hitter if the batter has failed to execute a sacrifice bunt.

The first-and-third situation occurs when a runner is on first base, a runner is on third base and second base is open. The goal in this situation is to generate a run or at least to advance the runner at first base into scoring position with a stolen base. Another motivation for the first-and-third play can be to move the runners out of a double-play situation. The play is also used to create pressure on the defense and possibly cause some kind of miscommunication or error that results in all runners advancing safely without the batter hitting the pitch.

 ## WATCH OUT!

The following circumstances might distract your athletes:

- The catcher throws immediately down to third base to pick off the runner who is taking a big lead.

- The pitcher cuts off the throw to second base from the catcher to attempt to pick off the runner on third. Some teams use a quick throw back to the pitcher to catch the runner on third off the base while the ball is in the pitching circle.

- The second-base player cuts off a steal throw to second base behind the pitcher's mound in an attempt to pick off the runner on third if she gets too far off the base.

- The catcher fakes a throw to second to draw the runner on third off the base and then throws down to third base to pick off the lead runner.

READING THE SITUATION

How can you and your players know when they are in a first-and-third situation? Teach your players to do the following:

- Be aware of the game situation, the inning, the score and your location in the batting lineup. This information will dictate the goal of the first-and-third play—whether it is to advance the runner on first out of double-play status or to create a rundown to attempt to score the runner on third.

- Be aware of the count on the batter in case the defense attempts a pitchout.

- The hitter and both runners should look for the appropriate signal from the coach, and all should be aware of the signals and the goal that the coach is looking for in the outcome of the play.

- Know the defensive coverage for the steal of second base. If the runners are able to see which defenders are moving to defend the first-and-third situation, then the coach and players have more information about how they might be able to expose a weakness during the play.

ACQUIRING THE APPROPRIATE KNOWLEDGE

To handle a first-and-third situation successfully, you and your athletes must understand the following:

Rules

You and your athletes need to know several main rules when you are in a first-and-third situation:

- Rules about interference and obstruction in case a rundown develops

REMINDER!

When in a first-and-third situation, your players must know your team strategy and game plan. Don't forget to consider the questions on page 128.

(continued)

- Rules about staying in the base path during rundowns
- Rules about the requirements for the runners when the pitcher has the ball in the pitching circle
- Rules about the batter's potential interference with the catcher's throw

Physical Playing Conditions

The physical playing conditions will significantly affect the game. Thus, you and your players must pay attention to the following physical conditions when in a first-and-third situation:

- The field conditions between first and second and third and home. Soft dirt or a wet, muddy surface makes it more challenging for runners to accelerate and change directions.
- The wind and sun could affect the ability of the defense to make and receive good throws. The wind could affect the speed and accuracy of throws, and the sun could make tracking the ball a challenge for the defense.

Strengths and Weaknesses of Opponents

You and your players must account for your opponent's strengths and weaknesses when in a first-and-third situation. Teach your players to consider the following about your opponents:

- Does the catcher have a strong and accurate throw to second base? The speed and accuracy of the ball traveling to second base will affect the amount of time that the runner on third base will have to score. The runner on third will need to wait at least until the catcher releases the ball before she attempts to steal home. If the catcher's arm is inconsistent or weak, the runner at third will have more time to score while the ball is traveling all the way down to second base and back on the throw by the infielder.
- How well does the catcher disguise her intentions? If the catcher has the ability to fake a throw to second using an aggressive arm swing, she may be able to draw the runner at third off base and then pick her off with a throw to the third-base player.
- Does the defense use the second-base player as a cutoff player to pick off the runner on third base? If so, then using a fake bunt can help freeze or delay her movement to the cut position. Because she first has to react to the batter's attempt and likely has the responsibility to cover first base, she may be caught leaning the wrong way—opposite the direction that she must move to cut off the steal throw to second.
- How strong and accurate is the shortstop's throw? When the shortstop receives a throw, she must be able to return the throw quickly and accurately to the catcher if the runner on third base attempts to score. Your runners may be able to take advantage of this weakness in the defenders by breaking for home immediately on the release from the catcher. So the time that passes from the catcher's release until the return throw arrives from the shortstop establishes the amount of time available for the runner on third base to run 60 feet.
- Where are the corner players positioned? If the corner players are positioned close to home plate to protect against the squeeze, the runner on third can increase her lead-off on the pitch and get closer to home. Because the third-base player is now farther from the base, she cannot keep the runner on third close to the base. The runner on third will be able to take a longer initial leadoff, which will reduce the distance that she will need to travel to score after the catcher releases her throw to second base on the steal.

Self-Knowledge

Besides being aware of your opponent's strengths and weaknesses, you and your players need to have knowledge about your own team's ability. When in a first-and-third situation, you and your players must be aware of the following:

- How strong is the hitter? If the player at bat is a good hitter with runners in scoring position, you may not want to open up first base for the defense to walk or pitch around her. With a big threat at the plate and first base open, the defense could take the bat out of your best hitter's hands and intentionally walk her. Therefore, you need to evaluate whether opening first base will be a positive move. If the defense walks the first hitter, the on-deck hitter will come to the plate with bases loaded. Evaluating the reverse situation is also important. If the batter is weak with runners in scoring position, then the risk of running the first-and-third play may pay off by scoring a run without the batter needing to do anything at the plate.

- Does the batter hit into double plays often? If the batter often hits into double plays because she is a slower runner, you may want to try to eliminate the double-play situation by advancing the runner from first base. Using the runner on third base as a decoy to draw the throw will allow the runner on first base to attempt to steal second and thus eliminate a potential double-play ground ball. Now a ground ball from the batter can score the runner on third even if the batter is thrown out at first base.

- Do your runners on first and third have good speed? In a first-and-third situation, speed can cause confusion and panic in the defense. If the runner on third is exceptionally fast and the defense knows it, they will likely try to rush their throws, which can increase the likelihood of throwing or ball-handling errors.

- Are the runners at first and third quick thinkers in rundown situations? The ability to change directions quickly is helpful if runners are caught in a rundown. To run the first-and-third play effectively, your runners need to be able to stay in a rundown for a while and possibly evade being tagged out at all. To do this, they need the ability to change directions quickly. The runner on first should know her role in case the ball beats her to second base. Getting into a rundown situation and not running into the out is paramount. The role of the runner on first base is to draw the throw to second base without being tagged out, but if the defense makes a good throw to second, the runner from first should get in a rundown to distract the defense from the runner on third base. If the runner from first can stay in a rundown long enough, the runner on third base may have enough time to attempt to steal home. If the defense does not make a throw to second base, the runner from first should be able to take the stolen base.

- How well does the runner on third read the throw from the catcher? A runner on third who can read the quality of the throw from the catcher can get a great jump on an attempt to steal home. If she reads a bad throw or high throw to second base, she can break for home as soon as the ball leaves the catcher's hand. Some catchers use a good fake throw to second base and then throw down to third base. Runners on third should be able to read the ball leaving the catcher's hand toward second base and not anticipate or guess when the catcher is going to release the ball to second base. Time is critical, and the time that the ball is in the air between defenders can determine whether the runner on third is safe or out at home.

- Do your players understand the signals used? Making sure that all players involved are confident in the play is crucial. If the player on first base is not clear about her role or what she is attempting to do by drawing the throw, the play will likely result in an out without giving the runner on third base enough time to attempt to steal home. Remember that giving up an out with a runner on third base decreases your opportunity to score with a sacrifice fly by the batter or the on-deck batter.

(continued)

Decision-Making Guidelines

When in a first-and-third situation, you and your players should be sure to consider the previous information. Also consider the following guidelines:

○ If the batter is walked with a runner on third base only, you could run a play in which the batter–runner continues to second base without stopping. The goal is to draw a throw or advance without a pitch being thrown. Coaches should have a signal or teach their players when to do this and when to hold at first base.

○ When runners are caught in a rundown, they need to stay in the rundown long enough to allow other runners time to advance, especially the runner who is in a rundown between first and second.

○ If your team has struggled to get hits and has not had much success against the opponent's pitcher, using alternative methods to create offense may be necessary. A good strategy on the first-and-third play can create an offensive threat without needing the batter to have success at the plate. By trying to draw the throw from the catcher down to second base, you may create enough of a diversion to cause an error or enough time for the runner on third to score. The risk is that you might give up an out, thus putting more pressure on the batter to get a hit to score the runner on third base.

○ If the game is close or in the late innings, the runner on third is critical. You need to decide how many outs you are willing to risk depending on where you are in your lineup. If the next two or three batters in your lineup are not strong and you do not have good pinch hitters to use off your bench, then attempting to create more offense with your baserunning may be a good option. If your next two or three batters are good hitters and can easily hit deep fly balls or base hits, then you may not want to risk the extra out at second base.

○ Ultimately, when running a first-and-third play, your players must not force the play by running into an out. Sometimes, the defense is able to execute a solid counter to the first-and-third play that will keep either runner from advancing. Offensively, you would like to advance at least one runner, but if the defensive coverage is good, your runner on first should make every attempt to end up safe back at first base. Explain to your athletes that ending up with no runners advancing is OK as long as they do not give up an out.

○ In many first-and-third situations trading an out by the runner going into second for a run scored is optimum. At other times your first-and-third play may be more about taking away the double-play situation for the defense. The runner on first base does not need to force the issue of advancing to second base if the defense is able to make a throw to second in time. So your runner on first needs to be able to read the throw from the catcher so that she does not automatically slide into an out at second.

○ You should train your athletes to stop in time to create a rundown between second base and first base. If a rundown occurs the runner should attempt to be safe at either base or stay in the rundown long enough for the runner on third to score. Giving away outs with a runner at third base only decreases the opportunity for a sacrifice fly or base hit by the current or on-deck hitter. The first-and-third play can be a useful offensive weapon, but the risk should always be evaluated.

At a Glance

The following parts of the text offer additional information on first-and-third situations.

ggressive base runners take advantage of bobbled balls or small mistakes by the defense because they are looking to take two bases when most runners focus only on being safe at the next base. Batters who look to take second base on balls hit in the gaps can force outfielders to make hurried and inaccurate throws, thus creating advantages for the offense and challenging the defense to react quickly and make multiple decisions when the ball is first hit.

⚠ WATCH OUT!

The following circumstances might distract your athletes:

- Defenses run pickoffs on aggressive offenses.
- Runners run with their heads down and do not pay close attention to the defense.
- Fake throws by the defense catch runners off base.

ACQUIRING THE APPROPRIATE KNOWLEDGE

To use aggressive baserunning successfully, you and your athletes must understand the following:

Rules

You and your athletes need to know several main rules when you are using aggressive baserunning:

- Rules about baserunning and the order that bases have to be touched in both directions
- Rules about force-outs
- Rules about switching directions or stopping in the base paths
- Rules about the dropped third strike with two outs
- Rules about infield flies and tagging up
- Rules about the ball in the pitching circle
- Rules about interference and obstruction
- Rules about contact with coaches
- Rules about being hit by a batted ball and what releases change that rule

READING THE SITUATION

How can you and your players know when to use aggressive baserunning? Teach your players to do the following:

- Be aware of the game situation. Always know how many outs there are and what the score is.
- Know where the ball is at all times. Leaving a base without knowing where the ball is can put you in a bad position.
- Watch the runners in front of you. Being aggressive is fine as long as you do not run into the runner ahead of you.
- Watch the base coaches for signals and signs and appropriately and immediately execute the signals that the coach gives.
- Always be ready for the defense to make an error and be prepared to act.

REMINDER!

When using aggressive baserunning, your players must know your team strategy and game plan. Don't forget to consider the questions on page 128.

(continued)

Physical Playing Conditions

The physical playing conditions will significantly affect the game. Thus, you and your players must pay attention to the following physical conditions when using aggressive baserunning:

- The surface quality of the infield. A soft or wet infield surface could cause the infielders to have problems getting to the ball quickly and fielding it cleanly. They may also have a hard time making accurate throws when pressured. On the other hand you should be aware of how the infield surface affects the speed of your runners. A soft or muddy field usually makes it difficult for runners to be as quick as they normally would be between the bases.

- The condition of the base paths. The base paths may be soft and or wet, which could slow a runner because of poor footing.

- The grass in the outfield. Long grass in the outfield will dramatically slow down a ball. If the ball is slowed down and the outfielders do not approach it aggressively, runners can take advantage of the extra time that outfielders will need to get to routine balls. If the grass is wet, outfielders may be unable to make accurate throws.

Strengths and Weaknesses of Opponents

You and your players must account for your opponent's strengths and weaknesses when using aggressive baserunning. Teach your players to consider the following about your opponents:

- Do the outfielders have strong throwing ability? Knowing the strength of each outfielder's throwing arm can give you useful information about how aggressive to be when running the bases on balls hit to the outfield. For example, if the outfielders have weaker arms, you can have your runners look to take that extra base on balls hit to the sides of the outfielders.

- Do the infielders adjust their starting positions based on the game situation? Pay attention to whether the infielders adjust their positions when runners are on base to achieve better coverage. Sometimes infielders will move closer to bases to protect against the steal. At other times infielders may fail to adjust when runners are on base and therefore will be extra vulnerable because they will need more time to cover on the steal.

- Do the infielders cheat a few steps in their coverage for a potential pickoff? Runners who know where the defense is before every pitch will be able to be more aggressive on the base paths. If you or your runners can read changes in the defense, then pickoff attempts or changes in defensive coverage will not surprise you. Aggressive baserunning is based on using team speed and being able to read the defenders' ability to cover the plays. The more you know about how the defense plays in every situation, the better you can take advantage of situations that come up when they make mistakes.

- Do the infielders maintain base coverage? Infielders often do not stay in good coverage responsibility when they think that a play is over. If the ball is still outside the pitching circle, it is live and runners are free to advance. Your players should watch throughout the entire game, from the dugout when they are not at bat or on the bases. Defenders have tendencies. The player who recognizes a vulnerability will be prepared if the infielders start to walk away from the bases before the ball is dead and back in the pitching circle.

- Does the catcher have a strong arm and a quick release? The strength of a catcher's arm can come into play whenever you are considering a baserunning strategy. If the catcher has a strong arm and a quick release, you may decide to rein in some of your aggressiveness when she is handling the ball. Every defender's ability comes into play, but the catcher is a critical player and often handles the ball on plays at the plate when your trail runners are trying to advance additional bases. On the other hand, if the catcher has a slow release or a weak arm, your team should always look to advance the additional base when throws go home for the lead runner.

- Where do the outfielders throw? If the outfielders throw toward the base where the runner is, runners may have a chance to take an extra base after the outfielder releases the ball to the infielder. For example, if the outfielders routinely throw to second base with runners on first and second base on a routine play, then the runner on second may be able to break for third base if the outfielders lazily toss the ball toward the middle infielder or toward second. By the time the infielder catches the ball, the runner could be halfway to the next base.

- In bunt situations, which runner do the corner players go after? Some defenses rarely go after the lead runner in bunt situations. This tendency can change the strategy and the aggressiveness of the base runners. In a sacrifice situation, many teams opt to go for the sure out at first base and do not risk going after the lead runner. In this situation, you may decide to be extremely aggressive and start the runners early or have them attempt to advance two bases on the bunt.

Self-Knowledge

Besides being aware of your opponent's strengths and weaknesses, you and your players need to have knowledge about your own team's ability. When using aggressive baserunning, you and your players must be aware of the following:

- How quick is your batter? If your batter is fast, you can adjust how aggressive you can be and whether you will go for extra bases. If the batter–base runner is quick, then you may work hard to draw throws with your lead runners to give your batter a chance to take an extra base on the play. If your batter–base runner is not fast, then being more aggressive with your lead runner will probably not help your batter advance an extra base without risking being thrown out.

- How well does your batter read the defense? If the batter is capable of picking up defensive miscues and reading the situation to take the extra base, you can use a more aggressive strategy. If the batter–base runner is expecting the defense to bobble the ball or make a mistake, then she will not be surprised when it happens. Batters are often satisfied when they get a hit and reach first base safely, so they are no longer watching the defense to see whether they have made a mistake. First-base coaches need to keep the athletes focused on the game until the ball is back in the pitching circle or time is called.

- How well do the runners read the defense? If the runners on base can read the defense well and be aggressive based on that knowledge, they will anticipate mistakes and not be surprised when they occur. Looking for the defense to make an error, miss the ball, throw the ball away, miss the cut with a throw, bobble a routine ground ball and so on are all things that runners can take advantage of the instant that they happen. Base runners who are looking for these mistakes can take full advantage. If they are expecting the defense not to make a mistake, they will not be able to react when the mistakes happen.

- Is the lead runner fast or slow? Be sure to avoid having a trail runner or the batter run into a slower or less aggressive runner ahead of her on the bases. The speed of a trail runner has nothing to do with the speed or aggressiveness of the runner ahead of her. The trail runner needs to adjust her aggressiveness slightly and read the defense and the lead base runner on the play. She must run with her head up, keeping her eyes up and always knowing where the lead runners are as well as what the defense is doing.

- How strong is the on-deck hitter? For example, does the on-deck hitter have strong ability when runners are on base with two outs? If the on-deck batter is a good hitter in clutch situations, you may choose to temper your aggressiveness and not risk running yourself out of an inning. If the on-deck batter is not strong in that situation, you may choose to go for more bases in hopes of causing the defense to falter and make mistakes.

(continued)

Decision-Making Guidelines

When using aggressive baserunning, you and your players should be sure to consider the previous information. Also consider the following guidelines:

- Aggressive baserunning should be used more often when your team is ahead and used consistently when you are behind. Being ahead offers a prime opportunity to be extra aggressive because the defense is generally feeling stress from the offensive production that your team has been exhibiting. When your team is behind you should continue to use the aggressive style of play that you normally play with. If you become conservative with your style when you are behind, then your team will likely not take advantage when the opportunity arises to take the lead. Overall, you should commit to the aggressive style of baserunning all the time, not just when you are winning. And when you are winning, you should step up the pressure on the defense with your team speed.

- Aggressive baserunning as a team is not an absolute requirement. Its application always depends on the players who are on base at the time of the play. Each player's aggressive style will be limited by her ability. Aggressiveness will not be the same for all players. A fast runner will attempt a more aggressive style of running versus a slower runner. Both can run aggressively, but different expectations will be in place for each runner, and no absolutes apply to every player.

- Batters must be willing to protect runners on steals with fake swings or fake bunts. Batters will need to feel comfortable taking a few strikes during the game to protect runners. To do this, they may have to start their at bat deeper into the pitch count. When your batters are comfortable doing this, you will be better able to employ your aggressive baserunning strategy.

- Your players should tag up only on fly balls that you believe they can advance on. Otherwise, runners should come off the base as far as they can without risking being doubled off by the defense. Some base runners tag up on fly balls that they will never be able to advance on and then fake that they are tagging up to advance. Instead, runners should come off the base as far as they can in case the ball is dropped but not so far off that when the catch is made the defense can throw back to the base and double them off.

- The runner should always come off the bag with the anticipation that she is going on the catch. But she must pick up the coach immediately as she is coming off the base in case the coach holds her up. Additionally, the coach must have clear signals that all players have practiced seeing when they are tagging up.

- Players should always tag up on any foul fly ball including pop-up bunts or soft line drives. A runner may be able to advance on a ball that the defense dives for in making a catch. Coming off a base to read whether the ball will drop is not necessary on a ball that is clearly foul. A runner can advance only on a fair ball that hits the ground. For all foul fly balls, the only chance to advance will be after a catch is made. Therefore, runners should immediately return to a base on any fly ball that is clearly in foul territory, even a short foul ball or a foul ball near the infield. If a fielder or catcher falls or dives while making a catch, the runners will be ready to advance.

- Runners on second base should always think about tagging up and advancing to third base on fly balls that are hit to the gap between right field and center field or down the right-field line. A ball caught in either location requires a difficult throw because the outfielder is usually moving away from home and must make a long throw to third base.

 As a runner prepares to score she should maximize the chance of being safe or at least draw a throw home. Beginning with the turn at third base, the runner can do several things to maximize her chance to score.

⚠ WATCH OUT!

The following circumstances might distract your athletes:

- Trying to avoid the defender covering third can cause the runner to make a wide turn toward home.
- Running with her eyes down can cause the runner to lose focus on the coach or the defensive players' positions when heading for home.
- Being tempted to turn her head to pick up the ball while rounding the base can cause the runner to slow down and hesitate.

ACQUIRING THE APPROPRIATE KNOWLEDGE

To approach home successfully, you and your athletes must understand the following:

Rules

You and your athletes need to know several main rules when runners are approaching home:

- Rules about obstruction and interference
- Rules about being hit by a batted ball
- Rules about when it is legal to leave the base on a catch
- Rules about the pitching circle
- Rules about the catcher and blocking the plate

Physical Playing Conditions

The physical playing conditions will significantly affect the game. Thus, you and your players must pay attention to the following physical conditions when runners approach home:

- The surface quality of the base paths. The playing surface in the base paths can affect the runner's speed and footing. A soft or muddy infield will also reduce the normal foot speed of a runner because of the lack of firm footing to push off against.

READING THE SITUATION

How can you and your players know how to approach home properly? Teach your players to do the following:

- Know how many outs there are and what the game situation is. As the player approaches third and rounds it for home, she should know the game situation.
- Be aware of defensive shifts in the infield and outfield before the pitch. Always knowing where the defense is playing can help the runner know which defender is closest to the ball when it is hit and whether that player will be in good position to make a solid throw home.
- The runner at third base must know the type of read that the coach is looking for.

REMINDER!

When approaching home, your players must know your team strategy and game plan. Don't forget to consider the questions on page 128.

(continued)

- The length of the grass may slow a ball hit on the ground to the outfield, thus giving the runner more time to score.

- Moisture and wetness in the outfield may challenge the outfielders' ability to make accurate and powerful throws.

- In addition, a wet outfield will cause the ball to skip and accelerate on hard-hit ground balls and line drives. This circumstance will challenge the outfielders' capacity to come up with the ball cleanly if it is hit in the gaps. Balls may get to the outfielders more quickly if they are hit directly to them.

- The location of the sun. The sun may become a challenge for the outfielders when they are trying to make a catch. A routine fly ball may end up falling safely to the ground. If the runner is prepared for this to occur, she can take advantage of it. Additionally, the sun could possibly be in a position that causes difficulty for the catcher when she is receiving a throw from a specific field. The coach and runner may choose to be more aggressive in this situation to challenge the catcher's ability to see the ball.

Strengths and Weaknesses of Opponents

You and your players must account for your opponent's strengths and weaknesses when playing the short game. Teach your players to consider the following about your opponents:

- How strong are the outfielders' throwing arms? Your players should know which outfielders have the strongest arms when they are throwing home on ground balls. Some outfielders can make a solid, accurate throw from a certain distance, but on a ball that is hit deeper they may not have the arm strength to deliver the ball home on the fly or on a single bounce. Each bounce of a throw dramatically slows the speed of the ball. Some outfielders do not throw as well when moving to the forehand side because they have difficulty changing directions to get the ball back toward home.

- How quick are the infielders? Knowing the range of the infielders and what balls they will be able to cut off and keep in the infield is helpful. Because the runner has her back to the defense when she rounds the base and heads toward home, she needs to rely on the coach's eyes and any knowledge that the coach and runner have about the infielders. If a shortstop is weak on balls hit up the middle and the runner is prepared, she will anticipate scoring on balls that are hit up the middle out of the range of the shortstop. Also, for a runner on third base who is in a read-ball situation, the range and speed of the infielders will directly affect what type of ball she will attempt to score on.

- How strong are the middle infielders' throws? A factor in a base runner's attempt to score from third may be the strength of the middle infielder's arm. Because middle infielders have to cover a large portion of the infield and are a long way away from home plate, the runner can benefit by knowing the strength of their arms when deciding whether to attempt to score.

- How strong is the catcher? How consistent and confident is the catcher at blocking the plate? Catchers who struggle with digging out a ball on a bad throw and have a hard time handling the ball and blocking the plate at the same time should be challenged. The play at the plate is a high-pressure situation for the catcher. If she struggles physically with a skill, the likelihood of an error increases when the pressure is on. If a catcher has a problem receiving the throw and blocking the plate at the same time, you can be more aggressive by sending the runner when you might normally hold her at third base. This aggressive strategy comes with more risk of having the runner thrown out, but the runner may force a difficult play and benefit from an error.

Self-Knowledge

Besides being aware of your opponent's strengths and weaknesses, you and your players need to have knowledge about your own team's ability. When runners are approaching home, you and your players must be aware of the following:

- How strong a player is the runner at second or third? The player at second or third will have to consider many things when preparing to approach home. For example, the player may be asked to read the speed and location of the ball before breaking for home. With the conservative approach, she should see the ball through the infield before breaking for home. She must be ready to score if the ball gets away from the catcher on a wild pitch or passed ball.

- How fast are the runners in scoring position? Speed has no substitute when a runner is attempting to score from second or third. Fast runners will always have the advantage. Because of pure time demands, a runner with great speed can travel from one base to the next faster than an average runner can. In the time that it takes for the ball to travel from contact with the bat into the field, for the defender to field the ball and for her to release the throw and get it into the catcher's hands, a faster runner will travel a greater distance than an average runner will. The time required for the defense to make the play does not change, but the time that it takes for a fast runner to advance versus a slow runner is dramatically different. Speed is the runner's greatest asset when attempting to score. For that reason, using pinch runners off the bench is important when runners get into scoring position.

- How strong is the batter? If the player at bat can make contact with the ball and hits lots of ground balls, you may choose to go with an aggressive ball-angle read, or contact play, with the runner on third base. If the batter tends to hit hard line drives, the ball-angle read can be risky because the ball will get to the infielders quickly and they may be able to double the runner off third.

- How strong is the on-deck hitter? When runners are in scoring position, knowing that your on-deck hitter has strong hitting ability may reduce the level of aggressiveness or risk that you take to score runners. You don't want to take the opportunity away from your best hitter because you get the runner thrown out trying to score. You will tend to be more aggressive with your runners when you are in the bottom of your lineup because they generally hit for a lower batting average. In that situation, being aggressive when the opportunity shows itself makes sense.

- How well can your runners read the catcher? A runner attempting to score must be able to read the catcher so that she can adjust her slide away from the play. Runners usually slide to the outside of home plate away from the catcher to avoid contact, but this technique ultimately gives the catcher more time to tag them out. If the runner is good at reading the catcher and can adjust her slide, she has a better chance to score on a number of different types of throws coming into home.

- How well can your runners read the ball? If a runner gets a great jump or can read the ball, then you will generally anticipate being more aggressive with your strategy when the ball is hit. Because runners who get a good read or jump on the hit will be moving toward home more quickly on the same ball than other runners will, they will have a valuable head start.

(continued)

Decision-Making Guidelines

When playing the short game, you and your players should be sure to consider the previous information. Also consider the following guidelines:

- As a rule, being aggressive early in the game or when you have a lead is generally more appropriate. Early in the game you should challenge the defense to make tough plays. You anticipate having more opportunities later, so why not take a little more risk to see whether you can take the lead? Similarly, when you are playing with a solid lead, you are able to risk having runners thrown out because each run is slightly less important. Still, you may want to take more risk by sending runners home late in the game when you are behind by a run or two. You may not get many additional opportunities before the end of the game, and you would regret never forcing the defense to make a play at the plate. This situation is a tough challenge: Do you force the defense to make a play at the risk of running your team into an out? Coaches should think in advance about what types of hits or situations would prompt them to send the runners at that point in the game. Coaches need to evaluate several things mentioned in this chapter before the batter even sees a pitch.

- Past success against the pitcher may help you gauge how aggressive you will be with runners in scoring position. The number of runners who have previously reached scoring position may determine how aggressive you and your players will be when the scoring opportunity arises. For example, if you expect to have many runners on base because your team hits a particular pitcher well, then you may be more confident about sending runners home on plays that you expect to be close.

- When you have a runner at third with less than two outs, you should consider where you are in the lineup. Knowing that your next two or three hitters have success with runners in scoring position will help you make decisions about sending runners. Additionally, if you have trail runners on first or second base, you may opt to be more aggressive with ground balls because the trail runners will likely advance into similar scoring position even if the lead runner is thrown out at home.

- Generally, the runner on third has three options. A conservative approach will be to make sure that any ball hit on the ground gets past the infield before the runner makes a move toward home. Conversely, the runner can be in an aggressive ball-angle read or contact play and break immediately for home on any ground ball or mis-hit that hits the ground. In this situation the player makes no judgment about whether she has adequate time to score if the defense makes a play. She simply breaks for home on first contact with a ball that is hit toward the ground. Thirdly, the coach can have the runner read whether the ball is going to be hit toward the middle infield as a slow roller or high chop. In this situation the runner is given the responsibility of making the judgment to break for home on ground balls that she believes will give her time to score because of the location and type of the ground ball hit.

The skills of hitting and base stealing can be combined to produce an effective offensive threat. This combination of the runner moving on the release of the pitch and the hitter swinging at the pitch is called the hit and run. When executed correctly, the hit and run creates an advantage for both the runner and the hitter.

The hit and run can create huge momentum for the offensive team. Creating momentum is a large part of softball, and a well-executed hit and run is a confidence builder for the offense and potentially a confidence destroyer for the defense. Because every base that a runner advances toward home creates greater pressure on the defense, a hit and run can often advance the runner several bases. In addition, the runner stealing on the release of the pitch can open up defensive holes if infielders vacate their positions early to cover the base. All these things combined can lead to positive momentum for the offense. The downside occurs if the hitter hits a sharp line drive at an infielder. A huge momentum switch can occur if the defense can double up the runner, which is likely because she was stealing on a pitch that a fielder caught for an out.

The hit and run is typically executed with a runner on first base, although the play can be done at any time and with runners at any base. For the hit-and-run play, the run or steal portion of play occurs first because the runner steals on the release of the pitch. The hitter then attempts to make contact on the pitch after the runner has started. This play is different than a standard straight steal because in this situation the batter is required to swing at the pitch and attempt to make contact with the ball if it is anywhere near the strike zone. The goal is for the hitter to put the ball on the ground, ideally in a location out of the range of the defense. If the hitter can drive the ball into a gap in the outfield, the result can be even better because the runner will have a good chance to move up several bases. As with any offensive strategy, the hit and run has risks, but good evaluation of the situation and correct execution can lead to great rewards.

READING THE SITUATION

How can you and your players know when to use the hit and run? Teach your players to do the following:

- Know the game situation, including how many outs there are, where the base runners are, where the defense is playing the batter, what the score is and so on. By being aware of the situations at all times, players can easily process the information when they receive the signal from the coach.

- Watch for the signal from the coach and know the expectations for your portion of the play. If you do not recognize the signals or do not understand them, poor execution on the hit and run is almost inevitable.

- Know the pitch count on the hitter. The pitcher typically throws hittable pitches when she is behind in the count, so this is a good time to use the hit and run.

- Know who has steal coverage responsibilities so that you can anticipate where the fielder will be when she attempts the tag.

WATCH OUT!

The following circumstances might distract your athletes:

- The defense communicates about whether they are anticipating the hit and run.
- A catcher tells her defense to hold their ground.
- Defensive shifts keep the infielders from breaking early on the steal.

REMINDER!

When using the hit and run, your players must know your team strategy and game plan. Don't forget to consider the questions on page 128.

(continued)

- Pitchers who have erratic or wild delivery patterns or speeds
- Pitches far out of the strike zone that hitters instinctively want to take for a ball but must attempt to hit
- Runners who try to get such a good jump off the base that they are called out for leaving early
- Runners who forget to peek back toward home while running to see where the ball is hit
- Runners who automatically stop at first base and thus forgo the potential for extra bases on the hit

ACQUIRING THE APPROPRIATE KNOWLEDGE

To hit and run successfully, you and your athletes must understand the following:

Rules

You and your athletes need to know several main rules when using the hit and run:

- Rules about the strike zone
- Rules about interference and obstruction
- Rules about contact with a batted ball
- Rules about the batter's box

Physical Playing Conditions

The physical playing conditions will significantly affect the game. Thus, you and your players must pay attention to the following physical conditions when using the hit and run:

- The condition of the base paths in front of the runner. Soft or muddy conditions may make it challenging for the runner to stop quickly and change directions if the ball is hit in the air.

THE RUN AND HIT

A variation on the hit and run is the run and hit. In this play the runner steals on the pitch just as she does with the hit and run, but the batter has two options. One is to swing away at a hittable pitch in the strike zone. The second option is not to swing at the pitch if it is far out of the strike zone. This variation falls somewhere between a straight steal and a hit and run, and it is generally used in the same game situations. You might want to use the run and hit instead of the steal or hit and run in these scenarios:

- With a fast runner at first you may be in a straight steal scenario, but you want to give the hitter the advantage of knowing that the defense could be moving early and opening up some holes. This gives you the same benefit of getting the runner going but also allows your hitter to have the green light to swing aggressively at any pitch in the strike zone.
- Your hitter or hitters have been overcautious in their at bats and have been taking too many good pitches in the strike zone. The run and hit encourages the hitter to be less selective and just swing at good strikes. This adjustment can have a huge positive effect on the hitter's approach to the at bat.
- Your hitters, in general, have been swinging late or not swinging with confidence. Sometimes the run and hit will put the hitter into a more confident and aggressive mental approach during her at bat.

- The condition of the infield. A soft infield will slow the ball down and force the defense to charge the ball more aggressively. A hard or fast infield will allow a solid ground ball to get through the infield faster and past any infielder in the area.
- The grass in the outfield. Moisture or dampness of the grass in the outfield is a condition to consider. Getting the runners going can cause the outfielders to make hurried or rushed throws if the ball is hit to them. This circumstance will increase the runners' chances of advancing several bases on the hit and run.

Strengths and Weaknesses of Opponents

You and your players must account for your opponent's strengths and weaknesses when using the hit and run. Teach your players to consider the following about your opponents:

- How effective is the pitcher at throwing her moving pitches? Will the batter have a hard time making contact with any or all of the pitcher's go-to junk pitches? To take advantage of the hit and run, the hitters need to understand the type of movement that the pitcher's ball has, as well as which type of moving pitch she throws most often with runners on base. Having this knowledge will help your hitters make the adjustments necessary to put the ball on the ground to advance the runner. The greatest threat to success on the hit and run is a caught fly ball or line drive, so if the pitcher throws lots of rise balls then the hitter will need to make sure to get on the top half of the ball.
- How strong is the catcher's arm? The hit and run becomes a straight steal attempt if the hitter fails to make contact on the pitch. Therefore, the runner's speed versus the catcher's arm strength and release could become a factor. The runner will already be committed to going and will be halfway between the bases. If she has better than average speed, she may still have a chance to be safe on the steal.
- What is the count on the batter? If the pitcher has been throwing lots of balls early in the count and is thus working from behind, the hitter will likely have the advantage of a hitter's count at some point during the at bat. A hitter's count is 2-0, 3-1, 3-0 or even 2-1 or 1-0 when considering the hit and run. One of these counts is a good time to put on the hit-and-run play because the pitcher will likely be throwing a pitch in or near the strike zone to avoid getting further behind in the count.
- Does the pitcher throw the first pitch to most batters for a strike or close to the strike zone? If so, the coach may want to call the hit and run on the first pitch to the batter. Conversely, the first pitch is not a good time for the hit and run if the pitcher rarely throws a hittable first pitch.
- What is the position of the defense? Sometimes middle infielders cheat and move a few steps closer to the base that they need to cover for the steal. This defensive shift allows the defender to hold her position longer. She is therefore less likely to leave her fielding position to cover for the steal when the runner takes off.
- How quick are the middle infielders? If they are quick, agile and able to change direction to react to a ball when they are off balance, then they will be able to recover and field the ball even if they have begun moving to cover the steal.
- Do the infielders keep their composure under pressure? Some players consistently rush their throws under pressure and therefore make throwing errors in crucial situations. With a runner moving on the pitch, an infielder may panic and rush her throw to attempt to get the lead runner. Because the lead runner is on the move with the release of the pitch, the infielder's attempt could be late or the infielder might be indecisive on the play and throw too late to retire the batter. With good speed on the bases and at the plate, the hit and run can create enough pressure to allow both runners to be safe even on routine ground balls.

(continued)

Self-Knowledge

Besides being aware of your opponent's strengths and weaknesses, you and your players need to have knowledge about your own team's ability. When using the hit and run, you and your players must be aware of the following:

- How good is the hitter at making contact with movement pitches in different locations around the plate? Hitters who struggle to make contact with certain movement pitches or pitches in certain hitting zones might not be good candidates for a hit and run. You will need to consider the hitter's strengths and abilities when matched up against the pitcher's style and tendencies. For example, a player who does not hit the rise ball well would be a poor hit-and-run candidate if the pitcher primarily throws the rise ball.

- How quick is the player at bat? If the batter has better than average speed, she will not hit into double plays often. This scenario is favorable for using the hit and run because a ground ball in the infield is unlikely to result in a double play even if the defense is able to get the lead runner. On the other hand, a batter who is not fast and regularly hits into double plays may not be a good candidate for a hit and run. Because the hitter is attempting to hit the ball on the ground as part of the play, if the defense is able to field the ball and get the lead runner out, the batter's lack of speed could lead to a double play.

- How fast are the runners on base? The hit and run becomes a steal attempt if the batter fails to make contact with the ball. A fast runner can often advance even if the batter does not make contact.

- How well can the runners on base read the ball off the bat? Some runners have exceptional ability to stop or read and react to the ball as it is hit off the bat. With runners on base who have the ability to read and react, the hit and run can be an excellent call because the runners will be effective on all types of balls hit.

- Where are you in the lineup? If the current batter is a much better hitter with runners in scoring position than the on-deck hitter, then the hit and run can be a strong option with a runner on first base. Rather than trade an out to advance the runner to second with a sacrifice, you can use the hit and run to maximize your hitter's ability and possibly end up with extra bases and no outs on the play.

- Does the batter put pressure on herself to get a hit instead of just focusing on making contact with the ball on the hit-and-run play? Knowing how your batter is likely to react when given the signal helps you determine whether the hit and run is a strong option.

- Does the batter commonly hit a lot of fly balls on balls outside the strike zone? Fly balls and pop-ups are definitely a huge negative in the hit-and-run scenario because the runner could be far off base when the ball is caught and the defender may be able to throw back to the base and double her off. Tread cautiously with the hit and run with batters who often hit pop-ups.

Decision-Making Guidelines

When using the hit and run, you and your players should be sure to consider the previous information. Also consider the following guidelines:

- Hitters should avoid panicking when the pitch is not hittable. Instead of popping up the ball, they should swing just to distract the catcher. Batters need to be able to evaluate whether they will be able to hit the pitch on the ground or into a gap. If they are not able to do that, their next best option to help the runner be safe is to distract the catcher by swinging at the pitch. The worst possible outcome on a failed hit and run is a double play that results from either a ground ball or a ball hit in the air to a defender who can throw the ball to the runner's original base before the runner can return to it.

- If the defense is expecting the bunt and the corners are playing close or moving in closer to home plate to attempt to get the lead runner on a bunt, the hit and run can be a strong option. The defensive setup in this scenario creates bigger holes in the 5-6 and 3-4 positions because the corners are playing closer and therefore cannot get to as many balls in those gaps.

- The hit and run is a good option in situations in which the pitcher does not throw many rise balls. For obvious reasons, the rise ball is a tough pitch for the batter to put on the ground and it leads to lots of fly balls on the hit and run.

- A good scenario for the hit and run occurs when your team has been consistently getting runners on base in a game but is leaving them stranded at second base. Using the hit and run instead of the sacrifice bunt may advance the runner all the way to third base. Because your team has been getting many runners on base, then even if the hit and run fails you will likely put more runners on base later in the game.

- Use the hit and run more often when your team has not had success using the straight steal. Combining the speed of the runner with the offensive potential of the hitter can lead to a good chance of advancing the runner compared with using the speed of the runner alone on a straight steal.

- Use the hit and run more often when your hitter has been slumping and has been tentative at the plate. Hitting is very much about the batter's mental approach when she steps into the box. If the hitter is not confident in her decision-making process about balls and strikes, taking the indecision out of the equation with the hit and run can sometimes give her a more confident approach to the at bat.

At a Glance

The following parts of the text offer additional information on the hit and run.

The hitter's ability to change or narrow the optimal outcome during a particular at bat because of the count, the location of the runners, the number of outs, and or any other variation in the game is called situational hitting. The biggest difference between batting practice and a game is that a game includes variables outside the mechanics of the swing and the ability of the pitcher. To prioritize the team's success above individual statistics is what keeps baseball and softball a team sport. Situational hitting is a combination of adjusting the approach to an at bat to optimize the team's opportunity and, ironically, adjusting the approach to an at bat to optimize the hitter's ability to be successful (i.e., get a hit).

 WATCH OUT!

The following circumstances might distract your athletes:

- The player at bat may be anxious and overanalytical. Or the batter may have a one-track mind about the outcome and not adjust well to the situation, perhaps because she is more concerned with her batting average or records than the team's success. Some ball players may just lack the maturity to understand how their at bat can help the team succeed.

- A player may fail to process all the options before stepping into the batter's box. This failure limits the chances that the batter will maximize her at bat and contribute to the team's overall success.

READING THE SITUATION

How can you and your players know how to hit based on the game situation? Teach your players to do the following:

- Know the number of outs and where the runners are.
- Know the pitcher's tendency to use specific moving pitches. Some pitchers have a specific go-to pitch that they use when they are in trouble or when they feel the pressure of runners being on base.
- Know how the pitcher has thrown to previous batters in various counts and situations.
- Keep an eye on the defense and be aware when changes occur in their movement or responsibilities.

ACQUIRING THE APPROPRIATE KNOWLEDGE

To hit successfully based on the game situation, you and your athletes must understand the following:

REMINDER!

When hitting based on the game situation, your players must know your team strategy and game plan. Don't forget to consider the questions on page 128.

Rules

You and your athletes need to know several main rules when hitting based on the game situation:

- Rules that govern the strike zone
- Rules about why a ball or strike is called against a batter
- Rules that deal with catcher's interference
- Rules that deal with batter's interference with the defense

Physical Playing Conditions

The physical playing conditions will significantly affect the game. Thus, you and your players must pay attention to the following physical conditions when hitting based on the game situation:

○ The condition of the infield. If the infield is soft or in some other condition that slows the ball down, dropping a bunt down can put a lot of pressure on the defense. On the other hand, a hard infield can allow ground balls to get past the infielders quickly or cause bad hops that can be challenging for the defense. These scenarios make trying to hit ground balls a better option than trying to hit fly balls.

○ The wind. If conditions are extremely windy, fly balls can be difficult for the defense to make plays on and get outs.

○ The position of the sun. The sun can be a huge factor for the defense to contend with at certain times of the day and at certain fields. Generally, the sun creates challenging situations on fly balls.

Strengths and Weaknesses of Opponents

You and your players must account for your opponent's strengths and weaknesses when hitting based on the game situation. Teach your players to consider the following about your opponents:

○ How effective are the corners and pitchers at fielding bunts, particularly the drag bunt? Corners may not expect certain hitters to bunt, and a drag bunt in that situation could put the batter safely at first base on a hit or an error.

○ How effective is the second-base player at covering first base on a bunt? The defense's weak link in defending the bunt may be the second-base player's ability to get to first base in time to handle the throw. When the second-base player is playing very deep or up the middle, she may be unable to cover first base in time to get the out on a drag bunt.

○ Does the catcher relay information about subtle changes that a hitter makes in the box? Learning that the defense does not communicate well is valuable because a hitter or the offense can take advantage of such teams. If a hitter makes adjustments at the plate to increase her ability to hit certain pitches or to hit to certain locations on the field and the catcher doesn't relay this information or adjust the defense, the offense can definitely take advantage of the situation. For example, the batter may move off the plate to try to hit the inside pitch better. If the catcher doesn't communicate or adjust the defense to shift off the right-field line, then the offense can take advantage by moving around in the box.

○ How strong is the pitcher? Against a dominating pitcher, the batter may alter her position in the batter's box to eliminate a particular pitch or alter her approach to take a particular pitch and focus on trying to hit a specific type or location of pitch.

○ For example, pitchers who have an outstanding rise ball might be easier to beat if the batters move to the very back of the batter's box and focus on not swinging at any pitches in the top of the strike zone because they will be moving up. Similarly, batters could combat pitchers with good drop balls by moving to the back of the box and being selective or moving to the front of the box and trying to make contact before the ball has a chance to break. Stepping off the plate or crowding the plate is an option that can be used against pitchers who rely heavily on the curveball or screwball.

○ What is the arm strength of the outfielders? Knowing which outfielders have weaker arms can alter how an offense chooses to hit in certain situations. Determining ways to take advantage of weaker arms is always part of a good game plan.

(continued)

○ What is the defensive coverage in specific situations? Knowing which players move to cover bases in certain situations can help the offense make decisions about executing in specific situations. When the defense shifts their starting positions, they create holes. Using any information about the opponent can give your offense an advantage.

Self-Knowledge

Besides being aware of your opponent's strengths and weaknesses, you and your players need to have knowledge about your own team's ability. When hitting based on the game situation, you and your players must be aware of the following:

○ How well does the hitter control the bat? The batter needs to have enough body awareness to make specific adjustments in the middle of an at bat. For example, in a two-strike count, many defenses shift out of a bunt defense. If your batter can still execute a bunt, she can contribute significantly to the offense. Additionally, all hitters should practice and train how to adjust their swings when the count changes. Success in situational hitting is not limited to getting a hit. Sometimes it is about moving runners. Sometimes it is about staying inside the ball and attempting to hit to the opposite field. The key to situational hitting is for the hitter to have confidence in her ability to adjust and alter her approach to maximize the chances for success.

○ What pitches does the hitter hit best? The player at bat needs to know her strengths and weaknesses as a hitter. More important, she should know what pitches to hit in specific counts. Pitch recognition and reaction are a product of isolating the optimal swing for particular pitch locations. For that reason, players should practice hitting off live pitchers or at least hitting different pitch locations, not just pitches thrown down the middle of the plate off a machine. The more confident the hitter is in her game plan and her ability to recognize the optimal pitch, the more success she will have at the plate in situational hitting opportunities.

○ What weapons does the hitter have in her arsenal? The more options a hitter has to call on and use in different situations, the greater her ability is to adjust to the demands of different situations in a game. Options include the ability to drop a drag bunt, to track the ball deeper in the zone and hit to the opposite field, to hit a ground ball to the right side, to hit a deep fly ball, to take several pitches and be able to hit successfully with two strikes, to foul off a large number of pitches and so on.

○ How well does the hitter know the strike zone? The player at bat needs to be able to adjust to the strike zone that the umpire is calling. If a hitter can trust what she sees and force a pitcher to throw more strikes, she will be able to succeed in a variety of situations during the game.

○ How well does the hitter comprehend the game situation? The player at bat must be aware of what the game situation is and what adjustments she should make. Experience is a huge part of learning what works and what does not work, but coaches should take every situational opportunity that comes up in a game and review it with their players after the game.

○ How well do the players on the bench focus on the pitcher's tendencies against their teammates? When players on the bench do not play close attention to other players' at bats, they have less information when their turn at bat comes. Situational hitting requires all players, including potential subs and pinch hitters, to be invested and involved at all times.

INDIVIDUAL HITTING STRATEGIES AND ADJUSTMENTS

Individual players, as well as teams, should have a hitting strategy when they are at bat. Hitters should step to the plate with a specific plan to create the greatest chance for success. Specific situations and scenarios that a hitter needs to be prepared for include the following:

- Hitting the first pitch
- Hitting when ahead in the count
- Hitting when behind in the count
- Hitting adjustments during the game

Hitting the First Pitch

When preparing for an at bat, your hitter should answer several questions before stepping to the plate. The answers to these questions will help your hitter focus on specific zones and pitches that she should be looking to hit and others that she should be looking not to hit.

- What location in the strike zone do I consistently hit best?
- What location in the strike zone do I consistently not hit well?
- What pitch am I looking to hit?
- What pitch am I looking to stay away from?

Hitting When Ahead in the Count

One of three things will happen after the first pitch—the hitter will hit the ball, be behind in the count or be ahead in the count. Hitting when ahead in the count should favor the hitter. Pitching counts that are considered in the hitter's favor are the 3-0, 3-1, 2-0 and 1-0 counts. Hitters should make educated decisions about what pitch the pitcher is going to throw, but they should also continue to look for the pitch that they earlier identified as giving them the best chance of success.

Hitting When Behind in the Count

When the hitter bats with a count in favor of the pitcher, she needs to make adjustments to increase her likelihood of success. Counts considered to be in the pitcher's favor are 0-2, 1-2, 0-1 and 2-2. In these situations, the hitter must open up the zone and go after pitches to protect against being called out on strikes by the umpire. In these counts, a hitter can still have a plan to protect herself if she has learned how to foul off pitches. When a hitter has two strikes, the ability to stay inside the ball and hit to the opposite field can extend her time at bat.

Hitting Adjustments During a Game

Hitters face many challenges during a game. Besides dealing with the pressure of the game, the hitter must contend with the pitcher's attempts to throw off her timing and ability to hit the pitch. An important principle that hitters need to grasp is that they cannot control everything, but they can control how they choose to deal with challenges placed in front of them. Following are a few of the basic strategies that players can use to adjust to certain hitting situations.

Adjustments to a Junk Pitcher   When facing a pitcher who uses a lot of movement but not overwhelming speed, the hitter can make a couple of adjustments. If the hitter is struggling with this type of pitcher, she should move up in the batter's box to attempt to make contact with the pitch before it moves. To adjust to the slow speed, the hitter should focus on

(continued)

(continued)

Individual Hitting Strategies and Adjustments *(continued)*

hitting to the opposite field. This approach will help the hitter watch the ball longer and track it deeper into the hitting zone. Another option is to move to the deepest portion of the batter's box and force the pitcher to throw a lot of pitches. If a junk pitcher has considerable movement on her pitches, then, in theory, the farther the hitter moves back, the greater the chance is that the pitch will move out of the strike zone when it gets to the hitting zone. Note, however, that this adjustment may not work for impatient hitters who struggle to stay off pitches.

Adjustments to a Power Pitcher   Power pitchers are generally successful against hitters who have a tendency to overswing. Hitters who can adjust their swing to stay compact and rely on using the pitcher's speed will have greater success. Hitters must learn that they can start their timing or their preparation to hit earlier without committing to taking a full swing. The easiest solution is to move to the back of the batter's box. The extra 2 to 3 feet can make a difference for hitters who are late with their timing. Hitters can also shorten up their swing by choking up slightly on the bat and starting with a slightly wider stance.

Adjustments to a Rise-Ball Pitcher   As a rule, rise-ball pitchers excel when they can get a hitter to swing at a pitch that is out of the strike zone. The first adjustment that your hitter should make is visual—she should adjust her strike zone and stay off any pitch that is starting above the waist. Additionally, a hitter can adjust the part of the ball that she is looking to make contact with. Tracking the ball into the hitting zone and focusing on the top half of the ball can help a hitter make solid contact. An additional adjustment is moving to the back of the batter's box. If a rise-ball pitcher struggles with throwing the low rise, she will have to adjust to keep the ball in the strike zone. Hitters need to be disciplined and patient to avoid chasing balls that are out of the strike zone.

Adjustments to a Curveball Pitcher   Against pitchers who like to work the inside and outside corners, your hitters may have to create a plan that eliminates one of the pitcher's pitches. Hitters who crowd the plate can dramatically affect some of these pitchers, so your hitter may want to do just that to increase her chance of hitting the outside pitch. In doing this, the hitter's goal is to challenge the pitcher to throw inside for a strike or risk hitting the batter.

Adjustments to an Off-Speed or Change-Up Pitcher   Against an off-speed or change-up pitcher, the hitter's adjustments may be more mental than physical. Hitters should approach the plate with a specific plan. For example, if the pitcher throws one or more change-ups to every batter, the hitter can plan to take the faster pitches and look to hit the change-up when the pitcher throws it. To use this option, however, the hitter will have to foul off the fastball to protect herself if she has two strikes. Another option is just the reverse—the hitter could commit to staying off the off-speed pitch or change-up until she has two strikes on her and then foul off those types of pitches until she sees a fastball in the strike zone. With either strategy, the hitter must completely commit to it to have success. Hitters can change their plan from one at bat to the next, but they should not switch in the middle of an at bat.

Decision-Making Guidelines

When hitting based on the game situation, you and your players should be sure to consider the previous information. Also consider the following guidelines:

- Make sure that all your hitters know how to hit pitches in every possible zone. Hitters who can only hit the ball pitched down the middle will make limited contributions because many pitchers never throw that pitch. A hitter needs to be able to succeed against all types of pitch locations, not just what they naturally do well.

- Teach all your players to execute all short-game skills including the drag bunt so that they have the option when the situation warrants. If the game situation calls for a specific play and your hitter cannot perform, you will have to substitute for her or forgo the opportunity to maximize your team's chance to succeed. Often, slower power hitters do not think that they need to know how to drag bunt, but the time may come against a vulnerable defense when the offense would benefit most to have the hitter drag bunt regardless of her foot speed.

- Make sure that your hitters are comfortable hitting behind the runner (to right field) with runners on second base. A runner at second base is much more likely to score on a ball hit to right field for two reasons. First, the runner does not need to hesitate to make sure that the ball will go through the infield when it is hit to the right side. Second, throws coming in from right field are more challenging for the catcher to receive while she tries to read the runner coming to the plate.

- Teach your hitters to be patient when a runner is on third base. Pitchers are cautious about throwing hittable pitches in this situation, so keep your players from being anxious and swinging at less than ideal hitter's pitches. Pitchers often throw pitches inside to try to get the hitter to hit foul balls and fall behind in the count. Many young hitters swing aggressively and early when a runner is at third base. A patient hitter has a strong game plan about what pitch she is looking to hit, and she will not deviate from that plan. Her game plan may vary depending on the pitcher, the umpire or the defensive alignment.

- Encourage your players to hit deep into the count when they are leading off an inning. This approach helps subsequent batters see a large number of pitches. The more pitches that a pitcher throws in a game, the more information all your hitters can gain about the pitcher. Hitters in the dugout or on deck often fail to pay attention to what the pitcher is throwing to other batters. If all hitters watch every at bat, then hitters who can hit deep into a count early in the inning can help provide more information to the rest of the team about the pitcher. Hitting deep into the count means swinging only at strikes, not chasing pitches out of the strike zone and fouling off pitches with two strikes. Technically, hitting deep into the count means making the pitcher throw a large number of pitches in a particular at bat.

- Teach your athletes to make adjustments going into their second at bats. Eight hitters have hit since a player's previous at bat, and each player should have gained a great deal of knowledge about the pitcher by then.

At a Glance

The following parts of the text offer additional information on situational hitting.

chapter 6

Defensive Tactical Skills

This chapter will cover the defensive tactical skills that you and your players must know in order to be successful. In this chapter, you will find:

When playing defense, infielders need to refocus one pitch at a time. Each pitch begins a new situation, and each fielder needs to take ownership of a specific set of responsibilities to maximize the team effort. The infield makes most of the plays in a game and has the responsibility of defending against the short game and dealing with the runners on base. Your four infielders, the catcher and the pitcher all contribute to the team's infield defensive effort. By working together as a unit, the team defense becomes more effective and makes it tougher for an opponent to score.

 ## WATCH OUT!

The following circumstances might distract your athletes:

- There are speedy runners on base. If infielders anticipate that a runner will be stealing, they may vacate their positions before the batter makes contact, creating holes where the batter can hit the ball safely through the infield.

- Batters take big swings. A big swing can distract your defenders from their focus on the runners. Infielders need to be able to keep sufficient focus on all responsibilities at the appropriate times.

- There are loud crowds or opposing teams. High levels of noise may disrupt defensive communication in crucial situations.

- Players may become distracted by opposing coaches' oral or visual signals.

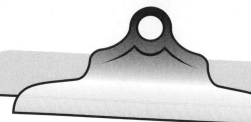

READING THE SITUATION

How can you and your players determine infield responsibilities? Teach your players to do the following:

- Know the game situation, the score, the number of outs and where the runners are. Informed defenders can be better prepared for the various situations that may come up during the game.

- Communicate to make sure that all infielders know their responsibilities.

- Move and flow together as a unit to be in the correct position to prevent the offense from gaining an advantage.

- Know the tendencies of the hitter at the plate and be prepared to respond decisively when the ball is hit.

- When runners are on base, infielders must be prepared for a steal on every pitch.

- Stay in base coverage until the ball is dead or back in the circle.

ACQUIRING THE APPROPRIATE KNOWLEDGE

REMINDER!

When determining defensive responsibilities in the infield, your players must know your team strategy and game plan. Don't forget to consider the questions on page 128.

To determine defensive responsibilities in the infield successfully, you and your athletes must understand the following:

Rules

You and your athletes need to know several main rules when you are determining defensive responsibilities in the infield:

- Rules about interference and obstruction
- Rules about force plays

- Rules about when a pitcher becomes an infielder
- Rules about the pitching circle
- Rules about receiving a throw when a runner is approaching the base
- Rules about dropped third strikes
- Rules about infield fly-ball outs
- Rules about balls thrown out of play

Physical Playing Conditions

The physical playing conditions will significantly affect the game. Thus, you and your players must pay attention to the following physical conditions when determining defensive responsibilities in the infield:

- The condition of the infield. Playing on either a soft, slow infield or a hard, fast infield will change how infielders prepare for and approach ground balls. If the infield is slow or soft, infielders need to attack or charge the batted ball aggressively to have a chance at throwing out the runner. Conversely, on a hard infield, infielders need to stay set and prepare for the ball coming quickly at them. Additionally, knowing whether any areas are wet or slippery will be helpful. Wet or soft spots on the field of play may affect how the ball comes out of that area. An infielder may choose to be more aggressive and get to the ball before it enters a wet or slick area.

- The position of the sun. Infielders should be aware of the sun's position so that no surprises occur during the inning. The sun may affect a fielder who is receiving or making a throw, or it can affect a ball hit by the batter. Fielders should try to avoid making plays from a position where the sun is in their eyes.

- The condition of the grass in the outfield. If the ball comes back into the infield wet, the infielders may have difficulty throwing the ball. A wet ball will be tougher to grip firmly and can slip out of the hand during a throw. If the infielders are prepared to handle a wet ball coming back into the infield, they can compensate by finding a seam or loosening their grip to maintain an accurate throw.

- The direction and strength of the wind. Balls hit up into the wind can be aided or moved. A wind-aided ball can travel substantially farther, and a ball held up in the wind will not travel as far as it otherwise would. Flight patterns of balls hit into calm air are consistent. The distance that the ball travels from the hitter to the peak of its flight defines the distance that it will travel before it contacts the ground. Good fielders use this knowledge to get to the spot where the ball will land without floating or drifting during the entire flight of the ball. Know which direction the wind is blowing can be extremely helpful. If the fielders know the strength and direction of the wind, they can be prepared for changes in the flight of the batted ball.

Strengths and Weaknesses of Opponents

You and your players must account for your opponent's strengths and weaknesses when determining defensive responsibilities in the infield. Teach your players to consider the following about your opponents:

- What type of hitter is at the plate? Infielders who can obtain information about the hitter or use experience with that hitter to know more about her ability and strengths can make defensive decisions. For example, if the hitter is a faster player who can drag bunt or slap hit, the corners can come in closer and the middle infielders can shift. Or, if a slower power hitter is at the plate, the defense can adjust accordingly and move back.

(continued)

○ How quick are the runners on base? The speed of the runners on base will help determine where the defense needs to play. Middle infielders will need to adjust their starting positions to cover second base or third base on the steal. With a fast runner on first base, the shortstop may need to move her starting defensive position slightly closer to second base so that she will be able to get to second on a steal by the runner. The same situation may apply with an extremely fast runner on second base if the shortstop is to cover third for the steal.

○ What type of offensive strategy does the opponent use? The opponent may have quick players and rely heavily on the short game and aggressive baserunning. Or the opponent might be extremely powerful and rely on big hits and swinging for power. Either way the more information that the defense has about the opponent, the better they can adjust.

○ Does the opponent run a conservative or aggressive style of play? If a team relies on the sacrifice bunt and a more conservative style, the defense can adjust accordingly. If the offensive team likes to get the runners started early in the short game or likes to try to take extra bases on routine plays, the defensive team can make sure that they are prepared and not surprised. The defensive team may want to use fake throws to try to catch lead runners off base. If the offensive team is aggressive and uses a risky type of play, the defense can prepare to take advantage of overaggressive base runners. Aggressive offensive play will have the runners on the move before the batter makes contact on bunts, slaps or batted balls. This approach is risky because the batter may fail to get the ball down on the ground. Therefore, the runner is at risk of being doubled off the base on a ball hit in the air.

○ Do the base runners take aggressive leadoffs? Is so, the defense has a prime opportunity to run pickoff plays or throws back to the base between pitches. If the opponent uses aggressive leadoffs, the runners will often be far off the base on every pitch. Good catchers can use a quick throw back to the base or even run a set play with a pitchout to attempt to pick off the runner.

Self-Knowledge

Besides being aware of your opponent's strengths and weaknesses, you and your players need to have knowledge about your own team's ability. When determining defensive responsibilities in the infield, teach your players to be aware of the following:

○ Do the middle infielders have enough range to cover second base on steals? If your middle infielders cannot cover the steal from their normal position, they will need to adjust a few steps closer to the base. If the defensive player is capable of covering the ground necessary to make a play, then she might be able to get away with moving farther from base coverage responsibility. Either overall foot speed or very good reaction time may permit the defender to cover more ground than another player can.

○ What kind of a pitcher is on the mound? If the pitcher throws a lot of drop balls that often result in mis-hit choppers or slow ground balls, then the infield may need to play closer to home to field the type of ball commonly hit off that pitcher. Similarly, if a pitcher throws a lot of rise balls and the outfielders are accustomed to the types of fly balls hit off that pitcher, then they can adjust their defensive positioning to increase their odds of making a successful play. If the pitcher throws a lot of drop balls that lead to a high number of ground balls, the infield may shift to cover the infield differently. Infielders and outfielders can shift their starting positions in a number of ways; they can move in, move out, move left or move right. In addition, by learning how the ball commonly comes off the bat—its spin, velocity and angle—with a particular pitcher, they can anticipate and prepare.

DEFENSIVE COVERAGE SITUATIONS

Although infield coverage for the game of softball is relatively simple, each player must remain active and engaged when the ball is in play. If we eliminate home plate coverage, a responsibility that falls solely on the catcher on balls hit into the infield, we have four infielders and a pitcher to cover three bases. Clearly, enough players are available to make a play on the ball and still have all the bases covered. Let's look more closely at defensive coverage in the infield.

No Runners on Base

If the ball is hit or bunted in front of the first-base player, then the second-base player covers first base. In fast-pitch softball, the pitcher almost never covers first base because the close proximity of the bases and the speed of the play make it difficult for the pitcher to get to the base, turn around and receive the throw. On plays when the second-base player covers first, the shortstop covers second base and remains there until the runner is called out at first or the ball is returned to the pitching circle.

On balls hit to second base, to the pitcher or to the left side of the infield, the first-base player covers first base for the force-out and either the second-base player or the shortstop covers second until the out is made or the ball is returned to the pitching circle.

Runner on First Base

For ground balls hit to the first-base player, the second-base player or the pitcher, the shortstop is the primary coverage at second base to turn the double play and the third-base player retreats to cover third base. Depending on which one fields the ball, either the first-base player or the second-base player covers first base. The catcher moves to back up the throw to first base and cover up any openings in the dugout, and the pitcher comes in to cover home in case an overthrow occurs.

For ground balls hit to the left side of the infield, the second-base player is the primary coverage at second base for the force-out or double play. Whoever did not field the ball, either the third-base player or the shortstop, moves to cover third base and remains there until the ball is back in the pitching circle. The first-base player retreats and covers first base for the force-out. The catcher moves down the line to back up the throw to first base, and the pitcher covers home.

Note, however, that with no outs or one out and a runner on first, the batter may be bunting, so refer to "Defending the Bunt" on page 182 to learn the coverage.

Runner on Second Base or Third Base or Both

For balls hit to the pitcher or the right side of the field, the third-base player retreats to third to cover for the force or tag play, depending on the situation. The middle infielders move toward second base and communicate which player will cover the base. The first-base player retreats to cover first base. In this situation, the catcher stays at home and does not run up the first-base line to protect against the overthrow.

For balls hit to the left side of the infield, whoever does not field the ball moves to cover third base. The second-base player covers second base in case of a throw to second, and the first-base player covers first base for the potential force-out. Again, the catcher stays at home in case of an overthrow or play at the plate.

Note, however, that with one out or no outs and a runner on second or third or both, the batter may be bunting, so refer to "Defending the Bunt" on page 182 to learn the proper coverage.

(continued)

○ How well does the pitcher perform as a fielder? If the pitcher has good range, the corners have more freedom in some coverages. You may be able to adjust the middle infield positions as well if the pitcher can defend well on balls up the middle.

○ How good is the range of each infielder? Knowing which infielders have the best range can help in adjusting the defense to maximize the coverage.

○ How strong are the infielders' arms? How quick are their releases? Knowing this can help when making decisions about how deep to play when certain hitters are at the plate.

Decision-Making Guidelines

When determining defensive responsibilities in the infield, you and your players should be sure to consider the previous information. Also consider the following guidelines:

○ The game situation may determine how you execute your defensive strategy. Late in a close game, the defense should play conservatively and make high-percentage plays that put more pressure on the offense. Earlier in the game the defense may play more aggressively and attempt to stop any momentum that the offense starts.

○ Play more aggressively and take more risk on defense if you are far ahead in the game. You may choose to play off the line more and play slightly deeper to increase range. Most balls are hit between the right-center and left-center gaps, so moving off the line puts the defenders where more balls are hit but increases the risk of giving up extra bases on routine hits down the line.

○ If you have a lead of several runs late in the game, continue to play for outs and do not always go after the lead runner. Conserving outs is the greatest challenge for the offense late in the game, so recording outs on every batter will eventually take the momentum out of a late-inning threat.

○ Shift the defense on pull hitters with no runners on base. Moving the defense to fill more holes can challenge a predictable hitter.

○ Use all the knowledge about the opponent, yourself and the situation to make high-percentage decisions about positioning the defense. Remember that every pitch brings a new situation, and you can make adjustments at any time.

○ Work as a team to communicate with one another. For example, use bench players to help when a runner is stealing. Communication can be a big help to your defense in defending the steal.

STEAL COVERAGES

One of most common flaws in the infield is that little or no communication occurs before the pitch about which players are covering the bases for steals in various situations. You may use option A when the offense does plan A and use option B for coverage if the offense does plan B. Practicing and communicating these defensive steal coverages is extremely important for your team's overall trust and comfort during a game.

Steal Coverage at Second Base

The traditional way to cover second base on a steal is to have your shortstop take the throw at second from the catcher. You can position the shortstop more up the middle closer to the base. Note, however, that this positioning leaves the defense vulnerable to a right-handed pull hitter or a left-handed hitter who hits to the opposite field. In a slap defense you may want to have your shortstop closer to the 5-6 hole. In this case the second-base player covers the base on a steal.

Here are some standard second-base coverage responsibilities:

Runner on First With a Right-Handed Batter at the Plate

In this situation, if there are two strikes on the batter or two outs in the inning, the first-base player is positioned deeper to receive the throwback from the catcher. This positioning frees up the second base player to cover on the steal. If the first base player is playing in for a bunt, then the second-base player shifts over toward first base to hold the runner and be ready for the bunt coverage. This situation requires the shortstop to be the coverage for the steal at second.

Runner on First With a Left-Handed Slap Hitter at the Plate

A common way to defend the left-handed slap is to move the third-base player in a few steps and have the shortstop shift over toward the hole between third and short, commonly referred to as the 5-6 hole. The shortstop will be in the baseline for the short slap. The second-base player shifts over toward second slightly and just behind the base path. The second-base player becomes the primary receiver at second for a steal. In this defense, however, the second-base player may be vulnerable if the offense puts down a bunt to the first-base side of the field. You can also choose to have the first-base player appear to be in for the bunt but then retreat to first base to cover for all bunts. In this case the third-base player and pitcher have primary responsibility for bunt coverage.

Steal Coverage at Third Base

At third base, there are two ways to cover on a steal. Both require communication among all players involved in the play—the third-base player, the shortstop and the catcher. One coverage is for the shortstop to move a few steps in her ready position so that she can cover the base. This way of defending the steal at third is done when the third-base player needs to defend against the bunt. The shortstop shifts toward third to gain an advantage against the runner so that she has enough time to catch the ball on the run, turn her body and tag the runner out. The third-base player must make sure that she is out of the view of the catcher and shortstop so that she does not block the throw.

Another way to defend the steal of third is to have the third-base player drop back and cover the bag. This method is common with a middle-of-the-lineup batter, with two outs, with two strikes on the batter or with a large lead. Note, however, that some offenses use a fake bunt to decoy the third-base player to come in, which leaves third base wide open on the steal. When using this defense make sure that your pitcher has bunt coverage responsibilities on the third-base side to keep your coverage at third base solid.

Outfielders are the last line of defense, so they above all others must anticipate fielding a batted ball or responding to an error. Many believe that the weakest players play the outfield, but these players must be the most mentally strong on the field. Infielders can more easily stay focused on the game because they have a greater chance of having the ball hit to them. Balls are far less likely to be hit to the outfield, especially against a good pitcher. The outfielder's job is to make a play on the ball and hold the base runners' advance to a minimum after the ball gets past the infield.

 WATCH OUT!

The following circumstances might distract your athletes:

○ Players fail to stay mentally prepared during the long interval between pitches and plays in the outfield.

○ Players overreact to a power hitter with a big swing. Outfielders may anticipate that the ball will travel farther or deeper if they watch the swing of the batter and do not watch and listen for the ball coming off the bat.

○ Players don't know when to dive and what balls to dive for. Attempting to make a diving catch is an acceptable risk in some situations. Making a diving attempt is always more appropriate when other outfielders can provide backup or support. Outfielders should rarely dive for balls hit down the foul lines in fair territory because the centerfielder is a long ways away and cannot provide good backup if the diving outfielder does not catch or stop the ball.

○ Players are afraid to fail, resulting in hesitation and belated decision making.

READING THE SITUATION

How can you and your players determine defensive responsibilities in the outfield? Teach your players to do the following:

• Know the inning, the number of outs, and the score. The game situation often dictates how aggressive the outfield should be on a ball.

• Know where the runners are on base. Outfielders should know before each pitch where they will throw the ball when various situations occur.

• Remember the previous at bats of each hitter. During the game, most batters come to the plate three or sometimes four times. If the same pitcher is throwing, then the outfield will be able to adjust to the hitter's tendencies.

• Know whether the game is on the line and whether the winning run is in scoring position.

REMINDER!

When determining defensive responsibilities in the outfield, your players must know your team strategy and game plan. Don't forget to consider the questions on page 128.

ACQUIRING THE APPROPRIATE KNOWLEDGE

To determine defensive responsibilities in the outfield successfully, you and your athletes must understand the following:

Rules

You and your athletes need to know several main rules when you are determining defensive responsibilities in the outfield:

- Rules about legal catches
- Rules about catching and carrying the ball out of bounds
- Rules about thrown balls going out of play
- Rules about breakaway fences
- Rules about ground-rule doubles
- Rules about the playing field and in-and-out-of-play issues

Physical Playing Conditions

The physical playing conditions will significantly affect the game. Many concerns are specific to the outfield position. Thus, you and your players must pay attention to the following physical conditions when determining defensive responsibilities in the outfield:

- The strength and direction of the wind. Outfielders must be aware of conditions that alter the trajectory of fly balls.

- The quality of the playing surface. The surface of the outfield can affect the speed of the ball as well as how it will bounce. The surface could also be a factor when athletes are diving for a ball. If the ground is relatively soft, outfielders can take a more aggressive approach because the ball will not travel as far on the ground. Players should take time before the game to survey the outfield so that they are aware of the characteristics of the playing surface as well as other conditions, such as bare spots, holes, sprinklers and so on.

- The length of the grass. Like surface quality, the length of the grass will dramatically affect the speed of the ball when it is hit on the ground. On long grass the ball will travel slower and over a shorter distance. Long grass could also affect the actual fielding and transition of the ball into the fielder's glove.

- The condition of the grass. Wet or damp grass can have a dramatic affect on the ball as it travels on the ground. A wet outfield generally slows down a rolling ball. The exception to this is a line drive that bounces on wet grass. If the outfield is firm but wet, the ball will tend to skip and maintain its speed out of the bounce.

- What kind of outfield fence is being used, and how does the ball play off the fence? Knowing how the ball will come off the fence is extremely important when a ground ball or fly ball hits it. Some chain-link fences or breakaway fences deaden the ball, whereas some wood fences or padded fences create a powerful rebound. In addition, the type and height of the fence will be a consideration for an outfielder who is trying to make a catch at or near the fence.

- What type of warning track, if any, is being used? The purpose of a warning track is to give outfielders more information as they run across it while trying to make a catch. A variety of surfaces and depths are used for warning tracks. Outfielders should know both variables so that they can feel the change in surface while looking toward the sky. Knowing how many strides they can take on the warning track before making contact with the fence helps outfielders prepare to make a catch.

- What is the position of the sun? Teach your outfielders to be aware of the sun's position in the sky so that they know when the sun may be a concern when backing up, when catching or tracking fly balls or when making throws. Knowing where the sun is at all times and what types of balls will be affected by it is important. If the outfielder knows what type of batted ball will pass near the sun, she can prepare by using her free hand or glove to block the sun from her sight line.

(continued)

Strengths and Weaknesses of Opponents

You and your players must account for your opponent's strengths and weaknesses when determining defensive responsibilities in the outfield. Teach your players to consider the following about your opponents:

o What is the location of the runners on base, and how quick are they? Knowing the location and speed of the runners on base will help your outfielders anticipate which bases to throw to on different types of balls. For example, if the runner on second is extremely fast, a play at the plate may not be possible, so the throw should go to make a play on a secondary runner.

o How powerful is the hitter? The strength of the hitter can determine whether the outfielders should move in or back. Good defensive players continually adjust as they gain more information. The outfield and the entire defense should make decisions about playing position based on the best information that they can get. The more times a defense plays a specific batter, the more information they should have about how the batter approaches her at bats and where she hits the ball.

o What are the hitter's tendencies? Some hitters use a specific type of swing that results in many balls being hit to the opposite field. Others tend to pull almost everything. You may find some players who hit to all fields.

o Does the opposing team use an aggressive baserunning approach? Being aware of this tendency will help outfielders make decisions about where to throw on different types of batted balls. Outfielders routinely throw one base ahead of the runner, but against extremely aggressive runners they may have to throw to a different base. Teams may also try to take advantage of outfielders who hesitate or delay their throws. For these types of teams, outfielders need to come up throwing without hesitation.

Self-Knowledge

Besides being aware of your opponent's strengths and weaknesses, you and your players need to have knowledge about your own team's ability. When determining defensive responsibilities in the outfield, teach your players to be aware of the following:

o What is the range of the outfielders, both individually and as a group? This consideration is important when positioning each outfielder. The range and distance that a specific player can cover in a given amount of time may vary. Speed and the ability to read a batted ball determine an outfielder's ability to get to balls hit away from her. Some outfielders may be strong going back on a ball but struggle to read a ball that is hit softly in front of them. Each outfielder's strengths and weaknesses in range are extremely important when trying to maximize team defense and starting positions during game situations. In addition, with runners on base you and your players need to know the strength and accuracy of the outfielders' arms so that the infielders and relays can compensate or adjust.

o What is the range of the infielders? If your infielders have great range on balls hit over their heads, the outfielders can play deeper because they do not have to make as many plays on balls hit just beyond the infield. If a particular infielder is exceptional at moving back and catching fly balls hit over her head, then the outfielder playing behind her may not need to play in as close.

o How well do the infielders and outfielders communicate with one another? Effective communication between the infield and outfield will help in positioning the outfield. The greater the trust and effectiveness of the communication system, the more effective the positioning can be. If communication between the infield and outfield is average or poor, then the outfielders will need to play close to the infield to protect against the in-between ball.

COVERAGE RESPONSIBILITIES ON HITS TO THE OUTFIELD

The outfield is the last line of defense, so the coverage responsibilities are important even if the ball is not hit to the outfield. Good outfielders take pride in being prepared if the infielders fail and being ready to pick up the pieces if they do. Another critical defensive coverage for the outfield occurs when balls are hit over the heads of the outfielders or in the gaps. The throw to the relay and solid communication between outfielders will make or break the outcome of the play and generally determine whether the defense can slow down or stop the offensive momentum. Let's take a closer look at defensive coverage in the outfield.

No Runners on Base or Runners on First Base or Second Base

For balls hit to the left side of the outfield, the left fielder is the primary fielder and needs to get to the ball aggressively and make the catch or keep the ball from going through to the fence. The center fielder moves aggressively toward the ball to back up the left fielder. For balls hit in the gap between the left fielder and the center fielder, the center fielder should generally take the more aggressive inside route in front of the left fielder to cut off the ball. The right fielder lines up for a throw coming into second base from where the ball is fielded in left field. If a throw goes to third base instead of second base, the right fielder shifts to provide secondary backup coverage of the ball being thrown by the third-base player toward second base.

For balls hit to the right side of the outfield, the left fielder lines up for the throw for the lead runner. If the lead runner is on first base, a ball hit to right field will likely be thrown to third base so the left fielder moves to back up that throw. The secondary responsibility is to cover a throw to third or second base from the infielder who received the primary throw. The center fielder moves aggressively toward right field either to make a play on a ball hit in the right-center gap or to back up the right fielder if she is the primary fielder. Secondary backup responsibilities are to back up throws going to second base from the infielder who receives the primary throw from the outfielder. Although she needs to worry about throws going to only one base, the ball can take three different angles on its way to second. The right fielder moves to field the ball or serves as the backup to the center fielder if she makes the play in the right-center gap. After the play is made and the ball is thrown back to the infield, the right fielder backs up any secondary throws back toward first base during the play.

Balls Hit to the Fence at the Left-Center or Right-Center Gap

The center fielder is involved as one of the primary fielders on balls hit to the fence at either gap. Depending on who gets to the ball quicker or who has the stronger arm, one outfielder calls for the ball and makes the play to the relay while the other outfielder acts as the eyes and the communicator to help the outfielder who is making the play. The flank outfielder, either the left fielder or right fielder depending on which gap the ball is hit into, should be as aggressive as possible to get to the ball and communicate with the center fielder about who will make the throw.

All outfielders need to keep their throws strong but low enough so that the infielder who is acting as the relay or cut is able to catch and throw the ball with ease. If an outfielder makes an errant throw or misses the cut or relay person, then the runner can advance extra bases and move that much closer to home. Strong arms in the outfield are valuable for the defense, but a strong arm that is inaccurate or misses the relay is of no value. Arm strength and accuracy allow the entire defense to work together to make the necessary play and ideally get the runners out.

For secondary backups on throws from the infield, outfielders must know where the runners are and anticipate where throws will be going in various situations. After the ball is back in the infield all outfielders continue to act as backups for any throws that come back to any of the bases. The right fielder is primarily responsible for backing up throws heading to first base and occasionally second base. The center fielder serves to back up throws to second base only, but the ball could come from several dramatic angles in the infield. The left fielder typically backs up throws going to third base after the ball is back in the infield and occasionally helps back up throws to second base.

(continued)

○ What type of pitches does the pitcher throw? Knowing how the pitcher is trying to get the hitter out can help the defense maximize their coverage. Having an idea what pitches the pitcher is throwing or how she will be selecting pitches to get a specific hitter out will provide additional information about what types of batted balls might be hit or what locations on the field the balls might be hit to.

Decision-Making Guidelines

When determining defensive responsibilities in the outfield, you and your players should be sure to consider the previous information. Also consider the following guidelines:

○ Stay on your feet as long as possible with slower runners on base to allow more consistent play. By staying on their feet and not diving for a lot of balls, outfielders can limit the runners' advance on a hit. When an outfielder dives for a ball, she may fail to make the catch. If that occurs, she will be on the ground and the ball will be loose, so runners will likely be able to advance extra bases.

○ Play more aggressively when your team is far ahead or far behind. Your rewards may be greater, and less risk is involved with every play. More aggressive play in the outfield includes diving for more balls and leaving the feet to cut off balls in the gaps. Additionally, outfielders can be more aggressive on their approach to ground balls and take tighter angles to cut off ground balls in hopes of reducing the gains of the offense. When the score is one sided, the entire team can take a more aggressive approach.

○ Protect the foul lines when the game is close to prevent extra-base hits down the lines. Because no teammate can provide backup on a hit down the line, an extra-base hit is likely to result if the left or right fielder misplays the ball in that area. So when the game is close, you may choose to have your outfield protect the lines even at the risk of giving up some balls hit in the gaps.

○ Play deeper late in the game when you have a small lead. This approach forces the opponent to string together several hits to score. Balls hit over an outfielder's head generally result in multiple bases for the batter or runners on base, so the offense has a greater chance to score on fewer consecutive hits. Playing deeper slightly increases the chance of giving up a single in front of the outfielders but significantly reduces the chance of giving up a big hit. So in this situation the offense will have to come up with several hits to score a run.

○ Play a few steps closer to the infield when the batter has two strikes. When hitters have two strikes against them, they tend to be in a defensive mode to protect against being struck out. Because they are less aggressive, they use a less powerful swing. In addition, pitchers who have two strikes on the batter rarely throw a hittable pitch to the batter. Consequently, you see lots of mis-hits and bloop singles by hitters who have two strikes on them.

○ Make accurate throws to the infielders in relay and cut situations to keep secondary runners from advancing extra bases. When receiving a throw, infielders should always line up between the outfielder with the ball and a base. This configuration gives the defense an automatic backup system should a bad throw occur because the infielder covering the base is able to act as a backup on an errant throw. If the infielder receiving the throw is not lined up with a base, an overthrow will travel randomly into the infield.

At a Glance

The following parts of the text offer additional information on outfield defensive responsibilities.

DIVING IN THE OUTFIELD

Many outfielders struggle with knowing when to dive and what balls to dive for. Many athletes hold back from diving because of the fear of missing the ball. By helping them to anticipate the path of the ball and building their belief that they have a chance to make a catch when they dive, you can prepare them to dive when the situation arises.

Your players should use these five cues to understand when they can and should dive for a ball:

- When a ball is hit in the gap between outfielders or a ball is dying (soft line drive or blooper that will not travel to the fence if it is not caught) and another outfielder is there as backup.

- When a low or shallow fly ball is hit between the infielder and the outfielder with no runners on base or a runner on first base. This ball is the most common one that an outfielder will dive for and is typically the best ball to dive for as well. The flight of the ball is just high enough that the player can time her dive and just low enough that the ball will not travel far if she misses it. In addition, on this play the outfielder will have a backup to help if the ball does get by her.

- On any ball in foul territory with no runners on base. For the right and left fielders, foul balls offer a great opportunity to dive. You want to stress to the wing outfielders that they should always dive for these balls if no runners are on base or if two are out. If they dive and make the catch with runners on base and less than two outs, the runners can tag up and advance on the play. In some situations, of course, the out is more valuable than giving up a base on the play.

- In a do-or-die situation with the game on the line. As mentioned previously, the outfielders are the last line of defense, so normally they should ensure that they have backup from another outfielder or that the path of the ball will limit how far it will travel on the ground if it falls. For a do-or-die play, however, the outfielder does not have to take into account these two factors—she just needs to know that if she does not make the catch, the game is probably over.

- With two outs and a runner on third base, an outfielder may dive for a ball (may depend on the defensive strategy). But with less than two outs, outfielders typically should not dive for a ball or make a catch in foul territory if they will be unable to throw out the runner at home on the tag up.

Defending the Bunt

A large part of the game of softball is bunting and playing the short game. Because most teams use the bunt extensively, a defense must be well prepared and practiced at defending the bunt. One of the big differences between softball and baseball is that the bunt is used far more often in softball. To defend the bunt effectively, your team needs the physical skills to execute the play as well as the ability to make decisions, communicate clearly and read the options. Defending the bunt is far more than just physical execution. Tactically, several variables affect how a team can choose to defend the bunt to maximize the odds of getting out of the inning without giving up a run.

Any time that the offense attempts to bunt, the defense should have one goal—to get an out on the play. By bunting, the offense is giving the defense an opportunity to get one of the valuable outs in an inning. With strong execution and a sound tactical approach to the bunting situation, the defense can take the momentum away from the offense by getting the lead runner out, but at the very least they should be able to get an out somewhere, a result that will take some advantage away from the offense.

READING THE SITUATION

How can you and your players know when to defend the bunt? Teach your players to do the following:

- Know where the runners are.
- Know the number of outs in the inning and the score of the game.
- Know where the offense is in the lineup.
- Read whether the batter has moved from where she started in the batter's box.

 WATCH OUT!

The following circumstances may distract your athletes:

- Too many players are communicating different messages on the bunt.
- A batter fakes a bunt and then pulls the bat back to swing or slap the ball.
- Defenders charge too aggressively and give the bunter the opportunity to push a bunt past the corners.

ACQUIRING THE APPROPRIATE KNOWLEDGE

To defend the bunt successfully, you and your athletes must understand the following:

Rules

You and your athletes need to know several main rules when you are defending the bunt:

REMINDER!

When defending the bunt, your players must know your team strategy and game plan. Don't forget to consider the questions on page 128.

- Rules about the 30-foot running lane for the runner along the first-base line
- Rules about catcher interference and obstruction
- Rules about interference and obstruction when fielding a bunt
- Rules about obstruction of the runner when receiving a throw at a base
- Rules about foul tips caught by the catcher
- Rules about fouling off a bunt with two strikes

Physical Playing Conditions

The physical playing conditions will significantly affect the game. Thus, you and your players must pay attention to the following physical conditions when defending the bunt:

- The slope of the infield along the foul lines. The slope can affect how a ball will roll when it goes up the line and whether it is likely to roll foul or stay fair.
- The condition of the infield in front of home plate. The surface characteristics of the field can dramatically affect the speed of the bunt and how aggressive the defense should be on bunts in front of home plate. If the playing surface in front of home is uneven or contains many ruts, the defense may need to prepare for bad hops and use their gloves more than their bare hands when fielding.
- The position of the sun. Catching the throw may be difficult if the sun is in the receiver's eyes.

Strengths and Weaknesses of Opponents

You and your players must account for your opponent's strengths and weaknesses when defending the bunt. Teach your players to consider the following about your opponents:

- How quick are the runners on base? Your defense needs to know the speed of the lead runner so that they are prepared to make the correct play if the batter bunts.
- How quick is the batter? Knowing how quick the batter is gives the corners an idea of how much time they have to make a decision about the lead runner.
- Does the offense or the batter square up for the bunt early or late? Some bunters square up or move late on the pitch, so your defense may have to play in closer in anticipation of the bunt.
- Does the offense attempt to bunt even with two strikes on the batter? If so, then your corners will not be able to move back with two strikes.
- Does the offense use the bunt at nontraditional times? Some teams drop a bunt at any time or in any count to catch the defense off-guard, so teach your players to be prepared for this possibility.
- Does the offense attempt to place their bunts up the lines or toward the center of the field? Some teams like to bunt along the lines to challenge the defense to make longer throws. Therefore, the corners need to prepare for bunts along the foul lines.
- Does the offense use the push bunt or the slap as part of their short game? If an offense uses the push bunt or slap off the sacrifice bunt, the corners need to hold their positions as long as possible to read the batter so that they can defend all options.

Self-Knowledge

Besides being aware of your opponent's strengths and weaknesses, you and your players need to have knowledge about your own team's ability. When defending the bunt, you and your players must be aware of the following:

- Do both corners have strong enough arms to throw out the lead runner at second base in a bunt situation? The throw to second base is a longer throw, so arm strength is important in deciding where to make the attempt.
- Does the catcher have good range when getting out from behind the plate to field a bunt? A catcher who can cover many of the bunts in front of home can affect how the defense covers and makes plays on bunts.

(continued)

BASIC BUNTING SITUATIONS

You and your team will encounter the bunt in a few basic situations. Consider the following defensive tactics in these situations:

Runner on First Base

With the runner on first base and either no outs or one out, the offense will likely be attempting to move the runner into scoring position. The bunt is the most common approach. Generally, your strategy should put your defense in position to get the lead runner if possible and get an out no matter what!

The basic defense has both corners playing close to home to be the primary fielders for the bunt. The pitcher backs up the corners in case the batter pushes a ball past them. The second-base player holds her position until the bunt is laid down and then breaks to cover first base for the force-out. The shortstop holds her position as well until the bunt is laid down and then breaks to cover second base for the force-out on the lead runner. She must step into the infield to give the runner room to round the base if the corners do not make a play to second base. Bringing an outfielder in to cover a base is not a good strategy because without a backup a bad throw will almost certainly result in a run. Therefore, coverage of third base should be prioritized in the following way. Ideally, the third-base player can get back to cover if she does not field the bunt attempt. If she cannot do this, then the catcher should move to cover third base. If the catcher cannot cover third, the pitcher should be close enough to provide coverage.

Another defensive approach for this situation is to have the pitcher and third-base player be the primary coverage for bunts. The pitcher covers bunts on the first-base side of the field that the catcher or third-base player cannot get to. The third-base player positions herself to cover as many bunts as she can. In this situation the first-base player stays back and covers the force-out at first. The second-base player covers the force-out at second base and covers second for the steal. The shortstop plays in and closer to third base and covers third base if the ball is bunted. This defense is effective against a left-handed slapper if your pitcher is capable of throwing good pitches away to the hitter.

Runner on Second Base

When a runner is on second base or runners are on second base and first base, the priority changes to getting the lead runner at third base if possible and if not then getting the batter out at first base. The same mentality applies—be aggressive but smart to make sure of getting an out.

The bunt defense will likely be similar to the basic setup. The corners provide primary coverage for the bunt. The second-base player holds her position as before until the bunt is laid down. She then breaks to cover first base for the force-out. But in this defense the shortstop holds until the bunt is laid down and then breaks to cover third base for either the force-out or the tag. In this coverage no infielder covers second base for the primary play. If a runner is not on first base to start the play, the second-base player releases from her coverage at first base if the corners make a play to third. The second-base player can then prevent the bunter who is safe at first from advancing freely to second base.

Another defensive alignment is to use the pitcher as one of the primary defenders, as before. In this situation you will likely have the third-base player stay back and have the first-base player and pitcher be the primary defenders. In this alignment the second-base player still covers first base on the bunt. The shortstop covers second base. This defense is best used when runners are on first and second instead of on second base only. This alignment is also useful if there is already one out because your defense can cover more situations than just the bunt.

Runner on Third Base

The bunt is a threat with a runner on any base, including third base. When a runner is on third base, several points are important. If the bases are loaded, there is a force play at home. If a runner is on third base and the bases are not loaded, a tag play is required to get the out at home. If there are two outs, the runner from third base who crosses home does not score a run if a force-out occurs at any other base, even if the runner crosses the plate before the force-out is made.

The offense may choose to use a suicide, or squeeze, bunt, which has the runner on third breaking for home on the release of the pitch. Alternatively, they may use a regular bunt, or safety squeeze, which has the runner on third breaking for home only after the defense makes a play or makes an error. To defend both options, the defense must have good communication from all players as well as from the dugout. Creating pressure is one of the key goals for the offense. A confident, unshakable defense can turn a bunt attempt with a runner on third into an out and take the momentum away from the offense.

A basic defense with a runner on third base with less than two outs is to keep both corners in tight to defend against the suicide bunt. The second-base player is responsible for covering the force-out at first base. The shortstop covers third base in case a rundown develops between home and third base. A second type of defense is to keep the first-base player back and rely on the third-base player and pitcher as the primary coverage players for the bunt. This scenario allows the first-base player to stay back for the force-out at first on a ground ball or safety squeeze bunt. The second-base player can play more up the middle to protect against ground balls.

- How well does your team communicate and read the bunt situation in attempting to get the lead runner? For the defense to get the lead runner, the corners must rely heavily on communication from other infielders and the catcher because they have their backs to the play when they field the ball.

- Is your pitcher a strong fielder? Using the pitcher to cover bunts on one side of the field can change your infield coverage. In addition, a good-fielding pitcher may be able to get the lead runner on a ball bunted to her.

- Does your team handle pressure well? The short game and bunting game can increase the intensity and pressure of the game. A defense that stays composed following a bobble or mishandled ball can go more aggressively after the lead runner and still get the out at first if there is no play on the lead runner.

- Does your pitcher throw a good rise or curveball? The hitter will have a tougher time executing a bunt on a high pitch or an away pitch. If your team commonly throws this pitch in a bunt situation, your corners can alter their strategy because the batter will likely hit a pop-up or foul on the bunt attempt.

Decision-Making Guidelines

When defending the bunt, you and your players should be sure to consider the previous information. Also consider the following guidelines:

- When the game is close, your team should always prepare to go after the lead runner but be willing to settle for any out.

- When playing with a big lead, always get an out and generally take the higher percentage play by getting the force-out on the batter. If your team has a big lead, limiting the number of batters who can possibly come to the plate is a sound strategy. The offense is ultimately limiting their opportunities by giving away outs, and the defense should take advantage of this offensive strategy.

- Establish a priority system for various scenarios when handling bunts. The catcher is the quarterback of the defense and should communicate the priority in every situation.

- Have your defense call a time-out if they are not all on the same page.

At a Glance

The following parts of the text offer additional information on defending the bunt

Fielding Balls on the Forehand or Backhand Side	67
Fielding Ground Balls in the Infield	72
Fielding Ground Balls in the Outfield	78
Infield Defensive Responsibilities	170
Outfield Defensive Responsibilities	176

The pickoff in fast-pitch softball is different from the one used in baseball. In baseball, a pickoff throw can be from a pitcher behind a runner on a leadoff. In softball the runner cannot lead off until after the release of the pitch, so pitchers have no opportunity to pick off a runner on base. Catchers therefore take on the bulk of the responsibility with the pickoff. A set pickoff play generally requires the pitcher to throw a pitchout or a pitch-up so that the hitter does not hit the pitch. Ensuring that the hitter does not hit the pitch becomes important if one of the defenders vacates her fielding position to sneak behind the runner who is leading off the base. Using the pickoff to catch an opponent's runner off base can lead to a huge momentum swing. Runners in fast-pitch are extremely valuable. Having a runner on base generally gives the momentum to the offense because they are putting pressure on the defense and pitcher. A successful pickoff can do two things—eliminate a runner on base and register an additional out during the inning. This dramatic play usually takes the wind out of the offensive team's inning.

The pickoff negates the offensive gain from a hit, an error by the defense or a walk that allowed the hitter to get on base. Even if a pickoff attempt does not yield an out, it can send a strong message to the runners and coaches that the defense is prepared to be aggressive and is not afraid to use the pickoff. A pickoff attempt usually causes the runner to be slightly more cautious in her leadoff, which might result in her being a step slower to the next base on a ball that is hit.

READING THE SITUATION

How can you and your players attempt a pickoff? Teach your players to do the following:

- Watch for runners who take a large leadoff.
- Take advantage of a pickoff if your pitcher is ahead in the count and can afford to throw a pitchout (ball).
- Be prepared to use a pickoff if the base coaches have not been watching the defense and helping the runners.
- Look for an opportunity to use a pickoff when the offense is starting to build momentum or has a big hitter at the plate.
- Watch for the runners to lose focus if the hitter takes the pitch. Sometimes runners walk back to the base or even look away from the catcher as they return to the base.

 WATCH OUT!

The following circumstances might distract your athletes:

- Pitchers are uncomfortable with throwing pitchouts because they have no glove target as they deliver the ball. A catcher cannot set up before the pitch with the glove exactly where she wants the ball thrown because doing so would tip off or give away the pickoff.
- Second-base players vacate their position too early because they fear getting to the base too late to receive the ball.
- Catchers throw before the receiver gets into position or throw the ball into the runner.

REMINDER!

When attempting a pickoff, your players must know your team strategy and game plan. Don't forget to consider the questions on page 128.

- Defenders who anticipate a physical tag play and are unprepared when the runner takes off to the next base on the delayed steal after the catcher releases the ball.
- Defenders who forget about the lead or primary runner when attempting to pick off a secondary runner.
- Runners who are decoying and trying to draw the pickoff so that they can attempt a delayed steal.

ACQUIRING THE APPROPRIATE KNOWLEDGE

To attempt a pickoff successfully, you and your athletes must understand the following:

Rules

You and your athletes need to know several main rules when attempting a pickoff:

- Rules about obstruction and interference
- Rules about the catcher's box and receiving a pitch
- Rules about deflected balls and foul tips
- Rules about catcher's interference
- Rules about batter's interference
- Rules about obstruction of the runner and blocking the base

Physical Playing Conditions

The physical playing conditions will significantly affect the game. Thus, you and your players must pay attention to the following physical conditions when attempting a pickoff:

- The condition of the base paths. A loose or wet surface can make it challenging for runners to change directions and can cause them to lose footing.
- The position of the sun. Your players should be aware of the position of the sun so that they will not have to look directly at it while receiving a throw, thus running the risk of losing track of the ball.
- The condition of the playing area in and around the catcher's box. Large holes or loose dirt can cause poor footing and affect where the catcher will step on the pickoff throw.

Strengths and Weaknesses of Opponents

You and your players must account for your opponent's strengths and weaknesses when attempting a pickoff. Teach your players to consider the following about your opponents:

- How quick are the runners on base? Do they have enough agility to change directions quickly? Agility is as important as speed in thwarting a pickoff. Runners who are extremely agile and can change directions quickly may have the ability to use a delayed steal on a pickoff attempt.
- How aggressive are the runners in their leadoffs? Both the intensity and the length of a runner's leadoff can work to the advantage of the defense when they attempt a pickoff. Runners who take larger leadoffs are more vulnerable to the catcher's throw to the base behind them.

(continued)

○ Does the offense use large leadoffs as bait for a delayed steal? Some teams like to bait the catcher into throwing behind the runner so that they can use a delayed steal to advance to the next base. Sometimes this is an offensive team strategy; other times an individual player uses this ploy. The defense needs to be prepared for this tactic so that they can react quickly when the runner breaks for the next base. The catcher might incorporate a fake throw to get the runner to lean the wrong way too early and therefore be vulnerable to being caught between bases.

Self-Knowledge

Besides being aware of your opponent's strengths and weaknesses, you and your players need to have knowledge about your own team's ability. When attempting a pickoff, your players should be aware of the following:

○ How strong and how quick is your catcher? When attempting a pickoff at first base, the quickness of the catcher's release is more important than her arm strength. When attempting a pickoff at second base, quickness and arm strength are equally important. Because the throw to first base from home is relatively short, a quick release will be enough to catch the runner off base. But second base is much farther from home, so the catcher needs to have a strong arm to catch the runner off base. Also, a catcher who does not have a strong arm is vulnerable to the delayed steal of third base because the pickoff throw to second must travel a long way across the infield.

○ Are your infielders quick? Infielders who cover the bag must have the quickness to get to the base behind the runner while she is off base. Defenders need to be sneaky and use exceptional timing to get behind a runner without giving away the pickoff to the runner or base coaches. The longer that the defender can maintain her position and still be able to get to the base before the runner does, the better the chance is that the pickoff attempt will work.

○ Does the outfield know that the pickoff is on? The pickoff is a risky play, but good communication and defensive movement can minimize the risk. Outfielders need to know that a pickoff is being executed so that they are prepared to act as a backup for an overthrow. They are the key to keeping the failed pickoff attempt from being hugely detrimental.

○ Does the pitcher have the ability to throw a pitchout? Because a defender will be vacating her position early before the pitch reaches the plate, the pitcher needs to be able to throw to a spot outside the strike zone but close enough to the strike zone that it does not appear to be a pitchout. A common flaw with a pitchout is throwing it so high that the catcher has to stand up to catch the ball. An effective pitchout is at the height of the strike zone but outside the strike zone by a foot to a foot and half. Pitchouts are common when the defense is attempting to pick off runners at first base or third base.

○ Does the pitcher have the ability to throw a pitch-up? Because a defender will be vacating her position early before the pitch reaches the plate, the pitcher needs to be able to throw to a spot above the strike zone, close enough for the catcher to catch it but not so close that the hitter can hit it. An effective pitch-up is at about the eye level of the hitter. Pitch-ups are generally more effective when attempting a pickoff at second base, a pickoff at first base with a left-handed batter up or a pickoff at third base with a right-handed batter up. In the last two situations, it is best to throw the pitch up, high and inside to the hitter. When attempting a pickoff at second base, the pitcher must throw a high pitch out of the strike zone but catchable for the catcher. The runner at second base should read the catcher's movement not as a pickoff attempt but as just a high pitch to the batter. The pitch-up protects the defender who is vacating her position and still gives the catcher a pitch that she can handle and throw to the base for the pickoff attempt.

Decision-Making Guidelines

When attempting a pickoff, you and your players should be sure to consider the previous information. Also consider the following guidelines:

- With runners on first and second, the runner on first is sometimes overaggressive and does not expect a throwback because she is not the lead runner. Your players should watch for the runner on first base to be taking a larger than normal lead or possibly being slow to return to the base after the catcher receives the pitch. When attempting a pickoff on the secondary runner, defenders need to be prepared for the lead runner on second base to attempt to steal third base on the throw. Generally, runners are not anticipating a pickoff attempt on the secondary runner, but awareness may vary by the team's or the individual players' skill level.

- Teach your catcher to read the play and hold the throw if the defender who is covering for the pickoff is not at the base in time. Sometimes the defender is there on time, but the runner was not fooled and is not far enough off the base for the catcher to attempt the pickoff. Some catchers make the throw anyway and inadvertently hit the runner or throw the ball away, thus giving the runner a chance to advance to the next base. The catcher should not force the play if she has no chance to get the runner out.

- Your catcher must be able to call the pickoff play and have a signal to inform all players on the team. You might also have some kind of a return signal from the infielder who will be covering on the pickoff so that the catcher knows that her signal was received. After they receive the communication from the catcher, the infielders should be able to relay some information to the outfielders behind them about the intended pickoff. An outfielder caught off guard may not be in position to back up the throw. Of course, to avoid giving away the play, the outfielders must not break too early.

- Be careful not to put your pitcher in a bad count situation with runners in scoring position. Pitchers who struggle to throw strikes are not good candidates for throwing pitchouts often.

- Look for undisciplined baserunning early in the game. Communicate with your catcher and infielders between innings about what you are seeing from the dugout. Defenders sometimes are so focused on the batter that they forget to think about using the pickoff as part of their defensive strategy.

- Just showing the pickoff attempt can be a way to get into the heads of the offensive players. Communicate your entire defensive strategy with your team before the game.

- Use a throwback instead of a pickoff if you do not want to risk throwing the pitchout or pitch-up (see "Defensive Coverage for Pickoffs" on page 190).

- Have your pitchers throw pitchouts and pitch-ups often during practice. If your pitchers are not consistent with pitchouts and pitch-ups, have them throw the pitches in every workout.

At a Glance

The following parts of the text offer additional information on pickoffs.

Throwing	56
Infield Throws	61
Fielding Balls on the Forehand or Backhand Side	67
Fielding Ground Balls in the Infield	72
Infield Defensive Responsibilities	170

(continued)

DEFENSIVE COVERAGE FOR PICKOFFS

Now let's look at a few coverage options for running the pickoff at different bases. Pickoff attempts require a specific defender to cover the base to try to catch the runner off base. Because several infielders can cover each base, you may want to consider a few of the following points when establishing the pickoff plays that your defense will run.

Pickoffs to First Base

Two ways to pick off a runner on first are to have the first-base player step back and take the throw or to have the second-base player come behind the runner to cover the bag. When the first-base player covers the bag, the catcher has not called for a pitchout but just uses a throwback or throw down to the first-base player when the runner takes a big lead at first. This play does not necessarily require the catcher to call a signal, but the first-base player must be ready on every pitch. The second-base player takes the throw from the catcher in two situations—when either the first-base player is up to defend the bunt or the catcher has called a pitchout and the second-base player is vacating her position to beat the runner back to first base.

Pickoffs to Second Base

When a pickoff to second is called, the second-base player must set up a few steps closer to the base without making it too obvious that she will be attempting the pickoff. Using a pitch-up may be more deceptive than using a pitchout because the catcher does not have to step out and vacate her normal position. The runner on second base can see the catcher take the step outside for the pitchout, but the pitch-up may simply appear to be a high pitch. Note that using the shortstop for a pickoff at second base is extremely uncommon in softball unless you are using a radically shifted defensive approach for the hitter. Because the runner cannot lead off until the pitch is released, the runner would see the shortstop moving toward second before she even takes her lead off the base. Also, do not attempt a pickoff to second with a runner at third base because two long throws across the infield gives the runner on third too much time to score.

Pickoffs to Third Base

As with a pickoff to first base, the coverage at third depends on the situation. If the third-base player moves in to defend the bunt, then the shortstop covers for the pickoff. The catcher and shortstop communicate this using a signal and a return signal. Again, the shortstop must cheat over toward third so that she can beat the runner back to the base. The normal ready position for the third-base player in softball is in front of the base, not behind it as in baseball, so if the third-base player is taking the pickoff, she does not try to get back to the base but instead moves toward the baseline and tries to tag the runner as she returns to third. This play does not require the catcher to call a pitchout or pitch-up as long as the third-base player is ready and covering the runner on every pitch. Note, however, that the pickoff at third base is extremely risky because the shortstop takes the throw when the runner is between her and the catcher. The runner could turn into or be hit by the catcher's throw, and would likely be able to score. Practice with runners or decoys in place so that the catcher can work on throwing to the inside part of the field and lead the shortstop accurately.

A rundown should be viewed as an opportunity to get an easy out without facing a batter. In general, the defense creates a rundown by catching a runner between bases. In this situation, the ball is live, so the runner is in jeopardy of being tagged out. The defense tries to keep that runner from reaching a base and get an out. Keep in mind that the offense may use a rundown as a diversion to allow another runner to advance or score. Teams that use an aggressive running game may attempt to use the rundown to cause the defense to falter or make an error. If the defense has worked on the rundown and practiced a sound strategy, then rundowns should result in an out or at least hold the runners to their original bases.

WATCH OUT!

The following circumstances might distract your athletes:

- Runners decoy or make a fake move with the upper body to draw a throw.
- Additional runners are on base when working on a rundown.
- Players rush because they are distracted by oral cues from the opposing team's players or coaches.
- Too many infielders become involved in the rundown, causing too many people to be operating in a small space.

ACQUIRING THE APPROPRIATE KNOWLEDGE

To perform a rundown successfully, you and your athletes must understand the following:

Rules

You and your athletes need to know several main rules when performing a rundown:

- Rules about interference and obstruction
- Rules about the pitching circle
- Rules pertaining to what the batter–runner is required to do after touching first base
- Rules about receiving a throw and blocking a base or home plate

READING THE SITUATION

How can you and your players execute an effective rundown? Teach your players to do the following:

- Know how many outs there are, what inning it is, and what the score is. All these factors can be important in determining which runners have priority. For example, working an effective rundown on a runner caught off between second and third base may result in an out, but if a runner on third base scores the tying or go-ahead run, the result is a negative for the defense. Before every pitch, your players should know whether getting outs or stopping a team from scoring is most important.
- Know where all the runners are and how fast they are.
- Keep an eye on trail runners who may be aggressive and take a large lead.
- Watch for runners who aggressively round the bases.

REMINDER!

When performing a rundown, your players must know your team strategy and game plan. Don't forget to consider the questions on page 128.

(continued)

Physical Playing Conditions

The physical playing conditions will significantly affect the game. Thus, you and your players must pay attention to the following physical conditions when executing a rundown:

- The condition of the base paths. A loose or muddy surface can make it difficult for the runner to change direction.
- The condition of the grass in the outfield. If a throw comes in from the outfield, the ball may be wet for the infielders when they work the rundown.
- The position of the sun. The sun can be a factor for one of the receivers in the rundown. The defenders should attempt to move the runner in a direction where the receiver does not have to look directly into the sun. The defenders may at times be unable to avoid the sun, so they should be sure to keep their throws low to minimize the effects of the sun on the receiver.

Strengths and Weaknesses of Opponents

You and your players must account for your opponent's strengths and weaknesses when executing a rundown. Teach your players to consider the following about your opponents:

- How fast are the runners on base? The speed of the runner in the rundown as well as the speed of other runners on base is important. When trying to trap a runner and keep the number of throws to a minimum, the player with the ball must know when to release the throw to the receiver so that the runner does not have enough time to stop, change direction and continue the rundown. Faster runners may require the thrower to release the ball slightly sooner so that the receiver will be able to get the ball and put the tag on before the runner is able to sneak safely back into the base.
- How agile is the runner in the rundown? Can the runner change direction with explosive quickness? This factor may determine which players you want to have the ball in the pursuit of the runner.
- Does the runner more often use a headfirst slide or a feet-first slide? Runners who use a headfirst slide can be difficult to tag out even when the ball beats them to the base because they will be able to reach around the tag with either arm. Defenders need to stay close to the base until they receive the throw to protect against the headfirst slide to either side of the base.
- Does the opponent use an aggressive baserunning style of play? An aggressive baserunning team rounds the bases farther and may be vulnerable to being caught off base. Against such an opponent, prepare your defense to take advantage of the offense and catch runners off base.
- Does the opponent use the rundown with a trail runner to create a diversion for the lead runner to score or advance? Your players must know the game situation and identify the priority runner. The defense may choose to use a fake throw to draw off the lead or priority runner, or they could use a cut. Most important, all infielders should be on the same page about how they will defend or execute the rundown before the pitch is thrown.

Self-Knowledge

Besides being aware of your opponent's strengths and weaknesses, you and your players need to have knowledge about your own team's ability. When executing a rundown, teach your players to be aware of the following:

- Are all the infielders aware of the team's rundown strategy and technique? Do not assume that all players who join your team know how to execute an effective rundown or know the oral or visual cues that your team uses to communicate. Communication and practice will help clear up any problems that may occur in the pressure situation of a game.

○ How strong are your infielders' arms? When a rundown occurs with two or three runners on base, your infielders may have to make a long throw across the infield to make a play on the lead runner.

○ Do all the infielders know how to make a dart-toss throw on the run? If some of the infielders struggle with or have not practiced making this kind of throw, then your team will probably not be able to execute an effective rundown. A dart-toss throw is aptly named. With the ball and elbow above the shoulder, the athlete extends the arm without swinging it backward first.

○ How well do the infielders make a tag at the base or block out the base? If some players are more competent at handling the ball and blocking the base when a runner is sliding in, your team may choose to run the runner in their direction more often. This tactic will give you better odds of making the out.

Decision-Making Guidelines

When performing a rundown, you and your players should be sure to consider the previous information. Also consider the following guidelines:

○ Limit the number of throws that your players make in a rundown. The more throws that they make, the greater the chance that an error will occur.

○ Use as few as players as possible in the rundown so that all the other bases are covered.

○ The player who begins the rundown should get the runner committed to running toward a base. If the runner is able to jog or jockey herself and change direction, she is dictating the rundown. If the first defensive player to make a throw can get the runner moving full speed toward one of the bases, then the defense is dictating the rundown, making it far more difficult for the runner to escape.

○ Players and coaches should always know which runner is the priority when the game is close or in the late innings. With multiple runners on base, the defense must never lose focus on the game situation. Sometimes a defense needs to focus on getting outs rather than preventing a run from scoring. If the runner on third base is the priority and another runner is caught between bases, your defense should keep the runner moving away from second base. A defender who is forcing a runner toward second has her back toward home and must make a long throw if she wants to throw to the plate. She may be able to get an out but could give up a run in the process. At other times in the game, getting an out may be the main concern. Knowing that an offense is limited by outs, a defense should at times be willing to give up a run to get an out, particularly when way ahead late in the game.

○ Never allow the winning or go-ahead run to move freely into scoring position in the late innings. A common situation occurs when a runner is on third base and the runner on first base represents the go-ahead or winning run. Here the defense should not allow the runner on first to steal second without making an attempt on her for fear that the runner on third might score.

○ Late in the game with a solid lead, getting a sure out from a rundown is more important than preventing the lead runner on third base from scoring. Here the defense must not allow the lead runner to distract them and should instead focus on getting an out on the runner in the rundown.

(continued)

○ A player with the ball who is running at the runner should be going fast enough to force the runner to go full speed in one direction. If the defense lets the runner go at a pace that allows her to sidestep or jog, the runner is controlling the tempo and the outcome of the rundown.

○ Defenders should vacate the base path quickly after releasing their throws so that the runner cannot make contact with them. Defenders should also follow the direction of their throws so that they can cover the base that they just threw toward if the rundown continues back in the other direction.

○ Defenders should always make quick tags with two hands so that they can react to other runners or plays that they need to make. By using both hands to make the tag, the defender does not have to waste time transferring the ball from the glove to the throwing hand.

○ Defenders who use fake throws while running at the base runner often fake out their teammates more than they do the runner. Runners usually do not react to a fake throw because they are not going to be catching the ball, but the faking arm action challenges the defender because she does not know which of the arm movements will actually result in a throw.

The first-and-third situation occurs whenever the offense has a runner on third base and a runner on first base with second base unoccupied. The first-and-third situation presents itself regardless of the number of outs, although the defense may alter how they defend it when two are out. A first-and-third situation may be the most difficult defensive skill for a team to execute because they must be disciplined and ready for a variety of options that the offense may use on the play. To run a good first-and-third defense, a team must have excellent team communication skills and be competent at executing a steal throw to second, a pickoff throw to third and an effective rundown.

The first-and-third situation has many layers of responsibility for each player, and it cannot be executed unless every player is on the same page. As a coach you may choose to limit the options that your team will attempt to a few set plays. The most advanced way to defend a first-and-third situation is to establish with your team the most important goal in the outcome and then let them react and adjust to the play that the offense puts on without a predetermined defensive play.

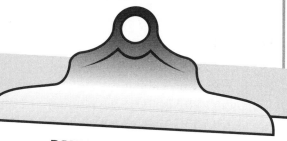

READING THE SITUATION

How can you and your players defend the first-and-third play? Teach your players to do the following:

- Know the number of outs, the inning and the score of the game. All pertain to how the situation will be prioritized.

- Know their primary and secondary responsibilities, especially when the first-and-third play is being run off a normal pitch versus a pitchout or pitch-up.

- Watch the batter at the plate for clues to what the offense will try to accomplish. For example, if the batter begins her at bat in the middle of the batter's box and then moves back on the next pitch, she may be trying to move the catcher farther from second base to increase the difficulty of the throw on the steal.

- Be prepared for errant throws because they can change the situation. For example, a runner breaking for home or stopping between bases needs to be read when throwing so that the defense can work as a unit for a common goal.

 WATCH OUT!

The following circumstances might distract your athletes:

- A fake swing or fake bunt by the batter distracts the defense from the runners who are attempting to steal.

- Poor communication by your players creates confusion on the field.

- Athletes are distracted by the runners and fail to focus on the location of the ball.

ACQUIRING THE APPROPRIATE KNOWLEDGE

To defend the first-and-third play successfully, you and your athletes must understand the following:

REMINDER!

When defending the first-and-third play, your players must know your team strategy and game plan. Don't forget to consider the questions on page 128.

(continued)

Rules

You and your athletes need to know several main rules when you are defending the first-and-third play:

- Rules about interference and obstruction
- Rules about the pitching circle and what runners must do
- Rules about fake tags and blocking the base
- Rules about multiple runners on a single base
- Rules about foul tips caught by the catcher

Physical Playing Conditions

The physical playing conditions will significantly affect the game. Thus, you and your players must pay attention to the following physical conditions when defending the first-and-third play:

- The condition of the playing surface. If the surface is extremely loose or wet, runners will be slower and be less able to change direction.
- The position of the sun. Because throws may be coming from various directions, every defender must know where the sun is and how it can affect her vision when throwing or receiving the ball.
- Moisture on the ball. If drizzle is falling or the playing surface is damp, the ball may be slick or wet when players throw it.
- The condition of the batter's box. The catcher or any other fielder who might be covering home on a tag play should be aware of the condition of the batter's box. If the surface is loose or the box has large holes in it, runners may avoid sliding directly into home to avoid the poor sliding surface.

Strengths and Weaknesses of Opponents

You and your players must account for your opponent's strengths and weaknesses when defending the first-and-third play. Teach your players to consider the following about your opponents:

- How aggressive are the runners on base? The time required for a runner to be safe between bases dramatically affects the quickness that the defense needs to have to react when a runner breaks for home on the steal. For fast runners the defense needs to make quick throws and cuts to get an out. For slower runners the defense has slightly more time to execute their throws and cuts.
- Does your opponent run first-and-third plays often? Some teams run first-and-third plays frequently and always try to score the runner on third. Other teams run the first-and-third play with regularity but rarely risk sending the runner on third base home. If you are aware of your opponent's tendencies, you may choose to run a specific play. Additionally, a defense that is aware that the offense may use a certain play is less likely to be fooled by a fake or trick play.
- Does the opponent use a fake swing or fake bunt to protect the runner? A defense that knows the opponent's tendencies will not be surprised when the batter fakes. If the pitcher does not deliver a pitchout, the first priority of the defense is to play the ball hit by the batter. If the defense knows that the offense is using the batter to fake the defense, they will be less likely to be fooled or drawn out of position by the batter's fake.

Self-Knowledge

Besides being aware of your opponent's strengths and weaknesses, you and your players need to have knowledge about your own team's ability. When defending the first-and-third play, teach your players to be aware of the following:

- How strong is your catcher's throw? The first and most important throw is the throw from the catcher. If that throw is weak or inaccurate, you may need to adjust your focus on the play. A strong, accurate throw from the catcher will start the play off right. If the catcher is not able to get a strong, accurate throw all the way to second base, you may choose to run a first-and-third play by having the catcher get the ball back to the pitcher quickly and letting her execute the play. You could also use a cut that is short of second base so that the catcher's throw will not put your team in a situation where they will be unable to get the lead runner. If the catcher's throw is strong and accurate, your team has a large number of options for the first-and-third play and usually has good success. The catcher is the key to the infield defense, and this situation is the most challenging one that the infielders will face.

- How strong and accurate are your middle infielders' throws? After the ball travels across the infield to second base, the middle infielder must make a powerful and accurate throw to the plate to have a chance to put out the runner on third when she tries to steal home.

- Do all the infielders know their primary and secondary responsibilities? Defensive roles and responsibilities change during the play, and each infielder needs to make adjustments as the play develops.

- Does your infield know how to execute an effective rundown? Without the ability to trap a runner in a rundown, the defense has few options for defending the first-and-third play. Generally, the goal of the offense is to create a rundown with the runner between first and second base to allow the runner on third base to score. If the defense is not competent at executing a rundown, the likelihood that they will get an out and not give up a run is extremely low. In this situation you may choose to have your pitcher receive the ball in the circle and hope that the offense makes a mistake. You could also choose to run a fake throw to second by the catcher and attempt a pickoff at third base.

- Is the pitcher an aggressive fielder who can handle bunts and squeezes? Your defense faces a big challenge to cover all scenarios, but having an outstanding defensive pitcher may allow you to adjust your defensive responsibilities slightly. Keeping your corners at normal depth allows them to be involved at their bases for the first-and-third situation. With a good-fielding pitcher, they can often cover a greater range of bunts or mis-hits in front of home. You may also choose to have one of the corners play back and use the other corner and the pitcher to cover all bunts. You can align your defense in various ways, but having a good-fielding pitcher allows more options.

- How well do your players communicate on defense? Communication from the dugout to the catcher and from the catcher to the infield is extremely important. To keep all the infielders on the same page, the specific play or priority must be communicated effectively and immediately between pitches. If this portion of the communication is not a strength, then calling a time-out may be the best option. After the pitch is thrown and play begins, the defense is under tremendous pressure to work precisely as a unit. The better the team can communicate what the offense is doing, the better they will be at achieving the desired outcome.

(continued)

Decision-Making Guidelines

When defending the first-and-third play, you and your players should be sure to consider the previous information. Also consider the following guidelines:

- All defenders must know which runner is the greatest concern or priority and which play is being run if several options are available. Generally, the central communicator for the specific play or the prioritizing of the runners is the catcher. The catcher either relays the play from the dugout to the entire team or calls the play herself, depending on the situation. If the call is for a specific set play that does not require reading the offense, each player should know her responsibility. If the call is to prioritize a specific runner as the primary focus and read the defense, a more advanced play, then the defense will have a primary responsibility. Then, depending on what the offense does, communication should occur to ensure execution of the appropriate play. In either type of situation, the catcher should be the single source of communication to the infield and pitcher. Communication requires practice and trust that everyone involved will fulfill her responsibility.

- If the score is close late in the game, you may not want to risk a play in which the catcher throws all the way to second base. Instead, you can use some sort of fake throw or cut throw to catch the runner on third off base trying to score. This fake or cut play is generally a conservative play that prevents the runner on third from scoring, but it generally results in giving up second base to the runner stealing from first base.

- If you have a solid lead late in the game, you should be playing for outs. In this situation you may be willing to give up a run to get an out, so your primary focus is the runner trying to steal second. Ideally, you can get the out on the steal play and avoid giving up the run, but if the runner stealing second is caught in a rundown, the defense should not be distracted by the runner on third base trying to score. Instead, the defense should execute a solid rundown that results in a valuable out late in the game.

- In most situations you and your team should put the priority on the runner at third base, but even so you will not always freely give up second base to the runner on first. Keeping the runner at first out of scoring position without allowing the runner on third to score is a positive outcome. So a successful first-and-third play from the defense's perspective could mean that the runners are kept at first and third even if no out is accomplished. Players on the defense often think that they must get an out for the play to be successful, but they should recognize that keeping the offense from advancing on the bases is a positive result. Scoring a runner from first base on a single hit is much more difficult than scoring a runner from second. Keeping the runners at first and third instead of allowing the runner on first to move into scoring position with a steal stops the momentum of the offense. Obviously, the standard goal of the defense in a first-and-third situation is to prevent the offense from scoring without getting a hit. Forcing the offense to earn every base with hits or walks puts pressure on their batters and keeps the defense in a solid situation.

- Use a pitchout or pitch-up when you suspect that the runner on first will be stealing or that the squeeze play might be on. Your pitcher needs to be careful with pitchouts so that she does not throw a wild pitch and give up a run. Of course, using a pitchout when the runners are not going puts your pitcher in a less advantageous count situation on the batter.

- If you are not using a pitchout, the defenders must hold their ground to read what the batter does, but they must expect the runners to be going if the batter does not hit the ball. Communication from the dugout and outfielders can be helpful when the runners are stealing.

- If you are using a quick throwback to the pitcher as a play for the first-and-third situation, she becomes the primary fielder in working the play. She should stay in the circle to freeze whichever runner she is not watching. If the runner whom she is not watching decides to jockey to draw the throw, she will be called out if the pitcher has the ball in the circle.

- The third-base player's primary move during the first-and-third situation is to go to the foul line and stay on the home plate side of the runner (similar to the position that she takes for a pickoff). After the catcher releases the throw toward second base, the third-base player can retreat to the base and get behind the runner. She is then in good position to receive a throw from the middle infielders if they attempt to pick off the runner at third.

- The first-base player's primary responsibility is to retreat to the bag as quickly as possible and expect a throw at any time. She needs to trust her teammates' communication about the runner on third base if she has the ball or is receiving the ball because she cannot see the move of the runner on third toward home.

- If the second-base player is in the cut position, her primary responsibility is to read the distance and movement of the runner on third as the catcher is releasing the ball. The second-base player is also the primary person to cut the ball from the catcher on a bad throw or a throw that will be difficult for the shortstop to handle. If the second-base player allows the throw through to the shortstop, she should circle back to second base and become the backup defender if the shortstop vacates the base to go after the runner.

- The pitcher's primary role after the catcher releases the throw is to communicate about the runner on third base to the entire defense. Reading the runner's distance and movement away from third base is important. If a rundown occurs between third base and home, the pitcher may need to break for either home or third base to become the backup.

At a Glance

The following parts of the text offer additional information on defending the first-and-third play.

Throwing	56
Infield Throws	61
Catching a Throw	84
Playing First Base	102
Playing Third Base	114

Planning for Teaching

Part IV helps you apply what you learned in the previous chapters to developing a plan for the upcoming season. By having a season plan that outlines your practices for the year and then creating specific practice plans that make up your season plan, you will be ready to coach and get the most out of your season.

In chapter 7 you learn how to create your season plan, which is a framework for the practices that make up your season. Besides teaching you about the six essential steps to developing the season plan, this chapter provides a sample games approach season plan. A sample traditional approach season plan can be found in the *Coaching Softball Technical and Tactical Skills* online course.

After you have your season plan, you must create what is called a practice plan, which outlines how you will approach each practice. Chapter 8 helps you do this by explaining the important components of a good practice plan and then providing you with a sample of the first eight practices of your season based on the games approach season plans. A sample traditional approach practice plan can be found in the *Coaching Softball Technical and Tactical Skills* online course.

chapter 7

Season Plans

John Wooden, the great UCLA basketball coach, followed a simple coaching philosophy that emphasized execution over winning. He felt that if his Bruins concentrated on executing the basics, winning would follow. In that regard, his well-planned practice sessions created a foundation for 10 national titles in a 12-year span in the 1960s and 1970s. As Wooden said, "Failure to prepare is preparing to fail." Before the first practice of the season, you should review your coaching philosophy and reflect on the upcoming year. By doing so, you can avoid the pitfalls of previous years and set goals for the one to come. No matter what the sport, a good coach makes plans.

Planning begins with formulating a sound coaching philosophy. Do you pursue a conservative approach to the game or an aggressive one? When a runner reaches first, do you bunt her to second, or do you have her try to steal the base instead? Will you let batters swing at the first pitch, or will you tell them to take that first pitch? These and myriad other considerations go into the building of a coaching philosophy.

How do you form a philosophy? First, you should always go with your gut feelings. You shouldn't try to adopt a viewpoint that goes against your personal beliefs. You will have difficulty selling something to players that you don't believe in yourself. At the same time, you can certainly borrow from successful approaches that have worked for others. Pay close attention to schools or teams that win often. What makes those teams successful? You shouldn't be afraid to ask other coaches how they prepare for a season, run practices or discipline players. A good coach will be flattered and more than willing to share information.

But as you know, gathering information from other coaches or from books provides only the raw material for an aspiring coach. The next step is to process this information and organize it into a useful plan. Good coaches are good teachers. Just as a teacher wouldn't think about walking into a classroom without a lesson plan, a coach shouldn't begin a season without a plan. You need to organize information into a working whole, or a season plan, by skillfully analyzing, observing and prioritizing.

Six Steps to Instructional Planning*

Chapter 1 of Rainer Martens' *Successful Coaching, Third Edition* provides a framework for creating and implementing coaching values. You may want to read that chapter and begin to refine your coaching philosophy.

After you have articulated your philosophy, you can begin planning for the season ahead by following a simple six-step procedure called "Six Steps to Instructional Planning," as shown here:

Step 1: Identify the skills that your athletes need.

Step 2: Know your athletes.

Step 3: Analyze your situation.

Step 4: Establish priorities.

Step 5: Select methods for teaching.

Step 6: Plan practices.

Step 1: Identify the Skills That Your Athletes Need

To help athletes become excellent softball players, you need to know what skills players need to play softball. Not all these skills will be within the reach of most high school players, so you must filter this all-encompassing list. First, you need to isolate the skills that the team needs to be successful, as shown in column one of figure 7.1.

Figure 7.1 provides an overview of the basic to intermediate skills needed in softball, based on the skills mentioned in chapters 3 through 6 as well as information on communication and physical, mental and character skills from Rainer Martens' *Successful Coaching, Third Edition.* At this stage, you should examine the list of skills and add others if desired. Step 4 of the planning process will explain further how you can put this list to work for yourself.

Step 2: Know Your Athletes

Before going into a season, you should be familiar with your athletes. If you trained the team the year before, you can just review the list of returning players and evaluate them—their strengths, their weaknesses, how much they still have to learn and so on. If you are a new coach with no knowledge of the skill level of a team, the process is more difficult. You should review the guidelines for evaluation discussed in chapter 2 before attempting this process. You may want to conduct a tryout camp on the first day of practice or before the season, if the rules allow. The camp could be conducted with the major skill components such as a test that provides a measure of a player's speed, balance and quickness using the first-to-third sprint as well as the sprint from home to first. Next, you could position players in deep center field

---

*Adapted, by permission, from R. Martens, 2004, *Successful coaching*, 3rd ed. (Champaign, IL: Human Kinetics), 237.

Figure 7.1   Identifying and Evaluating Skills

STEP 1	STEP 4							
	Teaching Priorities			Readiness to Learn		Priority Rating		
Skills Identified	Must	Should	Could	Yes	No	A	B	C
Offensive Technical Skills								
Hitting	M	S	C	Yes	No	A	B	C
Sacrifice Bunt	M	S	C	Yes	No	A	B	C
Slap Hit and Hard Bunt	M	S	C	Yes	No	A	B	C
Squeeze Bunt	M	S	C	Yes	No	A	B	C
Running Slap	M	S	C	Yes	No	A	B	C
Baserunning	M	S	C	Yes	No	A	B	C
Bent-Leg Slide	M	S	C	Yes	No	A	B	C
Pop-Up Slide	M	S	C	Yes	No	A	B	C
Headfirst Slide	M	S	C	Yes	No	A	B	C
Defensive Technical Skills								
Throwing	M	S	C	Yes	No	A	B	C
Infield Throws	M	S	C	Yes	No	A	B	C
Fielding Balls on the Forehand or Backhand Side	M	S	C	Yes	No	A	B	C
Fielding Ground Balls in the Infield	M	S	C	Yes	No	A	B	C
Fielding Ground Balls in the Outfield	M	S	C	Yes	No	A	B	C
Catching a Throw	M	S	C	Yes	No	A	B	C
Catching Fly Balls	M	S	C	Yes	No	A	B	C
Pitching	M	S	C	Yes	No	A	B	C
Catching	M	S	C	Yes	No	A	B	C
Playing First Base	M	S	C	Yes	No	A	B	C
Playing Second Base	M	S	C	Yes	No	A	B	C
Playing Third Base	M	S	C	Yes	No	A	B	C
Playing Shortstop	M	S	C	Yes	No	A	B	C
Offensive Tactical Skills								
Playing the Short Game	M	S	C	Yes	No	A	B	C
Stealing a Base	M	S	C	Yes	No	A	B	C
Protecting the Runner on a Steal	M	S	C	Yes	No	A	B	C
First-and-Third Situation	M	S	C	Yes	No	A	B	C
Aggressive Baserunning	M	S	C	Yes	No	A	B	C

(continued)

Figure 7.1 *(continued)*

STEP 1	STEP 4							
	Teaching Priorities			**Readiness to Learn**		**Priority Rating**		
Skills Identified	**Must**	**Should**	**Could**	**Yes**	**No**	**A**	**B**	**C**
Offensive Tactical Skills *(continued)*								
Approaching Home	M	S	C	Yes	No	A	B	C
Hit and Run	M	S	C	Yes	No	A	B	C
Situational Hitting	M	S	C	Yes	No	A	B	C
Defensive Tactical Skills								
Infield Defensive Responsibilities	M	S	C	Yes	No	A	B	C
Outfield Defensive Responsibilities	M	S	C	Yes	No	A	B	C
Defensive Coverage on Hits to the Infield	M	S	C	Yes	No	A	B	C
Defensive Coverage on Hits to the Outfield	M	S	C	Yes	No	A	B	C
Defending the Bunt	M	S	C	Yes	No	A	B	C
Pickoffs	M	S	C	Yes	No	A	B	C
Rundowns	M	S	C	Yes	No	A	B	C
Defending the First-and-Third Play	M	S	C	Yes	No	A	B	C
Physical Training Skills								
Strength	M	S	C	Yes	No	A	B	C
Speed	M	S	C	Yes	No	A	B	C
Power	M	S	C	Yes	No	A	B	C
Endurance	M	S	C	Yes	No	A	B	C
Flexibility	M	S	C	Yes	No	A	B	C
Quickness	M	S	C	Yes	No	A	B	C
Balance	M	S	C	Yes	No	A	B	C
Agility	M	S	C	Yes	No	A	B	C
Other	M	S	C	Yes	No	A	B	C
Mental Skills								
Emotional control—anxiety	M	S	C	Yes	No	A	B	C
Emotional control—anger	M	S	C	Yes	No	A	B	C
Self-confidence	M	S	C	Yes	No	A	B	C
Motivation to achieve	M	S	C	Yes	No	A	B	C
Ability to concentrate	M	S	C	Yes	No	A	B	C
Other	M	S	C	Yes	No	A	B	C

STEP 1	STEP 4							
	Teaching Priorities			Readiness to Learn		Priority Rating		
Skills Identified	Must	Should	Could	Yes	No	A	B	C
Communication Skills								
Sends positive messages	M	S	C	Yes	No	A	B	C
Sends accurate messages	M	S	C	Yes	No	A	B	C
Listens to messages	M	S	C	Yes	No	A	B	C
Understands messages	M	S	C	Yes	No	A	B	C
Receives constructive criticism	M	S	C	Yes	No	A	B	C
Receives praise and recognition	M	S	C	Yes	No	A	B	C
Credibility with teammates	M	S	C	Yes	No	A	B	C
Credibility with coaches	M	S	C	Yes	No	A	B	C
Character Skills								
Trustworthiness	M	S	C	Yes	No	A	B	C
Respect	M	S	C	Yes	No	A	B	C
Responsibility	M	S	C	Yes	No	A	B	C
Fairness	M	S	C	Yes	No	A	B	C
Caring	M	S	C	Yes	No	A	B	C
Citizenship	M	S	C	Yes	No	A	B	C

From ASEP, 2009, *Coaching softball technical and tactical skills,* (Champaign, IL: Human Kinetics). Adapted, by permission, from R. Martens, 2004, *Successful coaching*, 3rd ed. (Champaign, IL: Human Kinetics), 250–251.

and have fly balls and ground balls hit to them. Players would then throw to third base and home. This test gives you a picture of a player's arm strength and ability to read balls in the air. Finally, you could put all players at the shortstop position to field ground balls and throw to first, providing you with an indication of the players' footwork. Later, players with stronger arms could try out for specific positions like catcher or center field. Completing a form such as "Throwing Technical Skill Evaluation" on page 16 would give you a good idea of a player's throwing skills and potential ability. Armed with this knowledge, you could then reevaluate the skills identified in step 1 to ensure that they are the appropriate skills for the team.

Step 3: Analyze Your Situation

You also need to analyze your situation in preparing for a season. Before embarking on grandiose schemes like buying new uniforms or traveling great distances to play games, you need to consider the amount of help that you will get from the community, including parents and school and civic officials. You must be aware of budgetary concerns and have clear goals regarding fund-raising if any is needed. Practice facility availability is also a concern. A program self-evaluation form, as shown in figure 7.2, can help you with this process.

Figure 7.2　Evaluating Your Team Situation

How many practices will you have over the entire season, and how long can practices be?

How many contests will you have over the entire season?

What special events (team meetings, parent orientation sessions, banquets, tournaments) will you have and when?

How many athletes will you be coaching? How many assistants will you have? What is the ratio of athletes to coaches?

What facilities will be available for practice?

What equipment will be available for practice?

How much money do you have for travel and other expenses?

What instructional resources (videos, books, charts, CDs) will you need?

What other support personnel will be available?

What other factors may affect your instructional plan?

From ASEP, 2009, *Coaching softball technical and tactical skills,* (Champaign, IL: Human Kinetics). Reprinted, by permission, from R. Martens, 2004, *Successful coaching,* 3rd ed. (Champaign, IL: Human Kinetics), 247–248.

You must remember to consider many factors other than technical and tactical skills before planning for a season. Note that as the season progresses time available for practice diminishes. Be sure to teach all the basics early.

During the first 2 weeks of the season, practice is held six times a week, but during the following 8 to 10 weeks, only 3 days are open for training, subject to rainouts or rescheduling. Moreover, on any given practice day, key players may be absent for school-related reasons or fatigued and in need of rest. Any of these factors could necessitate a change of plans.

Step 4: Establish Priorities

You must institute a set of priorities before a season. Given the limited practice time available to most high school teams, you cannot do everything possible within the game of softball. You should also consider the abilities of the athletes before establishing priorities. Refer to figure 7.1, paying special attention to the column under "Step 4." Here you examine the list of essential skills and evaluate them to establish practice priorities for the season. First, you must give each skill a priority according to its importance. Ask yourself, "Is this a skill that I 'must,' 'should' or 'could' teach?" You should then ask, "Are my athletes ready to learn this skill?" The results from step 2 may help you with this phase. Finally, based on those two factors—the teaching priority and the athlete's readiness to learn—you can give each skill a priority rating in column 4. The A-rated skills would be those that you believe are essential to teach, so you should cover them early and often. Likewise, you should teach as many B-rated skills as possible. Finally, depending on the ability and rate of progression of the players, you could teach C-rated skills.

Although most of the skills have been tabbed as must-teach skills, circumstances may arise that make teaching some skills impractical at various times during the season. For example, you might feel that teaching the first-and-third play to your offensive unit is essential and that teaching your defense to defend against the double steal is vital as well. But the team may not be ready or able to learn the complicated assignments necessary to mastering these tactical skills. Players may have difficulty reading the play and picking up on the cues to execute the play properly. Some may be easily distracted or have trouble acquiring the necessary knowledge. Players at key positions may lack the physical ability to be effective. In this case, you might come up with a conservative approach to these two tactical skills and delay teaching complicated responses.

Step 5: Select Methods for Teaching

Next, you should choose the methods that you want to use in daily practices to teach the skills that you have decided are necessary. Take care in implementing this important step. The traditional approach to practice involves using daily drills to teach skills, interspersed with batting practice and infield practice. This approach emphasizes technical skill development, the thinking being that the more a player drills the little skills, the better she becomes at performing them in games.

This traditional method might cover the techniques of softball adequately and even approximate most of the tactical situations that a team will face during games, but it does have several glaring shortcomings. First, traditional practice sessions overemphasize techniques at the expense of tactics. Second, too much direct instruction occurs. Typically, a coach would explain a skill, show how to perform it and then set up situations in which players could learn the skill.

Recent educational research has shown, however, that students who learn a skill in one setting, say the library, have difficulty performing it in another setting, like the classroom. Compare this finding to the common belief among coaches that young players today don't have softball sense, the basic knowledge of the game that players used to have. For years, coaches have been bemoaning the fact that players don't react as well to game situations as they used to, blaming everything from video games to the increasing popularity of other sports. But external forces may not be entirely to blame for the decline in softball logic. Bookstores offer dozens of drill books to help coaches teach the technical skills of softball, and teams around the country practice those drills ad infinitum. If drills are so specific, numerous and clever, why aren't players developing that elusive softball sense? Perhaps just learning techniques and performing drill after drill creates not expertise, but only the ability to do drills.

An alternative way to teach softball skills is the games approach. As outlined in chapter 1, the games approach allows players to take responsibility for learning skills. A good analogy is to compare the games approach in sports to the holistic method of teaching writing. Traditional approaches to teaching students to write included doing sentence-writing exercises, identifying parts of speech and working with different types of paragraphs. After drilling students in these techniques, teachers assigned topics to write about. Teachers used this method of teaching for years. When graduating students could not write a competent essay or work application, educators began questioning the method and began to use a new approach, the holistic method. In the holistic method of teaching writing, students wrote compositions without learning parts of speech or sentence types or even ways to organize paragraphs. Teachers looked at the whole piece of writing and made suggestions for improvement from there, not worrying about spelling, grammar or punctuation unless it was germane. This method emphasized seeing the forest instead of the trees.

This forest versus trees approach is applicable to teaching softball skills as well. Instead of breaking down skills into their component parts and then having the athletes put the pieces back together, you can impart the whole skill and then let the athletes discover how the parts relate. This method resembles what actually occurs in a game, and learning occurs at game speed. These latter two concepts are crucial to understanding the games approach.

This method does not take you out of the equation; in fact, you must take a more active and creative role. You must shape the play of the athletes to get the desired results, focus the attention of the athletes on the important techniques and enhance the skill involved by attaching various challenges to the games played.

You can use the games approach to teach almost any area of the game. Instead of having pitchers and catchers throw to each other and simply chart their progress, you can create games around the pitchers' bullpen work and encourage competition. Instead of just holding an infield workout during a practice session, you can make the workout more gamelike by shaping, focusing and enhancing. Working on a double play, for example, might be more real if base runners were involved or if fielders were timed with a stopwatch each time. If infielders cannot complete the double play in 2.9 seconds or less, you will have to work on the infielders' positioning and quickness to ensure that they are capable of actually turning two.

Step 6: Plan Practices

At this stage of the planning process, you should sketch a brief overview of what you want to accomplish during each practice for the season. Using the information compiled in the previous five steps, you can sketch an outline for an entire season, both practices and games, which can be called the season plan. Figure 7.3 shows a sample season plan for the games approach, using a 12-week season plan that includes a 2-week period for postseason tournaments.

Figure 7.3 Games Approach Season Plan

		Purpose	**Skills**
WEEK 1 – (PRESEASON)	**Practice 1**	Introduce and review defensive technical skills.	Throwing, Infield Throws, Fielding Balls on the Forehand or Backhand Side, Fielding Ground Balls in the Infield, Fielding Ground Balls in the Outfield, Catching a Throw, Catching Fly Balls
	Practice 2	Continue review of defensive technical skills further; introduce and review hitting; introduce tactics of team defensive situations.	Pitching, Catching, Playing First Base, Playing Second Base, Playing Third Base, Playing Shortstop, Hitting
	Practice 3	Introduce the technical and tactical aspects of bunting (offense and defense).	Sacrifice Bunt, Slap Hit and Hard Bunt, Squeeze Bunt, Running Slap, Playing the Short Game, Protecting a Runner on a Steal
	Practice 4	Introduce aggressive baserunning in offensive and defensive situations.	Baserunning, Aggressive Baserunning, Hitting, Playing the Short Game
	Practice 5	Review the technical aspects of hitting with focus on the upper body.	Hitting
	Practice 6	Introduce the tactics of mixing pitches; review hitting and fielding basics; review decision making in the outfield; introduce pickoffs and the first-and-third situation.	Pitching, Hitting, Fielding Balls on the Forehand or Backhand Side, Fielding Ground Balls in the Infield, Fielding Ground Balls in the Outfield, Catching a Throw, Catching Fly Balls, Aggressive Baserunning, Pickoffs, First-and-Third Situation, Defending the First-and-Third Play
WEEK 2 – (PRESEASON)	**Practice 7**	Introduce situational hitting, slapper defense, and rundowns.	Situational Hitting, Slap Hit and Hard Bunt, Running Slap, Rundowns
	Practice 8	Focus on tactical skills related to stealing second; introduce team cohesiveness and mental and emotional toughness.	Playing Second Base, Stealing a Base, Protecting the Runner on a Steal, Infield Defensive Responsibilities, Defensive Coverage on Hits to the Infield
	Practice 9	Focus on tactical skills to prepare players for game day.	Playing the Short Game, Stealing a Base, Protecting the Runner on a Steal, First-and-Third Situation, Aggressive Baserunning, Approaching Home, Hit and Run, Situational Hitting, Infield Defensive Responsibilities, Outfield Defensive Responsibilities, Defensive Coverage on Hits to the Infield, Defensive Coverage on Hits to the Outfield, Defending the Bunt, Pickoffs, Rundowns, Defending the First-and-Third Play
	Practice 10	Focus on running tactics.	Playing the Short Game, Stealing a Base, Protecting the Runner on a Steal, First-and-Third Situation, Aggressive Baserunning, Approaching Home, Hit and Run
	Practice 11	Build pitchers' tactical awareness and strategy.	Pitching, Defending the Bunt, Pickoffs, Rundowns, Defending the First-and-Third Play
	Practice 12	Prepare for game day.	Review of skills identified in the game plan

(continued)

Figure 7.3 *(continued)*

		Purpose	Skills
WEEK 3 – (IN SEASON)	**[Game 1]**		
	Practice 13	Review bunts.	Sacrifice Bunt, Slap Hit and Hard Bunt, Squeeze Bunt, Running Slap
	[Game 2]		
	Practice 14	Review steals.	Stealing a Base, Protecting the Runner on a Steal
	[Game 3]		
	Practice 15	Review slides.	Bent-Leg Slid, Pop-Up Slide, Headfirst Slide
WEEK 4 – (IN SEASON)	**[Game 4]**		
	Practice 16	Review pitch selection and tactics.	Pitching
	[Game 5]		
	Practice 17	Review baserunning strategy.	Baserunning, Aggressive Baserunning
	[Game 6]		
	Practice 18	Review skills as necessary.	
WEEK 5 – (IN SEASON)	**[Game 7]**		
	Practice 19	Review options at third.	Playing Third Base, First-and-Third Situation, Approaching Home, Defending the First-and-Third Play
	[Game 8]		
	Practice 20	Review skills as necessary.	
	[Game 9]		
	Practice 21	Review skills as necessary.	
WEEK 6 – (IN SEASON)	**[Game 10]**		
	Practice 22	Review skills as necessary.	
	[Game 11]		
	Practice 23	Review skills as necessary.	
	[Game 12]		
	Practice 24	Review skills as necessary.	
WEEK 7 – (IN SEASON)	**[Game 13]**		
	Practice 25	Review skills as necessary.	
	[Game 14]		
	Practice 26	Review skills as necessary.	
	[Game 15]		
	Practice 27	Review skills as necessary.	

		Purpose	Skills
WEEK 8 – (IN SEASON)	**[Game 16]**		
	Practice 28	Review skills as necessary.	
	[Game 17]		
	Practice 29	Review skills as necessary.	
	[Game 18]		
	Practice 30	Review skills as necessary.	
WEEK 9 – (IN SEASON)	**[Game 19]**		
	Practice 31	Review skills as necessary.	
	[Game 20]		
	Practice 32	Review skills as necessary.	
	[Game 21]		
	Practice 33	Review skills as necessary.	
WEEK 10 – (IN SEASON)	**[Game 22]**		
	Practice 34	Review skills as necessary.	
	[Game 23]		
	Practice 35	Review skills as necessary.	
	[Game 24]		
	Practice 36	Review skills as necessary.	
	[Playoffs]		

For a sample traditional approach season plan, please refer to the *Coaching Softball Technical and Tactical Skills* online course.

This plan presumes that the first 2 weeks of the season will be devoted primarily to practice, with games beginning in the 3rd week. The early practices are more detailed and complete. After games begin, practice plans become more open ended so that you can focus on problems that may have occurred in past games and can develop practices according to the game plan (see chapter 9).

The game plan should include a review of the previous game, scouting reports and the team's overall strategy. Approaching practices in this manner helps you fine-tune practices to prepare for upcoming games. The main objective of practices at this point in the season is to focus on the game plan, but when time permits, you should revisit key skills so that the learning process continues all season long.

Although the plan in figure 7.3 is shown in isolation, you should employ both approaches when planning. You may feel more comfortable teaching bunting with the traditional approach but find that the games approach works better for you when teaching the first-and-third double-steal play. Remember to work through the six steps yourself to create a season plan best suited for your team.

After completing the season plan, you can further refine step 6 of the process by adding specifics to your individual workouts. The next chapter helps you in this procedure by showing the components of a good practice session and providing a sample of the games approach to practices.

chapter 8

Practice Plans

To get the most out of your practice sessions, you must plan each practice. Completing the season plan, as described in the last chapter, helps you do this. But you have to take that season plan a step further and specify what you will be covering at every practice.

As described in *Successful Coaching, Third Edition*, every practice plan should include the following:

o Date, time of practice and length of practice session
o Objective of the practice
o Equipment needed
o Warm-up
o Practice of previously taught skills
o Teaching and practicing new skills
o Cool-down
o Coaches' comments
o Evaluation of practice

The following games approach practice plans were developed based on the season plan from chapter 7 (as shown in figure 7.3 on page 211). Early practices focus on softball as a whole, including essential tactical skills. Then, as players need to refine technical skills, those skills are brought into the practices. When athletes' play is focused on games early in the season, they quickly discover their weaknesses and become more motivated to improve their skills so that they can perform better in game situations. For a sample traditional approach practice plan, please refer to the *Coaching Softball Technical and Tactical Skills* online course.

PRACTICE 1

Date:

Monday, March 13

Practice Start Time:

3:20 p.m.

Length of Practice:

2 hours, 40 minutes

Practice Objectives:

- Begin team conditioning.
- Players demonstrate basic throwing and catching techniques.
- Players demonstrate proper running form in running through first base.
- Begin to evaluate players for the varsity squad.

Time	Name of Activity	Description	Key Teaching Points	Related Skills
3:20–3:30	Prepractice meeting and team building	Review practice outline; make announcements; motivate players	• Hustle • Teamwork	
3:30–3:50	Warm-up	Warm up using dynamic movements and stretching for flexibility	• Full range of motion • Slow movements • Good form	
3:50–4:00	Conditioning	1-mile timed run	• Proper running form	• Baserunning, page 42
4:00–4:01	Water break			
4:01–4:20	Throwing and catching	Throwing progression through four stages: (1) proper arm action, (2) wrist snap, (3) leg drive and (4) footwork; centering when catching the ball	• Proper throwing form • 12 o'clock–6 o'clock rotation	• Throwing, page 56 • Catching a Throw, page 84
4:20–4:45	Everyday Drills for Catchers	Catcher Partner Drill as outlined in "Everyday Drills for Catchers"	• Quick hands • Receiving stance • Shifting in receiving stance • Framing • Blocking	• Catching, page 96
4:20–4:45	Everyday Drills for Pitchers	Pitcher Isolation Drill as outlined in "Everyday Drills for Pitchers"	• Spins, wrist • Balance • Arm motion • Linear and rotational moves	• Pitching, page 91

Time	Name of Activity	Description	Key Teaching Points	Related Skills
4:20–4:45	Everyday Drills for Infielders	Infielder Partner Drill as outlined in "Everyday Drills for Infielders"	• Fielding position • Watching the ball into the glove • Short hops (front, forehand and backhand) • Proper footwork	• Infield Throws, page 61 • Fielding Balls on the Forehand or Backhand Side, page 67 • Fielding Ground Balls in the Infield, page 72 • Infield Defensive Responsibilities, page 170
4:20–4:45	Everyday Drills for Outfielders	Outfielder Partner Drill as outlined in "Everyday Drills for Outfielders"	• Drop step and crossover • Catching above eye level • Blocking ground balls	• Throwing, page 56 • Fielding Balls on the Forehand or Backhand Side, page 67 • Fielding Ground Balls in the Outfield, page 78 • Outfield Defensive Responsibilities, page 176
4:45–4:46	Water break			
4:46–5:00	Baserunning	Gamelike drill to practice baserunning situations, such as running through first and rounding first	• Running form • Proper form for singles and doubles	• Baserunning, page 42 • Aggressive Baserunning, page 149
5:02–5:12	Cool-down	20-yard sprints out of batter's box, stretch main muscle groups	• Complete stretches	
5:12–5:20	Coaches' comments	End-of-practice comments; reminders	• General comments • Positive points • Motivate for next practice	
5:15–5:25	Team breathing and visualization exercises	Begin teaching breathing for relaxation; players lie on their backs	• Focus on inhaling • Work from feet up to head	
5:25–6:00	Coaches' meeting	Meet in coaches' office	• Assess the day's practice • Discuss next practice	

Date:

Tuesday, March 14

Practice Start Time:

3:20 p.m.

Length of Practice:

2 hours, 15 minutes

Objectives

- Continue conditioning.
- Continue training proper arm action in throwing.
- Players become more proficient in basic technical infield, catching, outfield and pitching skills.
- Through challenge games, players begin to understand and react appropriately to tactical defensive situations.
- Players learn proper defensive positioning in specific offensive situations listed in the playbook.

Time	Name of Activity	Description	Key Teaching Points	Related Skills
3:30–3:33	Prepractice meeting and team building	Review practice outline; make announcements; motivate players	• Hustle • Teamwork	
3:33–3:45	Warm-up	Warm up using dynamic movements and stretching for flexibility	• Full range of motion • Slow movements • Good form	
3:45–3:54	Conditioning	1-mile timed run	• Driving arms • Beating previous time	• Baserunning, page 42
3:54–3:55	Water break			
3:55–4:10	Throwing and catching	Throwing progression through four stages: (1) proper arm action, (2) wrist snap, (3) leg drive, and (4) footwork; centering when catching the ball	• Proper throwing form • 12 o'clock–6 o'clock rotation	• Throwing, page 56 • Catching a Throw, page 84
4:10–4:30	Everyday Drills for Catchers	Catcher Partner Drills as outlined in "Everyday Drills for Catchers"; catchers work in partners to develop framing, receiving and throwing skills	• Quick feet • Receiving stance and framing	• Catching, page 96
4:10–4:30	Everyday Drills for Pitchers	Pitcher's Challenge Drill as outlined in "Everyday Drills for Pitchers"; pitchers work together to focus on zones	• Work zones from close range • Arm motion and snap	• Pitching, page 91
4:10–4:30	Everyday Drills for Infielders	Infielder Partner Drill as outlined in "Everyday Drills for Infielders"; infielders work in partners or groups of three to develop fielding skills	• Short hops • Flip throws • Forehand and backhand into throwing position • Push through	• Infield Throws, page 61 • Fielding Balls on the Forehand or Backhand Side, page 67 • Fielding Ground Balls in the Infield, page 72 • Infield Defensive Responsibilities, page 170

Time	Name of Activity	Description	Key Teaching Points	Related Skills
4:10–4:30	Everyday Drills for Outfielders	Outfielder Line Drills with live bat or toss as outlined in "Everyday Drills for Outfielders"; outfielders work on drop step, crossover and blocking ground balls	• Think "First three steps hard and fast" on every ball • Direct route to the ball	• Throwing, page 56 • Fielding Balls on the Forehand or Backhand Side, page 67 • Fielding Ground Balls in the Outfield, page 78 • Outfield Defensive Responsibilities, page 173
4:30–5:00	Batting practice	Coaches throw or pitch; players move through five stations—tees, soft toss, swing trainer or Speed Stik, on deck and live	• Balance and weight shift • Hitting fundamentals • Evaluate swings	• Hitting, page 22
4:30–5:00	Battery practice	Pitchers, paired with catchers, rotate out of bullpen to throw 20 pitches to catcher; coach charts pitches, sets up situations	• Form • At 50% speed • Work inside, outside, up and down	• Pitching, page 91 • Catching, page 96
5:00–5:15	Defensive situations	Gamelike drill to practice defensive situations	• Emphasize fielding priorities • Every base gets covered • Every player moves on every play	• Aggressive Baserunning, page 149 • Infield Defensive Responsibilities, page 170 • Outfield Defensive Responsibilities, page 176 • Defensive Coverage Situations, page 173 • Coverage Responsibilities on Hits to the Outfield, page 179
5:15–5:20	Cool-down	Sprints from first to third for time; pitchers run foul lines	• Running form on sprints • Emphasize watching third-base coach • Tight turn at second	• Aggressive Baserunning, page 42
5:20–5:25	Coaches' comments	End-of-practice comments; reminders	• General comments • Positive points • Motivate for next practice	
5:25–5:30	Team breathing and visualization exercises	Continue breathing exercises from previous practice	• Long, easy breaths • Focus on exhalations	
5:30–5:45	Coaches' meeting	Meet in coaches' office	• Assess the day's practice • Discuss next practice	

PRACTICE 3

Date:

Wednesday, March 15

Practice Start Time:

3:20 p.m.

Practice Length:

2 hours, 20 minutes

Objectives:

- Catchers practice throwing.
- Players learn how to use cutoffs.
- Players learn how to read the bunt and respond to get one sure out.
- Put players in various defensive situations to improve their tactical skills.

Time	Name of Activity	Description	Key Teaching Points	Related Skills
3:25–3:30	Prepractice meeting and team building	Review practice outline; make announcements; motivate players	• Hustle • Teamwork	
3:30–3:40	Warm-up	Warm up using dynamic movements and stretching for flexibility	• Full range of motion • Slow movements • Good form	
3:40–3:50	Conditioning	1-mile timed run	• Proper running form	• Baserunning, page 42
3:50–3:51	Water break			
3:51–4:05	Throwing and catching	Same as previous practices; begin long toss	• Proper arm action and footwork • 12 o'clock–6 o'clock spin	• Throwing, page 56 • Catching a Throw, page 84
4:05–4:25	Everyday Drills for Catchers	Catcher Partner Drill as outlined in "Everyday Drills for Catchers"	• Quick hands • Receiving stance • Shifting in receiving stance • Framing • Blocking	• Catching, page 96
4:05–4:25	Everyday Drills for Pitchers	Pitcher Defensive Drill as outlined in "Everyday Drills for Pitchers"	• Spins and wrist • Balance • Arm motion • Linear and rotational moves	• Pitching, page 91
4:05–4:25	Everyday Drills for Infielders	Infield Defensive Drill as outlined in "Everyday Drills for Infielders"	• Short hops; front, forehand, and backhand • Push through	• Infield Throws, page 61 • Fielding Balls on the Forehand or Backhand Side, page 67 • Fielding Ground Balls in the Infield, page 72 • Infield Defensive Responsibilities, page 170

Time	Name of Activity	Description	Key Teaching Points	Related Skills
4:05–4:25	Everyday Drills for Outfielders	Outfield Defensive Drill as outlined in "Everyday Drills for Outfielders"	• Playing angles on ball off fence • Move through catch to crow hop	• Throwing, page 56 • Fielding Balls on the Forehand or Backhand Side, page 67 • Fielding Ground Balls in the Outfield, page 88 • Outfield Defensive Responsibilities, page 17
4:25–4:26	Water break			
4:26–4:46	Bunting	Gamelike drill to practice bunting situations, in which fielders must charge and react	• Bunting skills • Fielding skills	• Hitting, page 22 • Sacrifice Bunt, page 28 • Slap Hit and Hard Bunt, page 32 • Squeeze Bunt, page 35 • Running Slap, page 37 • Playing the Short Game, page 130 • Defending the Bunt, page 182
4:46–5:15	Offensive situations	Gamelike drill to practice offensive situations	• Batting skills • Short-game skills	• Hitting, page 22 • Sacrifice Bunt, page 28 • Slap Hit and Hard Bunt, page 32 • Squeeze Bunt, page 35 • Running Slap, page 37 • Playing the Short Game, page 130
4:46–5:15	Bullpens	Pitchers throw 40 pitches to catcher; coach charts pitches	• Power-line work • At only 75 to 90% velocity	• Pitching, page 91
5:15–5:25	Cool-down	Cone drill plyometrics; pitchers run foul lines; running downhill	• Lengthening stride in downhill runs	
5:25–5:30	Coaches' comments	End-of-practice comments; reminders	• General comments • Positive points • Motivate for next practice	
5:30–5:35	Team breathing and visualization exercises	Begin bringing in past performance recall	• Emphasize recreating a successful softball moment • Focus on all senses	
5:35–5:45	Coaches' meeting	Meet in coaches' office	• Assess the day's practice • Discuss next practice	

221

PRACTICE 4

Date:

Thursday, March 16

Practice Start Time:

3:20 p.m.

Practice Length:

2 hours, 20 minutes

Objectives:

- Incorporate tactical awareness into running.
- Incorporate tactical awareness into pitching challenges—working corners, throwing high in bunt situations and so on.
- Work on double-play tactics in infield games.
- Catchers react to tactical challenges in games.
- Incorporate defensive positioning tactics with aggressive baserunning.

Time	Name of Activity	Description	Key Teaching Points	Related Skills
3:30–3:35	Prepractice meeting and team building	Review practice outline; make announcements; motivate players	• Hustle • Teamwork	
3:35–3:50	Warm-up	Warm up using dynamic movements and stretching for flexibility; 1-mile timed run	• Slow movements • Good form	• Baserunning, page 42
3:50–4:15	Fielding balls in the outfield	Gamelike drill to practice fielding balls in the outfield, in which runners react to outfielders	• Fielding balls • Proper form when running the bases	• Fielding Balls on the Forehand or Backhand Side, page 67 • Fielding Ground Balls in the Outfield, page 78 • Catching Fly Balls, page 87 • Baserunning, page 42 • Aggressive Baserunning, page 149
4:15–4:17	Water break			
4:17–4:30	Throwing and catching	Throwing progression through four stages: (1) proper arm action, (2) wrist snap, (3) leg drive and (4) footwork; centering when catching the ball	• Proper throwing form • 12 o'clock–6 o'clock rotation	• Throwing, page 56 • Catching a Throw, page 84
4:30–4:40	Everyday Drills for Catchers	Catcher Partner Drills as outlined in "Everyday Drills for Catchers"; practice blocking and throwing	• Quick feet • Blocking • Quick feet to short throws	• Catching, page 96
4:30–4:40	Everyday Drills for Pitchers	Pitcher Isolation Drill as outlined in "Everyday Drills for Pitchers"	• Spins and wrist • Balance • Arm motion • Linear and rotational moves	• Pitching, page 91

Time	Name of Activity	Description	Key Teaching Points	Related Skills
4:30–4:40	Everyday Drills for Infielders	Infielder Partner Drill as outlined in "Everyday Drills for Infielders"; work in groups of three	• Fielding position • Watching the ball into the glove • Short hops (front, forehand and backhand) • Proper footwork	• Infield Throws, page 61 • Fielding Balls on the Forehand or Backhand Side, page 67 • Fielding Ground Balls in the Infield, page 72 • Infield Defensive Responsibilities, page 170
4:30–4:40	Everyday Drills for Outfielders	Outfielder Partner Drill as outlined in "Everyday Drills for Outfielders"; practice catching ground balls and fly balls and throwing to second	• Drop step and crossover • Catching above eye level • Blocking ground balls	• Throwing, page 56 • Fielding Balls on the Forehand or Backhand Side, page 67 • Fielding Ground Balls in the Outfield, page 78 • Outfield Defensive Responsibilities, page 176
4:40–5:05	Offensive and defensive situations	Gamelike drill to practice offensive and defensive situations; batters hit (bunt, swing away and so on) according to game situation, runners react to where ball is hit and fielders make plays on runners	• Aggressive running • Catcher throwing	• Hitting, page 22 • Baserunning, page 42 • Throwing, page 56 • Aggressive Baserunning, page 149 • Situational Hitting, page 162
5:05–5:20	Scrimmage	Divide teams; play two innings with three outs; rotate pitchers after three outs	• Coach evaluates players for later discussion	
5:05–5:20	Bullpens	Pitchers not throwing in scrimmage work on pitches; chart all pitches	• Visual focus on target	• Pitching, page 91
5:20–5:25	Cool-down	Run sprints from first to third and from second to home; coach hits fungoes to start	• Getting good jump when ball is hit	• Aggressive Baserunning, page 149
5:25–5:35	Coaches' comments	End-of-practice comments; reminders	• General comments • Positive points • Motivate for next practice	
5:35–5:40	Team breathing and visualization exercises	Continue teaching relaxation technique	• Focus and recall of past events while breathing • Introduce concept of visualization	
5:40–5:50	Coaches' meeting	Meet in coaches' office	• Assess the day's practice • Review practice plans • Discuss next practice	

PRACTICE 5

Date:

Friday, March 17

Practice Start Time:

3:20 p.m.

Practice Length:

2 hours, 30 minutes

Objectives:

- Players increase tactical abilities at all positions.
- Players work on reading the ball.
- Players execute pickoffs.

Time	Name of Activity	Description	Key Teaching Points	Related Skills
3:30–3:35	Prepractice meeting and team building	Review practice outline; make announcements; motivate players	• Hustle • Teamwork	
3:35–3:55	Warm-up	Warm up using dynamic movements and stretching for flexibility; 1-mile timed run	• Full range of motion • Slow movements • Good form	• Baserunning, page 42
3:55–3:57	Water break			
3:57–4:10	Throwing and catching	Throwing progression through four stages: (1) proper arm action, (2) wrist snap, (3) leg drive, and (4) footwork; centering when catching the ball; practice using long tosses	• Proper throwing form • 12 o'clock–6 o'clock rotation	• Throwing, page 56 • Catching a Throw, page 84
4:10–4:20	Everyday Drills for Catchers	Catcher Partner Drill as outlined in "Everyday Drills for Catchers"; practice reacting to bunts and catching throws from the outfield	• Fielding bunts with throws • Receiving throws from the outfield	• Catching, page 96
4:10–4:20	Everyday Drills for Pitchers	Pitcher Isolation Drill as outlined in "Everyday Drills for Pitchers"; focus on zones	• Spins and wrist • Balance • Arm motion • Linear and rotational moves	• Pitching, page 91
4:10–4:20	Everyday Drills for Infielders	Infielder Partner Drill as outlined in "Everyday Drills for Infielders"; focus on angles and footwork	• Route patterns to ball • Proper footwork for quickest angle	• Infield Throws, page 61 • Fielding Balls on the Forehand or Backhand Side, page 67 • Fielding Ground Balls in the Infield, page 72 • Infield Defensive Responsibilities, page 170

Time	Name of Activity	Description	Key Teaching Points	Related Skills
4:10–4:20	Everyday Drills for Outfielders	Outfielder Partner Drill as outlined in "Everyday Drills for Outfielders"; focus on catching fly balls	• Direct routes and angles • Running on balls of feet • Proper footwork	• Catching Fly Balls, page 87
4:20–4:40	Batting practice	Coaches throw or pitch; players move through five stations—tees, soft toss, swing trainer or Speed Stik, on deck and live	• Balance and weight shift • Hitting fundamentals • Evaluate swings	• Hitting, page 22
4:40-5:15	Situational hitting and short game practice	Coach throws or pitches balls; set up defense and add runners; use signals or have each athlete execute predetermined skills	• Advancing runners • Understanding situational priorities • Evaluating execution under pressure	• Playing the Short Game, page 130 • Situational Hitting, page 162
5:15–5:30	Cool-down	Run sprints from first to third and from second to home; coach hits fungoes to start	• Getting good jump when ball is hit	• Aggressive Baserunning, page 149
5:30–5:40	Coaches' comments	End-of-practice comments; reminders	• General comments • Positive points • Motivate for next practice	
5:40–5:45	Team breathing and visualization exercises	Continue breathing and focusing exercises; remind players to do exercises on their own several times daily	• Visualize for action	
5:45–6:00	Coaches' meeting	Meet in coaches' office	• Assess the day's practice • Discuss next practice	

PRACTICE 6

Date:

Saturday, March 18

Practice Start Time:

3:20 p.m.

Practice Length:

4 hours

Objectives:

- Build on tactical skills at all positions.
- Focus on cutoff executions with infielders and outfielders.
- Work with pitchers on moving the ball around the strike zone.
- Fine-tune sliding techniques.
- Work on first-and-third execution.
- Work on situational hitting and hit and run.

Time	Name of Activity	Description	Key Teaching Points	Related Skills
8:30–8:35	Prepractice meeting and team building	Review practice outline; make announcements; motivate players	• Hustle • Teamwork	
8:35–8:50	Warm-up	Warm up using dynamic movements and stretching for flexibility; 1-mile timed run	• Slow movements • Good form	• Baserunning, page 42
8:50–8:51	Water break			
8:51–9:05	Throwing and catching	Throwing progression through four stages: (1) proper arm action, (2) wrist snap, (3) leg drive, and (4) footwork; centering when catching the ball; practice using long tosses with one hop	• Proper throwing form • 12 o'clock–6 o'clock rotation	• Throwing, page 56 • Catching a Throw, page 84
9:05–9:15	Everyday Drills for Catchers	Catcher Partner Drills as outlined in "Everyday Drill for Catchers"; focus on tag plays at home from the outfield and fielding bunts with throws to first and second	• Form triangle with ball and approaching runner • Center ball between feet to field bunt • Stay low	• Catching, page 96
9:05–9:15	Everyday Drills for Pitchers	Pitcher Isolation Drills as outlined in "Everyday Drills for Pitchers"; focus on proper balance for pitches high in the zone	• Working the high zone • Shifting weight slightly back	• Pitching, page 91
9:05–9:15	Everyday Drills for Infielders	Infielder Partner Drills as outlined in "Everyday Drills for Infielders"; focus on fielding high hops, pop-ups in the infield and throws to first	• Charge high hops • Quick, accurate release to first • Going back on pop-ups	• Infield Throws, page 61 • Fielding Balls on the Forehand or Backhand Side, page 67 • Fielding Ground Balls in the Infield, page 75 • Infield Defensive Responsibilities, page 170

Time	Name of Activity	Description	Key Teaching Points	Related Skills
9:05–9:15	Everyday Drills for Outfielders	Outfielder Partner Drill as outlined in "Everyday Drills for Outfielders"; focus responsibilities based on game situations	• Decision making	• Throwing, page 56 • Fielding Balls on the Forehand or Backhand Side, page 67 • Fielding Ground Balls in the Outfield, page 78 • Outfield Defensive Responsibilities, page 176
9:15–9:45	Batting practice	Coaches throw or pitch; players move through five stations—tees, soft toss, swing trainer or Speed Stik, on deck and live	• Balance and weight shift • Hitting fundamentals • Evaluate swings	• Hitting, page 22
9:15–9:45	Battery practice	Pitchers throw 20 pitches to catcher; emphasize mixing zones; coach charts all pitches	• Getting ball in correct zones	• Pitching, page 91
9:45–10:30	Scrimmage	Divide teams; play two innings with three outs; rotate pitchers after three outs		
10:30–10:40	Bunting and baserunning	Gamelike drill to practice bunting and baserunning; focus on using pickoffs to get outs	• Getting good jump	• Hitting, page 22 • Sacrifice Bunt, page 28 • Slap Hit and Hard Bunt, page 32 • Squeeze Bunt, page 35 • Running Slap, page 37 • Baserunning, page 42 • Aggressive Baserunning, page 149
10:40–10:50	First-and-third situation (offense and defense)	Gamelike drill to practice first-and-third situations; focus on running the bases aggressively and defending the play	• Clear signs from catcher • Communication between fielders • Positioning • Cuts	• First-and-Third Situation, page 145 • Defending the First-and-Third Play, page 195 • Aggressive Baserunning, page 149
10:50–10:55	Cool-down	Four-corner sprints—straight steal at first, delay steal at second, tag and go at third, getting out of the box at home	• Jumps and hustle	• Aggressive Baserunning, page 149
10:55–11:00	Coaches' comments and team building	Coaches comment on practice; discuss rededicating attitudes for next week, remind players to practice breathing at home	• Progress made during the week Point out positives from the day	
11:00–12:30	Coaches' meeting	Meet in coaches' office	• Assess the day's practice • Discuss next practice	

Date:

Monday, March 20

Practice Start Time:

3:20 p.m.

Practice Time:

2 hours, 30 minutes

Objectives:

- Fine-tune tactical skills at all positions.
- Work with catchers and tactical skills for stealing.
- Work on tactical awareness and bunting.
- Continue to work on using the cutoff.

Time	Name of Activity	Description	Key Teaching Points	Related Skills
3:30–3:35	Prepractice meeting and team building	Review practice outline; make announcements; motivate players	• Hustle • Teamwork	
3:35–4:05	Warm-up	Warm up using dynamic movements and stretching for flexibility; 1-mile timed run	• Full range of motion • Slow movements • Proper form	• Baserunning, page 42
4:05-4:15	Throwing and catching	Throwing progression through four stages: (1) proper arm action, (2) wrist snap, (3) leg drive, and (4) footwork; centering when catching the ball	• Proper throwing form • 12 o'clock–6 o'clock rotation	• Throwing, page 56 • Catching a Throw, page 84
4:15–4:17	Water break			
4:17–4:30	Everyday Drills for Catchers	Catcher Partner Drill as outlined in "Everyday Drills for Catchers"; focus on reading signals and defensive positioning	• Accurately read signals • Proper positioning	• Catching, page 96
4:17–4:30	Everyday Drills for Pitchers	Pitcher Isolation Drill as outlined in "Everyday Drills for Pitchers"; focus on high pitches and full distance	• Shifting weight back • Full distance	• Pitching, page 91
4:17–4:30	Everyday Drills for Infielders	Infielder Partner Drill as outlined in "Everyday Drills for Infielders"; work in groups of four with focus on ground balls and quick throws	• Moving to path of ball • Squaring up to the ball • Good feeds at second	• Infield Throws, page 61 • Fielding Balls on the Forehand or Backhand Side, page 67 • Fielding Ground Balls in the Infield, page 72
4:17–4:30	Everyday Drills for Outfielders	Outfielder Partner Drill as outlined in "Everyday Drills for Outfielders"; focus on finding the cutoff	• Throwing to chest and head area of receiver	• Outfield Defensive Responsibilities, page 176

Time	Name of Activity	Description	Key Teaching Points	Related Skills
4:30–4:50	Situational batting practice	Coaches throw or pitch; players move through five stations—tees, soft toss, swing trainer or Speed Stik, on deck and live; make it a game by awarding points for successful execution; coach charts all pitches	• Reacting to the situation created • Swinging in the zone • Looking middle or away	• Hitting, page 22 • Situational Hitting, page 162
4:50–5:10	Defensive situations	Focus on ball between infield and outfield; two fungo hitters (LF and RF); team defense on cutoffs and relays	• Communication between infield and outfield • Hitting cutoff • Outfielder catching low and infielder catching high	• Infield Defensive Responsibilities, page 170 • Outfield Defensive Responsibilities, page 176 • Defensive Coverage Situations, page 173 • Defensive Responsibilities on Hits to the Outfield, page 179
5:10–5:25	Slapper defense	Gamelike drill to practice defense against a slap hitter; fielders take active role by reading the situation and responding	• Bunt defenses • Defending the slap hitter	• Slap Hit and Hard Bunt, page 32 • Running Slap, page 37 • Defending the Bunt, page 182
5:25–5:35	Duel rundowns	Gamelike drill to practice rundowns; focus on no throws after tag	• Communication • Rundowns • Keep switching runners	• Rundowns, page 191
5:35–5:40	Cool-down	First-to-third sprints from 8-foot lead for time; tag up and score from third; use outfielders and fungo hitter, no throws; stretch main muscle groups	• Economy of turn at second • Listening to the coach at third	
5:40–5:45	Coaches' comments	Introduce and define team strengths; reiterate season plans; remind players of relaxation drills; review the concept of team goals and formation of same by practice #9	• Importance of preparing for opponents • Evaluate correlation of team's technical skill and team tactical approach	
5:45–6:00	Coaches' meeting	Meet in coaches' office	• Assess the day's practice • Discuss next practice	

PRACTICE 8

Date:

Tuesday, March 21

Practice Start Time:

3:20 p.m.

Practice Length:

2 hours, 10 minutes

Objectives:

- Increase tactical skills at all positions.
- Continue to practice gamelike situations with situational hitting in BP and create running situations at the same time.
- Emphasize the importance of not playing the opposition but instead concentrating on getting outs.
- Begin preparation of the first game plan.

Time	Name of Activity	Description	Key Teaching Points	Related Skills
3:30–3:32	Prepractice meeting and team building	Review practice outline; make announcements; motivate players	• Hustle • Teamwork	
3:32–3:40	Warm-up	Warm up using dynamic movements and stretching for flexibility	• Full range of motion • Slow movements • Good form	
3:40–3:50	Conditioning	1-mile timed run	• Proper running form	• Baserunning, page 42
3:50–3:51	Water break			
3:51–4:00	Throwing and catching	Four corners—drill to practice throwing using multiple balls	• Proper form • Quick footwork • Focus and concentration	• Throwing, page 56 • Catching a Throw, page 84
4:00–4:10	Everyday Drills for Catchers	Catcher Partner Drill as outlined in "Everyday Drills for Catchers"	• Review blocking • Bunts • Signals • Passed balls with flip toss	• Catching, page 96
4:00–4:10	Everyday Drills for Pitchers	Pitcher Four-Zone Drill as outlined in "Everyday Drills for Pitchers"	• Location and speed in each zone	• Pitching, page 91
4:00–4:10	Everyday Drills for Infielders	Infield Defensive Drill as outlined in "Everyday Drills for Infielders"; focus on challenging plays such as slow rollers, balls in the hole and backhands	• Quick feet • Quick transfer to throw • Proper footwork • Communication	• Infield Throws, page 61 • Fielding Balls on the Forehand or Backhand Side, page 67 • Fielding Ground Balls in the Infield, page 72 • Infield Defensive Responsibilities, page 170

Time	Name of Activity	Description	Key Teaching Points	Related Skills
4:00–4:10	Everyday Drills for Outfielders	Outfield Defensive Drill as outlined in "Everyday Drills for Outfielders"; focus on long runs and long reaches	• Hustle • Proper footwork • First three steps hard and fast • Angles and getting to the ball	• Throwing, page 56 • Fielding Balls on the Forehand or Backhand Side, page 67 • Fielding Ground Balls in the Outfield, page 78 • Outfield Defensive Responsibilities, page 176
4:10-4:15	Throwing	Gamelike drill to practice throwing out a runner; focus on steals to second and sliding into second	• Hard first steps • Good sliding form • Catchers throw to second on steal attempt	• Baserunning, page 42 • Bent-Leg Slide, page 47 • Pop-Up Slide, page 49 • Headfirst Slide, page 51 • Stealing a Base, page 136
4:15–5:00	Playing defense	Gamelike drill to practice playing defense; coach hits various ground balls, line drives, bunts and fly balls to put players in pressure situations	• Team works together to stay positive and confident • Getting outs	• Throwing, page 56 • Fielding Ground Balls in the Infield, page 72 • Fielding Ground Balls in the Outfield, page 78 • Catching a Throw, page 84 • Catching Fly Balls, page 87
5:00–5:20	Battery practice	Pitchers in game setting; runners on base work on getting jumps to second and aggressive running strategies	• Pitchers work on rhythm	• Pitching, page 91
5:20–5:25	Cool-down	Sprints from first to third; stretches	• Looking in to plate after third step	
5:25–5:30	Coaches' comments and team building	Discuss positive aspects of practice, review season and game plans	• Progress made during the week; point out positives from the day	
5:30–5:40	Coaches' meeting	Meet in coach's office	• Assess the day's practice • Discuss next practice • Review season checklist	

Game Coaching

You can plan and practice all day long. But if your team does not perform to the best of its ability during your games, what good has all that planning done for you? Part V help you prepare for game situations.

Chapter 9 teaches you how to prepare long before the first game, including issues such as communication, scouting your opponent and creating your game plan. Chapter 10 teaches you how to be ready to make decisions during and after the game, such as how to deal with removing pitchers, making substitutions and setting a batting order.

After all the preparation that you have done, game day is when it really becomes exciting, especially if you and your team are ready for the challenge.

Preparing for Games

The performance of a softball team on game day reflects its preparation. A well-prepared team will be fundamentally sound, organized and efficient. The team will open the game with a strong attack and handle crucial situations effectively because the players have rehearsed relevant skills. Following are the areas that you should consider when preparing yourself and your team for a game.

Communication

As a coach, you must communicate well at many levels—with players, team captains, coaching staff, school and community officials, parents, game officials and the media. You must be aware of your nonverbal communication because it can be just as powerful as what you say out loud.

Players

When you communicate well, you engage your players in the learning process. When players become partners and have a stake in their own development, you become a facilitator, not merely a teacher. The players' participation in the learning process is the key to the games approach and what makes it such a valuable approach to coaching. Although shaping, focusing and enhancing play is difficult, it is ultimately more rewarding because it allows players to take ownership of their development.

TEAM EXPECTATIONS

- Exhibit the positive attitude of a team player. Be a team player. Never do anything that could destroy team morale.
- Conduct yourself with honor, dignity, humility and graciousness. Be humble in victory and gracious in defeat.
- Try to reach your potential consistently and set challenging goals for yourself each day, each week and each month of the season.
- Be on time for team meetings, practices, transportation departures and other team-related activities.
- Be at practice every day.
- Exhibit passion for the game and work hard each day.
- Commit yourself to the idea that we will be the hardest working team in the state.
- Respect fellow players, equipment, the game and yourself by having pride in our school, our team and your appearance.
- Be respectful to umpires, opposing players, coaches, fans and other field personnel at all times.
- Accept adversity and deal with it positively.
- Be able to accept criticism and practice self-discipline.
- Understand that no player is guaranteed playing time. The coaching staff will decide on playing time based on established criteria.
- Understand that everything that the coaching staff does has a purpose—to make the team better!
- Adhere to the school athletic code and all league, district and state policies and procedures.
- Prepare yourself mentally for each game. Focus only on the game or practice after you reach the field.

Before the season starts you should prepare a list of expectations that outlines the policies that you expect players to follow. The term *expectations* is preferable to the term *rules*, which conveys a sense of rigidity. The term *expectations* also communicates to players that they are responsible for living up to them. "Team Expectations" provides a list of basic expectations that you can adjust or expand to fit your own circumstances.

The coaching staff must reinforce expectations daily so that they become second nature to the team. Any breaches of discipline that arise should be handled immediately and evenhandedly. You must treat all players alike, starters no differently than subs. Finally, you should make sure that your list of expectations covers any exigency that may occur in your local situation.

Provide captains with opportunities to speak up during team meetings, because this kind of exchange can help teammates gain confidence in them. Keep captains informed on team issues, but do not put them in the situation where they have to keep secrets from their teammates. Captains are leaders, but they are also teammates. Respect the privacy of all players and do not put the captains in an awkward position.

COACH–CAPTAIN COMMUNICATION

Team captains are a liaison between the coaching staff and team, and you can use them for added support when communicating with the team. In choosing captains, you should select players whom you trust and who have the respect of the other players on the team. Following are a few questions that you can ask of your team to help determine the best players for the job:

- Who on the team works the hardest in practice?
- Who on the team do you think is the most consistent player?
- Who on the team has helped you through a bad day on the field?
- Who on the team do you think has the best attitude?

After choosing captains, you should communicate with them positively and consistently to help them be committed and supportive of your decisions. You can then use your captains to reinforce messages that you wish to send to the other players. Captains are often better able to get a message to their peers than you are as a coach. Regular meetings with your captains will encourage them to open up lines of communication that can be extremely helpful to you. You can use captains to get a read on the mood, motivation or concerns that the team may be experiencing. Coaches view things differently than their players do. Captains are the best way to gauge where a team is and what they are experiencing.

Parents

Before the season begins, you should schedule a preseason meeting with the parents of all team members. A few weeks before the season begins, you should mail a letter or send an e-mail to the homes of players to invite the parents to this meeting (see figure 9.1 on page 238 for a sample invitation). This personal touch will pique the interest of parents and make them feel valuable to the program. A special invitation letter should go to the superintendent, the principal and the athletic director, who should be present to explain school policies, athletic codes and general school issues.

You can prepare a simple agenda for this meeting and follow it to keep the meeting on track and to convey to parents a sense of your organizational ability. Besides setting an agenda, you should prepare and distribute a team manual and, in it, you should provide information on the team's philosophy, goals and season plan and outline the roles and responsibilities of parents, players and coaches (see "Team Roles and Responsibilities" on page 239).

Coaching Staff

Coaches need to communicate well with their assistant coaches and other team personnel. Each season, you should hold a formal preseason meeting with your coaching staff to outline expectations. Discuss your coaching philosophy and specific techniques that you will emphasize, especially if changes have occurred from the previous year or if new members have joined the staff. You should be clear on the roles and responsibilities of each staff member, including how to handle breaches of discipline and how to deal with parents. Additionally, you will want to make sure that all the coaches know what responsibilities they will oversee or

Figure 9.1   Sample Preseason Meeting Invitation

Date:_____

TO: Parents of Prospective Players

RE: Preseason Meeting

The coaching staff cordially invites you to be our guest at a preseason orientation meeting that will be

held on _____, 20_____ at _____.
　　　　　　　　　　　　　date　　　　　　　　　　　　　　　　　　　　　　　location and time

This informal meeting will give us an opportunity to share common concerns—our expectations for your daughter, what you may expect from us during the upcoming season and what we expect from you.

Please let me know if you will be able to attend by completing the bottom portion of this letter and returning it to school with your daughter. We look forward to meeting with you and promise to keep the meeting brief.

Sincerely,

_____

Name

_____

Title

✂ -

Parent's or guardian's name: _____

Athlete's name: _____

　　❑ Yes, I am planning to attend the preseason meeting

　　❑ No, I cannot attend the preseason meeting

Comments: _____

_____

_____

TEAM ROLES AND RESPONSIBILITIES

Coach's Roles

- To teach, encourage and motivate
- To be patient and enthusiastic
- To be positive, fair and consistent with players
- To set a good example for players and fans
- To use care in making all player-related decisions
- To conduct daily organized practice sessions in a safe environment
- To establish and keep channels of communication open with players and parents
- To make sure that players know expectations, procedures, policies and other requirements
- To provide updated game schedules throughout the season
- To help athletes set goals for themselves and the team

Parent's Roles

- To be positive and to support all team members
- To respect the decisions of the officials and coaches
- To respect the opponent's fans, coaches and players
- To contact the coach through agreed-upon athletic department procedures at the appropriate time and place—not on game day
- To understand that the coaching staff is concerned with making all players not only better athletes but also better people, a concern that may take precedence over winning
- To not criticize a coach or team member with destructive comments during a game

Player's Roles

- To exhibit good character both on and off the field, which includes being positive, having a good attitude, being respectful, being open to discipline, being honest, displaying good sporting behavior and being resilient
- To work and play hard
- To be a team player by understanding your role on the team
- To challenge yourself daily by going beyond what is expected
- To know and follow team and scholastic expectation
- To communicate with the coaching staff regarding any conflict or misunderstanding of expectations
- To be at practice every day or to notify the coach in advance of any conflicts
- To show pride

contribute to on the field. Ideally, all coaches will speak with the same terms or language so that the athletes receive a consistent message. The more similar the coaches are in terms of teaching methods, verbiage and mechanics, the more unified the message to the athletes will be.

Game Officials

Umpires are an important part of the game and must be treated as such. How a coach communicates with the umpires can send a huge message to the team. If coaches are disrespectful of umpires, players will think that they can react in the same way. When questioning a ruling, you should approach the official respectfully and attempt to communicate with the umpire face to face in a calm manner rather than yell from the dugout.

Community and Media

Involvement with the community and the media demands that you be a good communicator. You should be accommodating to the press and instruct players on tactics for talking to the media. Players need to understand that the role of the media may come in conflict with the goals and expectations of the team. Players should respectfully answer questions that deal with games, but they should defer questions about philosophy or game management to the coaching staff. Players must also be careful not to say anything derogatory about an opponent that might find its way onto an opponent's locker room bulletin board.

Scouting an Opponent

An essential step in preparing for games is to scout the opponent thoroughly and gain information about the opponent to eliminate the element of surprise from the game equation. Good scouting can help you with your practice plan in the days or week before a game and can make practices more engaging if you make players aware of the reasons why certain plays might be successful against an upcoming opponent.

Preparing to Scout

Scouting is less prevalent in high school softball than it is in some other sports, and coaches are often unable to scout all opponents because of scheduling conflicts and time constraints. Unlike teams in sports that play only one or two games a week, softball teams often play at least three games per week, making it difficult for a small coaching staff to do it all.

You can transform the liability of a small staff into an asset if you are willing to use parents or other volunteers as scouts. This approach helps make parents feel as though they are part of the team, perhaps enhancing the coach–parent relationship.

If scouting a team beforehand is not possible, a comprehensive record of the opponent's last contest can be extremely helpful. Alternatively, you can prepare much earlier and try to scout players who play in local summer leagues. Another effective approach is to watch an opponent during their pregame warm-up and observe their tendencies.

Scouting Report

Useful scouting includes information about the upcoming opponent such as the following: Are they aggressive on the bases? Do they like to bunt or steal? Do they like to get ahead with breaking pitches or fastballs? Does the opponent use any trick plays? You can use a scouting form to help you gather this kind of information.

Following is a list of important information that you should know about an upcoming opponent.

Defense

- What are the pitcher's strengths (What pitches does she throw? What is her best pitch? Does she throw a change-up?)
- Pitcher's weakness (Does she give up runs early? Does she tire late in the game?)
- What is the catcher's arm strength?
- How does the team defend against the short game, sacrifice, slap, squeeze and so on?
- How does the team defend the first-and-third situation?
- Which defensive players have the strongest arms?
- Does the team have any defensive weakness that can be exploited?

Offense

- Who is their fastest player? Which player has the most steals?
- Who has the most home runs?
- Who has the most RBIs?
- Who has the most strikeouts?
- Who walks the most?
- Does the team use the slap or push bunt?
- How many lefty slappers are in the lineup?
- In what innings do they score most of their runs?
- Do they like to run any trick offensive plays?

Developing a Game Plan

Although the methods that you use to scout your opponent, as we learned previously, are important, how you relate the information to your team is even more critical. Thus, after completing and analyzing the scouting report, the coaching staff must begin the process of developing a game plan for the opponent. The game plan, simply put, identifies the particular strategies that you have chosen to give your team the best chance for success against the schemes that the opponent uses. You formulate a game plan by carefully considering the scouting report, your overall strategy and your team's offensive and defensive capabilities. Your game plan should be specific to the opponent that you are playing and should be based on the overall strategy that you have established for the season.

The game plan should be clear and simple. It is often just a one-page listing of three or four plays for the offense, one to four important defensive tactics and any special situations that are apt to arise in the game and how you will play them.

At practice the day before the game, you should simulate your opponent's offense and defense in gamelike situations so that your team knows your game plan.

Besides developing the game plan, coaches also need to set up a practice plan for the days leading up to the game, based on the scouting report from the opponent and the team's mental and physical state. Practices may be set up to focus on different parts of the game, or they may be set up to have varying degrees of difficulty. Light, medium and hard workouts can be combined to peak your team at different times during the season. Drills that focus on technical skills need to be combined with drills or situations that focus on the game plan or tactical skills.

Controlling a Team's Performance

In preparing a game plan, you need to remind players that they can manage only their own play and that they have no control over the officials, the fans and the way that the other team plays. But as the coach, you can control some things in the performance arena, particularly the game routine. Established routines, such as pregame meetings and warm-ups, help players relax before competition.

Pregame Meeting

The pregame meeting, which should take place before the warm-up to embed the players' focus for the day, should emphasize the points worked on in practice and meaningful items from the scouting report. You need to tell players beforehand the uniform of the day and when they need to arrive at the field.

Also, for home games, you should address postgame and pregame field preparation responsibilities. Because most teams do not have grounds crews to do the work for them, items such as who puts in the bases, who lines the field and who rakes before and after the game should be spelled out, using a simple field maintenance checklist as shown in figure 9.2.

Pregame Warm-Up

The pregame warm-up should do more than just loosen up your players' arms and prepare their muscles for activity. It should touch on all basic plays and techniques that your team might use in a game. Make sure that all players, both starters and reserves, are prepared for the types of balls that will be hit to them and the types of throws that they may need to make during the game. You will not be able to cover everything in a pregame warm-up, but creating a routine is important. You should be sure that players at each position have time to warm up based on their specific needs. A well-organized and structured warm-up will give your athletes a sense of consistency and confidence before the pressures of the game take over.

Team Building and Motivation

Softball is a team game. A malfunction by any part of the whole can destroy the rhythm of the entire team. You should therefore spend quality time each day motivating players to behave as a team.

One method is to include some fun elements during practice sessions. For example, after practice on one day of the week, you can conduct a nonsoftball

Figure 9.2   Field Maintenance Checklist

Game: _____   **Date:** _____

Stow and plug bases	_____	_____	_____
Sweep home dugout	_____	_____	_____
Sweep visitor dugout	_____	_____	_____
Empty trash	_____	_____	_____
Put equipment in storage closet	_____	_____	_____
Rake mound	_____	_____	_____
Tamp mound	_____	_____	_____
Rake bullpens	_____	_____	_____
Rake batter's box	_____	_____	_____
Police warning track	_____	_____	_____
Rake first-base line	_____	_____	_____
Rake third-base line	_____	_____	_____
Line field	_____	_____	_____

From ASEP, 2009, *Coaching softball technical and tactical skills* (Champaign, IL: Human Kinetics).

activity such as going to a movie or out to dinner as a team. You can make practices fun by incorporating games to stimulate players, or you can allow players to plan activities for a parents' day. You may want to think about pairing returning players with new players during the first week of practice; this approach will help the rookies learn the drills and routine more easily and help them gain confidence. Instilling a sense of pride in the players and making them feel a part of the process give them self-esteem. Rewarding the whole team every once in a while can be effective, especially after a difficult week of practice. These special activities help build camaraderie. You should also use daily practices to motivate players. Don't wait until the pregame pep talk to do your motivating. Rah-rah talks and "Win one for the Gipper" speeches are rarely effective.

Another area in which you should play a direct role is setting individual and team goals. Tell players in advance that you expect them to write out their personal and team goals before the end of the first week of practice. To give players a concrete focus for their goals, you should create and distribute a simple fill-in-the-blanks form with space to list individual and team goals. But you cannot expect players to formulate realistic goals without assistance. You should spend a few minutes explaining the characteristics of goals—that they should provide direction, be specific, aim high but be achievable and be measureable. After players submit their goals, you should discuss them individually with the players.

Make it clear that the team is always emphasized above the individual when talking about goals. Individual goals help athletes contribute to team goals and therefore have value. You should never single out individual players as being more important than others to achieving team goals; doing so can lead to animosity and destroy team unity. Every athlete contributes to the team in different ways. Your bench players need to feel valued even if they do not get to contribute on the field as often as others do. Try to develop in team members the belief that they have ownership and that their individual efforts count.

chapter 10

During and After the Game

You, your staff and your players need to know what will happen before, during and after a game. All must know what their individual responsibilities are to ensure your best possible chance for success. Preparation is important for both athletes and coaches, and having a good understanding of what will happen on a game day will help in that preparation. Sit down with your entire staff and discuss the priorities of the areas covered in this chapter. In addition, you may have other areas specific to your program or team that you need to address.

Before the Game

On a game day, the coach needs to be prepared in several areas. These are the starting lineup, the batting order, field inspection and the pregame warm-up.

Lineup

Your first tactical move of the game is to create a lineup. Many factors pertain to this task. You need to consider not only the athletes on your team but also the opposing team and their strengths. Another key to creating a winning lineup is assembling the combination of players on your team who will work best on the field as a unit. The more thought and time you put into the lineup, the easier it will be for your team to support your decision.

In softball we have the luxury of using a DH or DP, depending on the rules that you play under. The lineup will also include the starting nine defensive players and the batting order for the starting players. All other players will serve as substitutes and can have specific roles to fill for the team during the game. Every player should understand her role and how she might be expected to contribute to the team's success.

When you begin creating your lineup, ask yourself the following list of questions:

- Who will be the starting pitcher in this game?
- Who is in relief?
- Who is the best catcher to catch that pitcher?
- Who is the best defensive player at each of the other seven positions?
- Without looking at the defensive players, who are the best nine offensive players?
- Do I focus more on offense or more on defense in this game?
- Will this be a close, low-scoring ball game or a high-scoring game? If the game will be a close, low-scoring game, then focus your lineup on defense to limit your opponent's offense. If it will be a high-scoring game, then focus on an offensive lineup to increase your chances of scoring more runs.
- Depending on the DH or DP rules, who will be able to be in that position?
- If I do not need to use the DH or DP spot offensively, will I need the DH or DP position if the relief pitcher enters the game? If the answer is yes, then you must make a plan based on the substitution rules of your association.

After you have answered the preceding questions you are ready to start making out your lineup and evaluating your substitutes' roles. Use any knowledge that you have about your opponent when finalizing your starting lineup and consider how you can use your subs. As a rule it is best to put your best offensive team in the starting lineup without sacrificing defensive play. Use all the information that you have to put the team on the field that will perform best as a unit and under the pressure of a game.

Batting Order

After finalizing your defensive starters you need to figure how to put them in the batting order that maximizes your scoring opportunities. You can choose from among several strategies. Depending on your team's offensive strengths and weaknesses you will need to formulate a plan and strategy for the lineup card. Evaluating performances in recent games can help you make educated decisions about the lineup. You may want to plug in a few key players in the batting order first rather than go down the list sequentially. For example, you may choose to fill in the number 3 and 4 hitters first because your biggest RBI producers should fill those slots. Listed here are some basics about the batting order that you can use to start making decisions.

- 1st (leadoff)—speed, high on-base percentage, has a good eye and is selective with pitches
- 2nd—bat control and good bunting ability, as well as strengths similar to those of the leadoff hitter; possibly a slapper to advance runners

- 3rd—generally your most consistent hitter, clutch with runners on base, many RBIs
- 4th—also a strong RBI hitter, may be more of a power hitter but not always
- 5th—generally the next highest RBI player and someone who can protect the 4th hitter
- 6th and 7th—strongest hitters remaining among the last four
- 8th—generally the weakest hitter in your lineup
- 9th—good to great speed, good on-base percentage

Field Inspection

Before the game starts, you should inspect the playing area for any problem areas. Players' safety is paramount, and any areas of danger should be addressed with officials before game time. In addition, if you take time to inspect the field you can inform your athletes about specific playing-area issues that may affect the ball or the game. Knowing as much as possible about the playing area helps teams react appropriately during the game.

Field Openings

Most fields are not completely enclosed and have areas that are out of play. All players should know where those openings are so that they know where balls could leave the field of play and result in extra bases for the offense. If you are playing on an unfamiliar field, players should use the time before the game to look for areas of concern. Examples of a few places to observe and point out are dugouts, sidelines or holes in fences.

Outfield

Outfield fences vary in construction type and distance from home plate, so you and your players should learn a few things about the fence at the facility where you are playing. Here are some questions that you should answer:

- What is the distance to the outfield fences down the lines and to center field? This information is important when your team sets up to work a relay from the outfield fence. Your outfielders should always make the longer throw, so your infielders need to know the outfield fence distances to set up correctly. Offensively, you will want to know whether the outfield alleys are extra deep so that your team can consider taking extra bases on balls hit in the gap.
- Can the ball get through any holes in the outfield fence? Outfielders should know where the ball may leave the field of play.
- Is the fence permanent, or is it a breakaway, or safety, fence? Outfielders can use this information to decide how they will approach or play the ball off the fence. A breakaway fence will give way if an athlete crashes into it. For a permanent fence, the outfielders will have to figure out how best to use the fence when trying to catch a ball that is hit just over it.
- How will the ball react when it hits the fence? Some fields have plywood signs or panels that cause the ball to ricochet significantly; others are a loose chain link that will cause the ball to die and fall straight down. Poles or angles on the fence may deflect the ball in unpredictable directions.

- Does the outfield have a sideline fence? A sideline fence can alter how the outfielders back up throws from the infield. Additionally, the type and style of fence can alter the path of fair balls that travel down the fence line, so outfielders should be aware of that issue before the game starts.

- Is a warning track present? If so, how many steps can the athletes take at full speed before they make contact with the fence? The purpose of a warning track is to give the outfielders an indication that they are approaching the fence. Teach your athletes to be aware of changes in the surface. Outfielders should practice approaching the outfield fence at full speed and count the number of steps that they can take before they would run into the fence.

Pitching Area

The pitcher's mound can vary considerably from field to field. Obviously, pitchers cannot change the pitching area, but by examining the mound they may learn what adjustments they need to make during the game. They should check the surface to see whether it is solid and stable. The accuracy of the pitching distance is another often overlooked issue. Large holes or muddy areas can be extremely difficult for a pitcher to deal with. Inspection can help limit those issues.

Batter's Box

Batter's boxes may be worn or overused. Large holes in the right-handed batter's box may affect a runner who is sliding into the plate. Check the dimensions of the batter's box to make sure that your team is not disadvantaged. Although the dimensions will be the same for both teams, a team that is prepared and aware of the field conditions may gain an advantage.

Playing Area

There are many different types of infield dirt. Different infield surfaces will cause the ball to react differently. Some are considered fast, others slow. The surface can affect the signals that you use or how you will play the short game. Defensively, the team must know how the ball will react. For this reason, you should be sure that the infielders get some ground balls on the infield before game time.

Finally, address any safety issues with the officials (watering boxes, sprinkler heads, muddy areas, holes and so on). Also, note whether any obstructions are present overhead. Trees, wires or structures over the field of play might be a factor for your athletes in catching fly balls.

Backstop

Most backstops are made of some kind of fencing or chain link. Some backstops have concrete, wood, brick or block walls as part of the structure as well. Catchers should be aware of these features so that they can predict how the ball will react. On passed balls or overthrows that hit the backstop, the ball may react in different ways. Concrete, block, brick or wood backstops can create a fast rebound that can shoot past the catcher. Other types of backstops may have poles or structures that will cause the ball to ricochet at odd angles. During the warm-up for a game, coaches should have their catchers stand at home plate and throw several types of balls into the backstop so that they will know how to react during the game. Catchers should also know how far or how many steps it is from their position to the backstop. Knowing the distance from her position to the backstop can help the catcher when she is going after a pop fly and is not able to see the backstop.

Pregame Warm-Up

At the beginning of the season you should establish a warm-up routine that you will use before each game. The pregame warm-up will not only get the team warmed up but also create a consistent routine for your players for the entire season. Routines help create confidence in your players. They know what to expect, and they become comfortable with how things happen. Although creating routines is helpful for your players, they should learn not to rely on routines to gain confidence.

Following are types of activities that you should include in your pregame warm-up:

Team Stretching

- Light jogging before beginning a stretching session
- Instruction on proper stretching techniques
- Led by an assistant coach, strength coach or team captains

Offense

- Batting practice for pitchers and catchers (hitting first so that they can begin their pitching warm-up)
- Warm-up dry swings for all players
- Hitting off batting tees, a machine or a live batting-practice pitcher
- Side-toss hitting drills
- A game of pepper to warm up players' hand–eye coordination
- Players throwing balls for practice bunting

Throwing

- Warm-up throwing drills for all players with specific numbers of reps
- Specific throws for position players to warm up all throwing needs before the game (i.e., long throws for outfielders, steal throws for catchers, warm-up tosses and short, quick throws for infielders)

Defense

- Footwork practice and running catches for outfielders
- Fielding technique practice and glove work for infielders
- Fly-ball practice for outfielders
- Ground-ball practice for infielders

During the Game

Coaches can make tactical decisions during a game, but most decisions happen on the field. The games of baseball and softball are similar in that the tactical decisions generally occur in a few areas—defensive alignment, offensive strategy through signals and the pitching approach. Baseball and softball are quite different from sports that use a game clock and flow from offense to defense without changes in personnel. The areas listed earlier are the specific areas where coaches can make some tactical decisions. Much of the game of softball is about reacting to your opponent, so having dynamic tactical influence during actual play is extremely difficult. Coaches must make tactical changes on defense or offense when the ball is dead. When tactical changes need to be made, the best approach is often to call a time-out to make sure that the players are all on the same page. Minor tactical changes such as moving defensive players, calling pitches, shifting outfielders or prioritizing specific runners can happen between pitches without calling a time-out. The ability to adjust and read the game as it develops is a critical application of the tactical triangle, which was detailed earlier in this book on page 5.

The three-step tactical triangle approach to analyzing a game situation creates a blueprint for you and your players to follow in making decisions during a game. While the game is in progress, you must accurately read the cues presented, apply technical and tactical knowledge on the spot, adjust the game plan accordingly and make decisions immediately. The logical format of the triangle helps you slow the speed of the game and apply organized, logical thinking to any situation. The following sections show how to apply the tactical triangle to several key situations that commonly occur during games.

Time-Outs

Coaches need to know several strategies for calling time-outs so that they can use them to their advantage.

To start, coaches need to know the time-out limitations under the game rules. You can clarify this in the pregame meeting with the umpire if you have a question. Coaches are typically allowed a limited number of time-outs per inning or per game. After you know how many time-outs you can use and how often you can call them, you can choose how best to use them—as informative time-outs or as time-outs to break the momentum of the game.

When you call a time-out to relay information to the team, you should be ready to communicate a clear, concise message. Although not every player on the field needs to be involved in a time-out, make sure that the players who need to be in the meeting are present. Some common things to discuss during an informative time-out are the following:

o   The strategy for the upcoming situation

o   The type of pitches that you would like to see thrown

o   Specific trick plays or adjustments to the game plan that you want to make

o   Reminders to players of situations and their choices

Time-outs can also be used to break momentum, refocus energy or calm athletes down. As you view the game from the sidelines, you will note many apparent momentum swings. Encourage players to handle these situations on the field so that they learn to play the game mentally and physically, but be ready to use a time-out to regroup in a pivotal situation.

In these types of meetings, how you communicate is more important than what you communicate. Calm, confident and positive language and body language will go a long way in alleviating the situation. Making eye contact with an athlete helps bring her focus back to the present and can give you an idea of where she is and whether you need to make a change. Keeping the mood light and using humor can often be a good way to redirect negative energy. Sometimes these kinds of time-outs can be used to break an opponent's momentum as well. To keep a situation from getting out of hand, you may choose to stop play. Momentum changes occur many times during a game, and a time-out can be one way to effect a change. Time-outs can also create additional pressure on the opponent. These types of time-outs can be called by field captains or leaders just as easily as by coaches. Ideally, you can teach your leaders to sense these opportunities and call time so that you do not have to burn one of your limited time-outs.

Substitutions

Making substitutions during the game is a major responsibility for the head coach. You need to be thinking constantly about how you can use the players on your bench to win the ball game. When to make changes can be as important as whom to change. For that reason you should have a game plan for your substitutes. When will you pinch hit, pinch run, make defensive changes? Most important, when will you make a pitching change? These questions plague every coach. You can reduce the pressure by preparing before the game. Create a list of situations that may come up during a game and the ideal options to use as you make substitutions.

Handling substitutes is not only about making changes but also about keeping track of the substitutions that you have made. You should create a consistent system to keep track of these changes. Some coaches like to have a lineup card or cheat sheet in their pocket. Others like to use dugout cards to keep the information straight. One of the most frustrating situations for a coach is forgetting or losing track of which subs are eligible to go into the game. Lost opportunities can be exasperating for both coaches and players. Bench players will learn to trust the coach's decisions when consistent utilization of subs occurs.

Basic substitution rules allow the starters to leave the game once and then return to the game once (reentry rule). Bench players, on the other hand, are allowed to enter the game, but after they leave the game they are not eligible to reenter. Here are some key ways to use bench players:

Pinch runners

- Use speedy runners who are faster than a current base runner.
- Use them when they can affect the outcome of the game.
- Be careful about using pinch runners early in the game.
- Be willing to lose that player for any other role for the remainder of the game.

Pinch hitters

- Use pinch hitters when they can affect the outcome of the game.
- Use a hitter's strength against specific types of pitching.
- Get extra at bats for hitters when the game is one sided.
- Pinch hit for starters who have been unsuccessful in the game.

Defensive specialists

- Use players on the bench who can be more consistent or stronger on defense than one of the starters.
- Use these players later in the game when your team is ahead and offensive production is less important.

Relief pitchers

- Designate which pitchers are in relief before the game so that they can prepare.
- Give relief pitchers as much warning as possible before making the switch.

- Make changes when the starter has lost her control or ability to get hitters out.
- Make changes when the defense has been struggling to make plays and the team needs a strikeout.

Game Plan

Coaches have a big responsibility in implementing the offensive game plan. You should establish a game plan before the game using information about your team's ability and the opponent's style of play. You will need to make many adjustments to the game plan during the game. When a good game plan is not working, you might need to make adjustments without completely abandoning the plan. At other times, you may need to implement a completely new strategy. In any case you must communicate with the team about changes to the game plan. Players need to be committed to the plan for it to be effective and successful, and they will feed off your confidence in regard to the game plan. Give the game plan a chance to succeed but do not be afraid to adjust or alter your plan if it is not working.

Offensively, coaches need to be observant of their hitters and be ready to relay information about making adjustments. The time to teach mechanics is not during the game, but the game is the best time to teach the art of making adjustments. Hitting is a game of adjustments, and many players become so concerned with their failures that they do not consider making adjustments. One of the best times for a hitter to learn about what a pitcher does well or does not do well is to watch her teammates' at bats. Hitters need to learn how to gather information from the hitters who go before them.

Coaches can educate hitters about pitchers' tendencies. Hitters can then start making adjustments that will help them succeed. Helping athletes adjust to the pitcher can pay huge dividends. Many failures of a hitter may relate more to how a pitcher is throwing to her than to a flaw in her hitting mechanics. Pitchers tend to use a consistent pitch to get hitters out.

Observing an opponent's defensive weakness during the game can create an opportunity to score later. Be aware of defensive tendencies and figure out how to take advantage of them. Sometimes adjustments need to be made to the game plan based on what the defense or pitchers are giving your team to work with. This cat-and-mouse game is part of what makes softball a fun game to coach.

After the Game

After the last play of the game, the coach's job does not end. Areas to be prepared for after the game include good sporting behavior, the postgame routine, the coaches' meeting and the postgame meeting.

Good Sporting Behavior

Win or lose, coaches need to send the right message to their athletes. You must keep your interaction with the officials, opposing coaches and opposing players courteous even if emotional situations occurred during the game. Learn to let go of issues that happened during the game quickly. Many things are said or done in the heat of competition, and nothing will be gained by overreacting.

During the postgame handshake, when tension is high, rely on common courtesy and keep interaction to a minimum. A simple handshake and saying, "Good job" is sufficient; nothing more needs to be done. In the heat of the moment, further comments can be seen as provocative or patronizing.

The same policy is best with the officials. Even when the officiating was not to the standard that you would have liked, a simple handshake and a thank-you will be the best action to take. Competition can create intense emotions, and coaches need to set the example for athletes and fans.

Postgame Routine

Coaches need to create a consistent postgame routine that the athletes understand. The routine may be different for home games versus away games, but a postgame routine for each situation should be established. A routine after each game will help make life easier for parents, players and coaches. When players know exactly what to expect and when they will have a chance to see parents and friends, confusion and anxiety will be lessened.

The first task is to develop a list of items that need to be accomplished after the game and then prioritize how and when they will be executed. Here is a list of common types of things that need to happen in the postgame routine. Note that some items may not be relevant to all teams.

- Give a postgame cheer for the opposing team. This item will vary greatly with the level of play and the age of the athletes, but at the very least a simple oral acknowledgement or a clap should occur before the postgame handshake.
- Courteously shake hands with the opposing team.
- Take care of officials' and opposing team's needs.
- Pick up equipment.
- Break down the press box and scorer's table.
- Rake out the field, batter's box, pitcher's mound, bullpens and batting cages.
- Clean and sweep the dugouts.
- Ice injuries.
- Do media interviews.

Coaches must be consistent with the expectations of all players. You may decide to allow a designated time after the game when players may visit with fans, friends and parents before they take care of the postgame routine. This approach is generally a good idea because it keeps parents and friends from standing around waiting for players to be released. After this designated time, all players should complete their postgame routine responsibilities. You can assign these responsibilities each game or for the entire year.

During the completion of postgame routine items, players should have some type of cool-down or postgame stretch. This cool-down does not need to be lengthy, but it will help give the athletes time to unwind from the tension of the game.

Coaches' Meeting

Coaches may want to meet with their staff and assistant coaches while players are meeting with family, completing routines or stretching. You can use this meeting to debrief and prioritize the key points that you want to stress during the postgame meeting with your players. Assistant coaches are a great resource, and their view of things can sometimes make a big difference when evaluating game issues. During the game some coaches keep a list of mistakes or key issues that they want to talk about at the end of the game. Writing things down ensures that they will not be forgotten or overlooked.

Postgame Meeting

The postgame meeting, or debriefing, is a great opportunity for the coach to have an effect on players' learning. Postgame talks should remain fairly consistent regardless of the outcome of the game.

Logistically, you can do several things to ensure a good meeting and the attentiveness of the athletes. Make sure to communicate your expectations for these meetings. All athletes should sit so that they can make eye contact with coaches; players should not be using this time to change shoes or ice down, for example. All eyes should be up and not looking at the grass.

When covering topics during the postgame meeting, only one person should speak at a time. You should try to cover all necessary topics, including the following:

- Acknowledge and discuss team mistakes and missed opportunities.
  - Avoid singling out individual players, but talk about specific situations that happened.
  - Use the list that you created during the game.
  - Talk about what should have happened or what needs to happen.
  - Include a constructive comment with every mistake noted so that athletes can learn.
- Acknowledge and discuss positive team play and adjustments made.
  - Note good executions.
  - Mention improvements from previous games.
  - Note effective adjustments that players made to the opposing pitcher.
- Evaluate execution of the game plan.
- Acknowledge contributions by team members, large or small.
- Include a team exercise.
  - Ask for feedback and observations from team members.
  - Encourage team members to talk about what they experienced during the game and how they felt in certain situations, good or bad.
  - Discuss taking responsibility for failures without pointing the finger at others.
  - Always discuss failures with the intent of helping players learn and grow.
- Reinforce season goals and team goals.
  - How can the game help move the team toward their goal?
  - What can they take from the game?
- End the meeting with something positive or motivational to give your players something to strive for.
- Give the team details about the next day or next meeting time.
- Always end the day with a team cheer, win or lose.

index

Note: An f or t following a page number refers to a figure or table, respectively.

about ASEP

Coaching Softball Technical and Tactical Skills is written by the American Sport Education Program (ASEP) in conjunction with softball coaching legends Kirk Walker and Mona Stevens.

ASEP has been developing and delivering coaching education courses and resources since 1981. As the nation's leading sport education provider, ASEP works with national, state, and local sport organizations to develop educational programs for coaches, officials, administrators, and parents. These programs incorporate ASEP's philosophy of "Athletes first, winning second."

Contributing author **Kirk Walker** drastically improved the Oregon State softball program when he became head coach in 1994. Walker has become Oregon State's all-time winningest softball coach with a 462-347-3 career record. Each season his team has improved—they've had eight seasons of winning 40-plus games. In 2005 Walker earned his second Pacific-10 Conference Coach of the Year Award after winning the Pac-10 title for the first time. Walker also coached in the Amateur Softball Association, where he led his team to four consecutive women's major fastpitch national titles. Currently he is coaching in the Pro Fastpitch Xtreme Tour. He also edited and contributed to *The Softball Drill Book* (Human Kinetics, 2007).

Contributing author **Mona Stevens** was a University of Utah softball stalwart, coaching from 1996 - 2005. She led her team to three NCAA Tournament appearances, three Mountain West Conference Tournament titles, and one regular-season championship. Throughout her coaching career, Stevens amassed a 281-239-1 (.540) record. In addition to coaching at the collegiate level, she has served as a coach for national and international competitions. In 1989 she created Mona Stevens Enterprises, conducting workshops, clinics, and camps for thousands of coaches and players annually. Stevens is the author of *The Fastpitch Softball Drill Book: A Coaches' Guide to Common Problems and Corrections*. She also coauthored the *Softball Coaching Bible* (Human Kinetics, 2002).

THE NATIONAL FASTPITCH COACHES ASSOCIATION

HELPING FASTPITCH SOFTBALL COACHES BE THE BEST THEY CAN BE

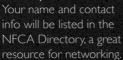

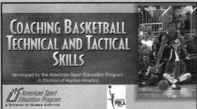
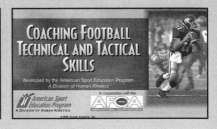